EARLY HUMANS AND
THEIR WORLD

This book presents a breadth of scholarship not found in previous books on the evolution of early hominids. This wide-ranging account creates an accessible introduction to the development of humankind, suitable for students at all levels and the interested non-specialist. The re-evaluation of existing conventions and their replacement with convincing alternatives provide the basis for the study of early hominid evolution for years to come.

The author combines biological and humanistic perspectives to provide a synthesis of the latest palaeo-anthropological and biological research on early human origins and evolution, from the split with the apes some six million years ago to the rise of early modern humans. He focuses on how early humans evolved, lived and organised themselves, whilst signifying the relevance of that advancement for the understanding of modern social life.

The deconstruction of current thought on early hominid evolution continues as the author applies critical scrutiny to the biological theory of kin selection and its relevance for the evolution of human morality and the behaviours of inbreeding avoidance and infanticide. He also examines other key issues such as the origin of cognition, spoken language, morality and typical human sexuality, as well as diet and population density.

In a discussion on the present lack of a coherent evolutionary explanation of bipedalism, the author also draws our attention back to the idea of a possible semi-aquatic environment for our early ancestors that is otherwise seldom given a fair account. He gives further consideration to the evolutionary instruments used in creating bipedalism, as well as the modern human skull and face and the special human traits of curiosity and creativity.

The author accesses research by the world's leading scholars of early hominid evolution and primate behaviour to create a landmark exploration of human origins.

Bo Gräslund is Emeritus Professor of Archaeology at Uppsala University, Sweden. Among his many research areas are biological-cultural evolution and ecology in prehistory.

EARLY HUMANS AND THEIR WORLD

Bo Gräslund

 Routledge
Taylor & Francis Group

LONDON AND NEW YORK

First published 2005
by Routledge
2 Park Square, Milton Park, Abingdon, Oxon OX14 4RN

Simultaneously published in the USA and Canada
by Routledge
270 Madison Ave, New York, NY 10016

Routledge is an imprint of the Taylor & Francis Group

© 2005 Bo Gräslund

Typeset in Garamond by Book Now Ltd
Printed and bound in Great Britain by
St Edmundsbury Press, Bury St Edmunds, Suffolk

Translated by Neil Price

British Library Cataloguing in Publication Data
A catalogue record for this book is available from the British Library

Library of Congress Cataloging in Publication Data
Gräslund, Bo.
Early humans and their world/Bo Gräslund.
p. cm.
Includes bibliographical references and index.
1. Fossil hominids. 2. Human evolution. 3. Social evolution. I. Title.
GN282.G73 2005
599.93'8–dc22
2004020988

ISBN 0–415–35345–9 (pbk)
ISBN 0–415–35344–0 (hbk)

CONTENTS

Preface   vii
Acknowledgements   ix

1   The tangible past   1

2   The evolution of human social life   12

3   Next of kin   41

4   Traces of the early humans   47

5   Becoming human   64

6   Evolutionary tools and the path to humanity   81

7   A new sexual pattern   89

8   Intellect and language   106

9   Ways of life and social structure   136

Bibliography   165
Index   175

PREFACE

Imagine how different it would have been if human beings had been delivered ready-made with an instruction book, well thought through, simple and un-complicated. In reality the opposite occurred, and we must write the manual ourselves. We are only able to do this if we follow the strands of our biology and culture back into the most distant past. It was with this in mind that I began this book.

In the first instance the book deals with humankind's origins as a species, and with our biological, social and cultural development at and after the 'creation'. I have tried to bring together recent results from a broad range of research fields, and to combine them in an over-arching interpretation. There can be no question of an exhaustive survey. I have primarily worked with issues that I myself find exciting, important or unjustly neglected.

In recent years several scholars have brought great insight to the difficult and sensitive matter of innate and culturally acquired elements of human behaviour. It is my hope that this book on human origins can contribute to a continued discussion of these and other questions of our evolutionary inherit-ance. I have time and again gone off at tangents of this kind, only to rein myself in in order to return to the main theme of the book.

A critical chapter is devoted to the dominant biological theory on the evolution of elementary social order, and its maintenance among the higher animals – a question of decisive importance for our perspectives on both early and modern humans.

I am conscious of the problems inherent in attempting to combine and interpret the findings of a range of different disciplines in which one lacks direct research experience. If any reader should find their blood pressure rising as a result of this book, I offer my apologies. In my defence I would say that multi-disciplinary syntheses would never be written by a single individual if scholars always kept to their own narrow specialisms. The alternative, a number of researchers working together across a broad front, appears more secure but often loses out through lack of co-ordination and an appreciation of the whole.

The immediate source material for the study of early humans consists first of the more-or-less fragmentary remains of their bones, of the environmental data that illuminate the world in which they lived, and the simple objects that they made. This material has deficiencies that make it hard to interpret, and in the light of this we can note that the frequent disagreements between researchers are in fact a healthy sign. We should remember that the sources will remain mute until we ask questions of them. When some kind of answer is received, it is more often than not in the form of an obscure pronouncement that differs according to who is asking and how the question is phrased. This is, in turn, linked to the fact that we cannot come to an understanding about anything in the past – whether it be a matter of culture, nature, human or animal – unless we can relate it first to something that we believe ourselves to understand already. In this way, all interpretation is coloured by the researcher's frames of reference and prejudices, so that even the most serious research receives an intravenous dose of subjectivity, limitations and circumstance. This general dilemma of theoretical knowledge rarely emerges more clearly than in research into the origins of the human race and its earliest development. This, naturally, is true of the present book.

The necessary background information on important finds, find-spots, dating, research histories and similar matters has been collected in a single chapter.

Wherever practicable, professional jargon has been avoided, even if this has only been possible to a certain extent. Hopefully whatever remains is adequately explained. For the guidance of interested readers, I have provided a bibliography of selected books and journals at the end of the book.

To conclude, it is perhaps unnecessary to point it out, but I shall do so anyway, the term 'evolution' is used here in neither a positive nor negative sense, but only as a synonym for biological change. There is likewise no value judgement implied in the expressions 'higher' and 'lower' animals that I have sometimes rather lightly employed to distinguish mammals and birds from other creatures.

Bo Gräslund

ACKNOWLEDGEMENTS

This book is an English version of my Swedish original, *De första stegen: Urmänniskan och hennes värld*, that was published in 2001 by Atlantis Press in Stockholm. For the English edition I have made a few minor changes and additions.

The book has been translated by Dr Neil Price, my colleague at Uppsala. Neil has also made valuable comments on the content and supported me with good advice. The same applies to a large number of colleagues, friends and associates – none named but none forgotten. I owe them all many thanks.

I am also grateful to Routledge's two anonymous referees for their constructive comments on the text. One of them also expressed some mild surprise at the occasional colloquialisms in this book, and I feel I should point out that these are faithful renditions of my Swedish.

That we know so much about the earliest origins of humankind is due to the dedicated efforts of numerous researchers working with great care in the field and in the laboratory, within the various specialist fields that shelter under the broad umbrella of palaeoanthropology. Here I can mention only a few: Berhane Asfaw, Robert Broom, Michel Brunet, Ronald Clarke, Yves Coppens, Raymond Dart, Yohannes Haile-Selassie, F. Clark Howell, Glyn Isaac, Donald Johansson, Kimoya Kimeu, Louis Leakey, Mary Leakey, Meave Leakey, Richard Leakey, David Pilbeam, Martin Pickford, Brigitte Senut, Gen Suwa, Phillip Tobias, Alan Walker, Tim White and Bernhard Wood. Of great importance for this book, and for me personally, has been the contribution of modern primatology with its systematic studies of wild apes and monkeys. This especially applies to our closest relatives among the former. Here too I can mention only a select handful of scholars: Christophe Boesch, Hedwige Boesch-Ammermann, Richard Byrne, Diane Fossey, Biruté Galdikas, Jane Goodall, T. Hasegawa, M. Hiraiwai-Hasegawa, William McGrew, Takayoshi Kano, Linda Merchant, Toshisada Nishida, Vernon Reynolds, Susanne Savage-Rumbaugh, Carel van Schaik, George Schaller, Craig Stanford, Yukimaru Suguyama, Randall Susman, Geza Teleki, Michael Tomasello, Caroline Tutin, Frands de Waal, Francis White, Andrew Whiten and Richard Wrangham. The work for this book has also required a number of excursions into several other disciplines, including evolutionary biology and evolutionary psychology. I owe a debt of thanks to all the researchers, whether named above or not, whose findings and discoveries I have been able to employ for this volume.

The translation has been funded by *The Royal Academy of Letters, History and Antiquities*, Stockholm and *Dagmar och Sven Saléns Stiftelse*, Stockholm, to whom I wish to express my gratitude.

1

THE TANGIBLE PAST

Time perspectives

Every breath we draw, every step we take, every emotion we experience reflects our past. As the youngest link in an evolutionary chain many hundreds of millions of years old, every person is a wandering exhibition of her or his biological history.

This insight presses itself upon us unlooked for when we study a subject such as the evolution of the human race. This prompts me to begin this book with a few reflections on humanity's evolutionary background.

To make an open-minded journey through the past is an exhilarating experience, worth any amount of effort. But there are also other reasons to listen to what has gone before. All over the world those in power demonstrate their ignorance of history. To the extent that they have a historical perspective at all, it is often so narrow that it mostly tempts them to abuse the past. Unless we take a long view of the past, then we will never be able to think more than a few years into the future – at best a few generations, rarely the necessary centuries, millennia and millions of years. Never before has it been so important to place the present and future in a larger temporal context.

Our ancestors living in more traditional social patterns had close emotional and cultural relationships to their past. Now those connections are mostly passive in the sense that they are maintained by a few experts on behalf of the majority. For most people today, the past appears to them as an abyss.

During the long period when the human brain evolved to what it is today, there was hardly any evolutionary need for reflection on a broad spatial, social and temporal scale. Humanity's natural understanding of time and social space has thereby become ever more confined to the narrow horizon of the individual's own lifetime. To this we can add our difficulty in imagining that which we cannot relate to our own experience. The ability to think far-sightedly into the future does not seem prominent among our gifts.

Many people experience the time reckoning of history books – years, millennia and millions of years – as abstractions, almost as difficult to grasp as the distances of inter-stellar space. With this in mind, let us try to find a more concrete measurement of time. Human beings generally produce about three generations every hundred years. Instead of placing Genghis Khan about 800 years ago, we can say that he lived about 24 generations before the present. Twenty-four people: about the size of a school class. So we can use the timescale of parents plus children, or parents plus children and grandchildren, family units with which most people are well familiar. At once the distance shrinks to 12 two-generation or 8 three-generation families in straight descent. It doesn't sound very much, and the point is that it isn't.

Consider the fact that only 60 or so generations of people or 20 three-generation families separates us from the time of Jesus Christ; that the Stone Age in northern Europe lasted until 135 generations or 45 three-generation families ago; that my home country of Sweden has not even been populated for more than 400 generations or 133 three-generation families; and that what we call civilisation began as late as 350 generations ago.

On the other hand, biologically modern humans have more than 6,000 generations behind them, and our ancestors have been walking upright for something approaching 250,000 generations.

Talking about time in this way brings the past closer, and the present into focus. It lets us understand that our history and culture are not very old at all, and that in some sense the threads that bind us to the past are very short.

Ever since we began to till the soil, keep domestic animals and live in settled communities, some 350 generations ago, we can see how population pressure and economic growth have been instrumental in the drive for techno-logical, cultural and social development. Today the global society is as depen-dent on growth as an addict on a drug. As long as the growth mechanisms function then most things eventually get sorted out, but as soon as expansion stagnates or is reversed then society is shaken to its foundations. In this way the concept of growth has come to stand for progress and positive develop-ment to the point at which it has superseded all other ideologies, including those of religion.

The Western understanding of history is saturated by the notion that evolution has led from lower forms of culture and society to ever-greater heights of civilisation. The more developed is seen as automatically superior to the less developed, and the past as inferior to the present. Despite the fact that our belief in the future has become somewhat ragged around the edges, the devaluation of the past is still etched firmly in the popular consciousness. Not many would be attracted by the idea of time-travelling 10,000, 20,000 or 100,000 years back into history, at least not on a one-way ticket.

With an evolutionary weakness that makes it hard for us to deal with the future, we allow short-term problems to overshadow those of the long-term. Our globe has finally become a crawling ant-heap which every hour adds another 100,000 people to its population. While only a small proportion of this mass of humanity enjoys anything approaching adequate welfare, the earth's resources are still being depleted, its diversity of plant and animal life is being reduced, and the environmental conditions for life are declining rapidly.

The history of our civilisation has thrown up many examples of enlightened cultural efforts, impressive social achievements and individual human greatness. But all the while this picture is dimmed by a collective stupidity and shallowness of truly appalling dimensions. This is a paradox that is only intelligible in the light of a very long evolutionary perspective. However, to blame our ancestors for all this would be meaningless. The paths of history have been marked by combinations of cultural, social, biological and environmental factors that neither individuals nor groups have ever before been able to perceive, understand or control. In fact it is possible that humans like us may never actually acquire this talent, as our intelligence has inherited limitations which impair our ability to survey, analyse and counteract the long-term effects of our collective activities.

For the greater part of humanity's time on earth, cultural change has proceeded at a snail's pace, to such a degree that even relatively recent generations of modern humans must have understood the world as essentially static. The winds of change have now become a hurricane. In the short space of a human life a person can now experience greater technological and social evolution than once occurred over thousands of generations.

As a norm for a good society, most people would probably put forward notions such as democracy and welfare for all, a high material standard, comfort, good health, good medical care, a long lifespan, and good food and drink, not forgetting the joys of culture and sport. The problem is that this vision has not so far been reconciled with another, equally self-evident dream: a world without hunger, epidemics and ruined environments, a life without war, violence, torture, sexual assault, oppression, stress, anxiety and loneliness.

We have had to take the bad with the good. Both of these aspects of reality in fact derive primarily from the effects of one and the same event – the moment when we became settled, socialising farmers. This process began as late as 350 generations ago in the Near East and Asia, and 180 generations ago in Central America. But the modern human is infinitely older. As far as we know at present, about 6,000 generations have passed since we emerged in Africa; in the Near East we appeared 3,000 generations ago; in Australia, 2,000; in Europe, 1,500; and in America some 500 to 1,000 generations have elapsed.

For a species with such a sluggish cycle of generation, evolution works slowly. There is nothing to suggest that the people of late prehistory were in any way intellectually or neurologically different from you or me. In other words, the modern human is not modern at all. We are children of the early Stone Age.

This means that in the essentials we evolved for a quite different environment than that of the industrialised world, which is just a few moments old. In evolutionary terms, we are therefore poorly equipped to meet many of the demands placed upon us by a modern society. There is no doubt that many of our current and historical problems – social, psychological, medical and political – stem from this imbalance between inherited qualities and needs, and cultural development. A lack of insight and knowledge of this permanent opposition is a threat to the future of humanity. This is one of several reasons to improve our acquaintance with the evolutionary history of our species.

Family ties

Although all living organisms are perhaps not related at the cellular level, they nevertheless belong on the same family tree. In this sense we have a collective inheritance with insects, plants and bacteria. We in fact share something like 40 per cent of our genes with a relative as far removed as the banana. To some animals we stand very close indeed.

Even so, we are keener to speak of what separates us from other creatures than of what unites us with them. We prefer to think in terms of 'us' and 'others', and it is only rarely that our comparisons favour the animals. The feeling of communality and humility in relation to animals, nature and the rhythm of life, which characterised more traditional societies, was slowly transformed into its opposite through the population pressure of agrarian subsistence and its need for control over the environment. From this arose the notion that human beings stood higher than other creatures, made ruler over 'the beasts of the field and the fowls of the heavens'.

To define the modern human as a species is not problematic. But when did we actually become *people*? Is it possible to find some point in the chain of evolution when our animal ancestors became . . . us? This question cannot be answered at a stroke, because the more we learn about animals the more indistinct this border becomes.

For many years the only true criteria for increasing 'human-ness' were defined in terms of culture, as expressed in the manufacture and use of tools. However, we now know that even common chimpanzees in the wild deliberately prepare and employ tools, and to some extent teach these skills to their young. They can also treat stone objects in such a way that the resulting debitage differs only in the most minor ways from the earliest finds of stone tools made by humans. Their tools and even their way of using them are also culturally variable. Many other animals also use tools. In the same way, many other animals have a discernible intelligence, a considerable ability to understand concepts, an elementary capacity for abstraction and a basic consciousness of personality. We are unique in having an articulated, complex language, but we are not alone in possessing a functioning communication system. The problem is that opinions differ considerably as to when this level of complex language was achieved.

It has sometimes been suggested that the real watershed between animals and humans came into being when our ancestors began to overcome self-interest with regard to those who were not their close relatives, for example by dividing food equally within a group. Unfortunately we have only the slightest grasp of when this could have been and when a truly human altruism began to

4

emerge. Naturally, this kind of behaviour is not easy to recover archaeologically. As an aside we can note that our close relatives in the wild, such as chimpanzees and some groups of orang-utans, also share their food, albeit unsystematically.

Researchers with a more pessimistic view of human nature have argued that we are at least unique in our ability to wage war against our own species. However, we are forced to share even this miserable claim with others, at least with common chimpanzees and some social insects, such as certain kinds of ants.

When so many differences between animals and modern humans are more a matter of degree than outright opposites, it is not strange that we should find it so hard to isolate signals of a true humanity that would separate the earliest hominids from their closest ancestors among the contemporary apes. Time and again we have been forced to retreat, in order to formulate new definitions of the human concept.

I personally believe that anatomical features are a better way to trace an early 'humanity' than intellectual, social, cultural and moral criteria, which are all hard to define, perceive and date. A bipedal gait with all its implications seems more than enough to characterise the early humans. If we do not accept this, then we must place the origins of humanity much later in time, according to our idea of what it is to be human. Seen in this light, if we instead seize upon such advanced accomplishments as the use of fire, the cooking of food, the practice of religion, the creation of symbolic art, the use of a complex articulated language or other, safer signs of humanity, then we have come so far forward that this line of argument becomes quite irrelevant for the problem of the early hominids.

A lot of fuss has been made about the notion that our culture has to some extent been instrumental in our biological evolution. But this is nothing unique for us, as many animals also exhibit cultural behaviour that can be important for selection. The decisive factor is that evolution cannot move along anything other than a genetic path. As evolutionary products humans are and always will be purely biological beings. The term 'cultural evolution' should be reserved for the process of cultural change.

Biological heritage

Our biological inheritance was certainly determined long before the emergence of anything resembling civilisation as we know it, and in certain important respects long before the origins of humans themselves. For 50 million years our ancestors lived as apes in the trees of tropical forests, after that for another 15 million years as anthropoid apes in trees and on the ground, and after that for several million years more as early humans, mainly on the forest floor. In evolutionary terms, it was during this incomprehensible span of time in the tropical forests that the greater part of our physical make-up and much of our psychological and elementary social behaviour were formed. Neurologically, physiologically and anatomically we are to a very large degree children of this remote forest age.

Truly radical changes in the circumstances of human life first came with the industrial society. For a species with such a long reproductive cycle, this is far too short a time to result in any perceptible biological alterations. Quite simply, the many new demands placed upon us by our new lifestyles have left no significant mark on our genes.

Many mammals have rather poor eyesight, and thus rely primarily on their outstanding sense of smell. With human beings the opposite is true. We have nothing much to boast of in the way of olfactory skills, but we have excellent stereoscopic vision and a good colour sense. We also possess articulated shoulders, arms and hands that can be rotated, mobile fingers with an opposable grip, and a brain that is uniquely good at co-ordinating sight and dexterity. All these qualities are things that we take for granted. Granted is also exactly what they are, granted to us as a biological inheritance from our fruit- and plant-eating ape ancestors during that very long period in the tropical canopy. As we raised ourselves to stand on two legs and our intelligence later increased, this anatomical and physical toolkit became the functional key to our entire cultural development. Without this inheritance we would have been literally incapable of making and using tools and machines, making fire, cooking food, domesticating animals, tilling the soil, building houses, producing metal, sewing clothes, writing words, printing books, playing a piano, pole-vaulting or using computers. So, if there is anything to which someone who values civilisation should send a grateful thought, it is our inheritance from the apes and monkeys.

Exactly like our nearest animal relatives we are typical creatures of daylight. We have little free will when it comes to our daily biorhythm. The fact that we normally sleep at night and are active during the day has not been noticeably affected by access to artificial light. The day-dweller within us is also revealed by our poor night-vision, by the fact that drastic changes in shift-work make us physically and psychologically ill, by our frequent fear of the dark and the depression that often comes with long periods of winter gloom. The fact is that we have exactly the same inner biological clock as other mammals, even the humble fruit fly.

Another concrete example is that of hearing. In the tropical forest, powerful vibrations are so unusual that our ancestors' auditory organs and nervous systems never needed to develop any real protection against loud noise. This is why we damage our hearing with machine sounds, rock concerts and Walkmans, while hunter-gatherers maintain perfect hearing all their lives. This is a simple example of how cultural development is speeding away from its biological counterpart.

Dependent upon climate and environment, indigenous peoples today can differ considerably as to height, body form and skin colour. But these physiological differences are marginal. All modern humans have essentially the same poor defences against a cold climate. We have no fur, no layer of blubber and no decent system to prevent heat loss. By contrast we possess excellent mechanisms for disposing of excess heat. A naked person, motionless in the shade, is already beginning to shiver when the air temperature goes below 28 degrees centigrade, when the bodily cycle activates itself to cope with the loss of warmth. Not so strange when we consider that more or less all our biological evolution took place in the tropics. The fact that, in spite of this, human beings managed to colonise every climatic zone of the globe by the end of the early Stone Age can only be understood in the light of our cultural abilities.

Humans are very much herd animals. Our extreme need for company, our mobile and hierarchical social structures, our noticeable propensity for group cooperation, our patterns of aggression and conciliation and our collective territoriality are all in their essentials an inheritance from our ape ancestors.

Still, for many people the 'primitive' herd instinct is something embarrassing, to be spoken of in an undertone. Certainly this inheritance has its negative sides, but it is easy to forget that the herd instinct also contains the evolutionary codes for mutual tolerance and consideration between unrelated individuals, the very seeds for human morality, solidarity and love. The herd instinct is the key to our complex social life, the toolkit that enables different human beings to combine in functioning societies. To deny this biological inheritance is to deny almost everything that we see as positively human.

We would very much like to see human feelings as something specific to our own species. However, the lie to this is given by the fact that most of our fundamental emotions are regulated by the oldest parts of the brain, the hypothalamus and the limbic system. In fact we share much of our emotional repertoire with other higher mammals. Anger, fear, anxiety, respect, happiness, the joy of reunion, parental love, sorrow, sadness, loneliness, apathy, friendship and sexual frustration, perhaps also melancholy, longing, jealousy, hate and a lust for revenge are all things that we encounter in some form among several other higher animals.

Without our inherited herding behaviour we would never have been able to tame the animals that gave the Old World's early agricultural communities their dynamism and capacity for development. Only herd animals like us have the ability to domesticate, and even then we can only do this to other herd animals. It is no coincidence that dogs, cattle, horses, pigs, sheep, goats, camels and chickens are all hierarchical creatures of the flock, with an instinctive tendency to subordinate themselves to that which seems most dominant.

It is now more than 250 years since Carl von Linné – Linnæus – defined humanity's close family ties with the higher simians, and nearly 150 years since Charles Darwin explained the basic mechanisms for biological evolution. Even now, many turn from the thought that we are related to such simple and furry characters as the great apes, without pausing to wonder for whom the comparison might be most embarrassing. The common chimp is not always the best behaved of individuals, but we could still learn a thing or two from the gentle gorilla and the socially adept bonobo.

Sociobiology

Charles Darwin was one of the first to assert that human behaviour is to some extent determined by inherited tendencies. Later, Sigmund Freud, C. G. Jung, Konrad Lorenz and others made their own contributions to our understanding of the undercurrents of human social interaction and mental response that we carry with us from birth.

The biosocial perspective has many components. Advances in biology have been of particular importance for our understanding of the social life and intellectual capacity of the higher animals, not least the primates. To this we can add studies of human universals that have emerged from genetics, cognitive research, neuro-physiology, psychology and anthropology, and of human behaviour and reactions. These transcend boundaries of culture, religion and race, and therefore should have a collective biological foundation. In the same picture we find the classic socio-biological assertion – somewhat dubious but undoubtedly influential – that social life in the animal world is largely steered by an instinctive attempt to maximise the individual's reproductive success.

To oppose such a biological view of human behaviour on the grounds that this is to drag the human spirit down to a bestial level, or with the argument that these ideas can be abused, is like dealing with a difficult reality by claiming that it does not exist. In passing we can note that biological research has in no way made people more animal-like, though it has possibly made animals more human.

While few people today deny the connection between body and soul and between brain and physiology, and even though most accept the thought that anatomically and physiologically we are the result of a long biological process, many of us still have difficulty in swallowing the idea that this should also apply to our behaviour. We would prefer to think of free will, of a general liberty in our social activity and in our construction of society and culture. But if human behaviour completely lacked biological programming then it would be a total chaos, utterly unpredictable and quite impossible to characterise from a species viewpoint. It is not. Despite all our individual and cultural variety, human behaviour clearly follows certain basic patterns. The very fact that we can consider particular types of behaviour to be typically human depends upon their repetition independent of cultural and environmental conditions, and this is because they ultimately rest on a collective biological foundation.

If by free will we mean the capacity for cultural and individual variation, then we undoubtedly possess this. But it is easy to forget how limited cultural behaviour can be. Even though in theoretical terms there are many possibilities for varying the manner of our clothing or our way of eating a meal, we still follow narrow cultural patterns. Thus much of the will that is free of biology is quickly gobbled up by cultural traditions. From this perspective, if we want to speak of free will then we should talk in terms of parole or temporary permission.

This does not mean that everything we do is predetermined, far from it. When put together, variation in the biological, environmental, cultural and individual components leaves significant room for manoeuvre. It is still an open question as to what extent or in which respects our behaviour is directly or indirectly biologically predisposed. It is hard to see clearly in the grey zone where nature and culture meet, because they partly obscure each other. The same is true to some degree for certain of the higher animals, and not just our closest relatives.

In any case there is no doubt that all people are the bearers of a collective biological inheritance that does not just affect our anatomy and physiology but also provides the framework for our psychological, social and intellectual qualities. Indirectly it also is present in our cultural behaviour.

All too often we meet the pessimistic view that brutality, cruelty and war are normal expressions of human nature. But in normal terms such behaviour is exclusively a reaction to evolutionary conditions that have *deviated* from normality.

There is a widespread fear of so-called biologism, that observations of biological differences between the sexes can be socio-politically abused. But closing our eyes to biological variations does not solve any problems. There are no unavoidable or fated social effects of biological inheritance. There is nothing to say that we must accept problems and injustices that we have essentially caused ourselves, by developing a culture and society that in some ways conflicts with our inherited patterns of behaviour. Just as for anatomical and physiological differences, eventual sexual variation in terms of dominance behaviour, reactions and thought patterns is no argument for giving women reduced opportunities in the job market, or in any other social context, on the grounds of giving 'nature' free rein.

The fact is that we do not watch impassively when any other aspect of inherited behaviour becomes exaggerated under cultural pressure. Nobody suggests that male violence should be tolerated or encouraged, just because in indisputable biological patterns males totally and violently dominate all primate communities throughout the world. Nor would we claim that lies are generally acceptable merely because people of both sexes have inherited a capacity for deception from our ape ancestors. Quite the opposite, as we use every means available for dealing with such problems.

Another argument against biologism is the knowledge that, even if in some respects the sexes think and react somewhat differently, when intelligence is measured in terms of mental dexterity, the capacity for association, analysis and interpretation then it is clearly the same for women and men. Biology provides us with the important detail that the same is true for the animals.

The origins of the historical oppression of women lie among other things in the way our civilisation patterns – newborn in evolutionary terms – have corrupted our reactions to biological differences between the sexes, especially with regard to dominant behaviour. But since we cannot turn back the clock, we must instead try to understand the mechanisms that are in operation here. If we seek greater insight into the genetic factors that ultimately regulate destructive impulses such as aggression, violence and hierarchical oppression, including the oppression of women, then this is not to unleash dangerous, primitive forces or to argue in favour of biologism. Quite the opposite – the more we know about the inherited motors that activate, release and nullify such behaviour, the greater possibilities we have to control and defuse it.

As a humanist I also have difficulty in seeing how a deeper knowledge of humans as biological beings should obscure the picture of our intellectual, mental and cultural achievements. To distance ourselves from a biological perspective on humanity, with the argument that human behaviour is cultural to the core, or that everything good is culture whereas everything bad is nature, is to promote an anti-intellectual attitude that is quite alien to the human sciences. Not least, we cannot even know what is culture if we do not understand what is nature.

Interest in the biological components of human behaviour has not always been welcome. In 1975 the Harvard entomologist Edward O. Wilson met with an especially strong reaction with his book *Sociobiology: The new synthesis*. Typical for its time was the book's emphasis on reproductive strategies as the social drive for all living things (kin selection – see the following chapter), and many people were challenged by the author's rather vague statements on the ethical consequences of such a viewpoint. The intense critique with which the book was received is still with us today as an almost reflexive rejection of biological perspectives on human behaviour that is common among non-biologists. Through Wilson's book the term sociobiology became the general label for the evolutionary study of human behaviour. Now we prefer to employ terms such as biosociology, evolutionary psychology, human ethology, behavioural ecology and so on.

In the following year, 1976, the Oxford biologist Richard Dawkins published his influential book *The Selfish Gene*. With a steady stream of work since then, Dawkins has emerged as the leading spokesman for classic sociobiology. To underline his contention that biological selection takes place not at the level of species, groups or even individuals, but actually through genes, Dawkins coined the dramatic phrase with which he titled his book. This concept is the core of the sociobiological narrative genre that imaginatively illustrates how social behaviour, in line with the theory of kin selection, is intended to favour the continuance of one's own genes. The notion that every creature is living proof that its ancestors were evolutionarily programmed to provide well for their descendants is here re-written to indicate that parents care for their children in order to promote the future of their own genes. Behaviour that is the unintentional result of a combination of evolutionary conditions is here depicted as the fruit of particular genes' and individuals' selfish purpose, as if genetic success were the deepest meaning of life. Workers among social insects such as termites, ants and bees are at times described as almost happy that they cannot reproduce themselves, but must instead be content with spreading their genes indirectly through a close relative.

This sociobiological jargon, which from theories of kin selection describes social behaviour in terms of intention and human values, is more a reflection of the modern Western dream of individual achievement than basic principles of evolution. More than anything else this has discredited the sociobiological perspective by raising the spectre of democratic values and humanistic lifestyles being pushed aside by a cynical biological determinism, valuing human beings only by their capacity to compete through their own reproduction. Many had difficulty here in seeing any space for moral responsibility, individual creativity and the freedom of thought and will. It was remembered how in the late 1800s and early 1900s biological research had been misused to discriminate against other races, women, particular social classes, the mentally ill and other groups, in a similar fashion to the Nazis' biological motivations for racial extermination.

But scientific data does not include value judgements, which instead spring from human thought. The lesson we should draw from this is that we should not undertake less research on humanity's biological background, we should instead undertake more; we should not suppress its results, we should instead give them a wider dissemination.

The social theory of classic sociobiology, as it was formulated in the 1970s from the thesis of kin selection, has paralysed the dialogue between biology and the social sciences, not so much due to its cynicism as to its contradictions. The problem is that we cannot completely understand elementary social patterns among modern, historical or prehistoric people without a grasp of the mechanisms that regulate the essentials of social life among the higher animals. This is why I will here subject the theory of kin selection to closer scrutiny. It will be seen that the animal world does not manifest the mechanisms that in theory are supposed to regulate kin selection. My conclusion is that this theory lacks scientific credence as a means of understanding the evolution of higher social life. I contend that it is in fact one of the greatest scientific myths of modern times. This, in turn, forces me to attempt a definition of the evolutionary mechanisms that operate in place of kin selection.

2

THE EVOLUTION OF
HUMAN SOCIAL LIFE

The theory of kin selection

In 1930, based on Darwin's theory of natural selection and the laws of inheritance set out by Gregor Mendel, the Oxford scholar Ronald Fisher formulated his idea that animals' social behaviour is primarily steered in evolutionary terms by their ability to generate a vigorous and sizeable progeny. He called this capacity *reproductive fitness*. Individuals whose behaviour improves their chances of successful reproduction thereby increase the spread of their genes, and in turn the propagation of the behaviour that produces such a result.

It remained unclear as to how such strong self-interest could be combined with the assistance that animals could nevertheless be seen to render one another. It was in response to this that in 1963 and 1964 the Oxford biologist William Hamilton presented his famous theory on the evolution of altruism – unselfish behaviour – and how this primarily concerns individuals who are closely related.

Hamilton proceeded from the fact that siblings, as with parents and children, share roughly half their genes. Half-siblings share a quarter, as do grandparents and grandchildren, while cousins have an eighth in common and second cousins a sixteenth. He suggested that individuals who face danger and even death in helping a relative might nevertheless be promoting the interests of their own genes. A prerequisite here is that the genetic cost must not exceed the collective gain, in other words the more numerous and closer the relatives are, the better. In this way the ability to promote one's own genes at the expense of others, expressed through aiding one's relatives, should become an inherited characteristic.

Naturally, all individuals within a population and a species have most of their genes in common. The genes that Hamilton meant were those few that are not generally shared, but which are still sufficient in number to give selection something to work with. To emphasise his primary focus on unselfishness outside the sphere of direct parental care, Hamilton coined the term *inclusive fitness*. Soon researchers were following John Maynard Smith in speaking also of *kin selection*.

12

But many problems remained. It was known that even animals that were in no way related sometimes helped each other, which contradicted the theory of kin selection. Still, the theory was little doubted. In their eagerness to make everything match up, a few researchers even took a metaphysical line. In all seriousness it was claimed that animals that receive assistance from others, with whom they are unrelated, in some way give off signals that convince their helpers that they *are* kin.

In 1971 the American Robert Trivers at last came to the rescue with his concept of *reciprocal altruism*. With reference to the fact that assistance between non-kin animals is often returned, if not immediately then at least later on, Trivers argued that this behaviour would in the long term benefit all parties' reproductive success. The process was essentially just genetic selfishness regulated through kin selection, and altruism could thus be evolutionarily explained in exactly the same way as egoism. With this the path was cleared for interpreting all basic social behaviour among animals as an expression of genetic self-interest – and this is exactly what happened.

Now there was only one serious contradiction left: human beings themselves. In 1975 Edward O. Wilson suggested in his book *Sociobiology* that in theory we cannot speak of genuine altruism among humans, as even our behaviour must have evolved in accordance with Hamilton's and Trivers' laws. On the other hand, he did not deny that true altruism does in fact occur among humans. The equation did not balance, and Wilson openly admitted the dilemma by citing human altruism as sociobiology's greatest theoretical problem. However, the original point of departure, the theory of kin selection, was not called into question. Wilson was then bitterly criticised for what many saw as biological determinism in his view of humankind. So, after only a few years he retreated, together with Charles Lumsden, into the assurance that humanity was above the laws of kin selection that applied to the animals. Our capacity for a little genuine altruism was instead due to our species' unique evolutionary dialogue between genes and culture.

Similar ideas were being put forward at the same time by Richard Dawkins in Oxford, in his 1976 bestseller *The Selfish Gene*. Dawkins also introduced the term *mem* for the evolutionarily active component in this supposed interaction of culture and genetics. Few seemed to worry that this was merely an unsupported hypothesis, as it fulfilled its purpose in discretely filling what was seen as the last crack in the theory of kin selection.

It now appeared that all decisive opposition to kin selection had been overcome, and its fundamental premise established once and for all. Thereafter interest was mostly focused on cosmetic problems, as with the American political scientist Robert Axelrod's introduction of games theory into the debate in 1981.

Back in 1966, George Williams had criticised the notion that selection primarily operated with groups and individuals, and suggested instead that it worked at the level of separate genes. This idea agreed well with the theories of kin selection, and was now taken up anew by Dawkins with considerable energy. More than anything else, Dawkins' elegant metaphor of the 'selfish gene' has contributed to the consolidation of Hamilton's hypothesis on extended kin selection.

The classic social theory of sociobiology was thus laid out. With kin selection and selfish genes as its chief tools, it also influenced the way in which human behaviour was viewed. Thereafter a great deal of ink was spilt about evolutionary self-interest, and if anyone found the word altruism on their lips it was accompanied by a flush of embarrassment.

Despite one or two critical voices, the theory of kin selection is still regarded as a powerful scientific instrument for understanding the evolution of helping mechanisms and elementary social order. It is generally seen as one of the most important contributions to evolutionary theory since Darwin.

Neither Wilson nor Dawkins specified more closely how and when in the evolutionary process human culture should have contributed to the creation of true altruism. It was in an attempt to understand precisely this problem that I began to analyse the background of this notion and the theory of kin selection.

General critique

These are no small demands that the theory of kin selection places on those involved. Firstly, an animal must be able to recognise its own kin. Then it needs to be able to understand the degree of such a relationship. After that it must decide to positively discriminate in favour of its relatives, and further-more along a sliding scale of closeness. Next it must be able to judge whether helping several relatives is genetically sensible or not, by estimating the pros and cons of its social actions in the light of the entire reproductive situation of the animal itself and of its relatives, including the possible loss of its own life.

Of course, animals are not supposed to behave like this through considered thought but instead by instinct. However, the assumption is still made that they are in general able to correctly and instantly react in situations that are often so complex that researchers themselves must employ advanced mathe-matics to – at best – arrive at a conclusion.

The crucial question is therefore to ask which mechanisms are actually capable of regulating functions as complex as these, and more often 'correctly' than not.

In its exact sense, kin selection makes a choice of genes for positive discri-mination, based on direct or indirect signs of genetic relationship. The fact that many proponents of classic kin selection have regarded true altruism as a theoretical problem confirms that this is how they view the matter, for it is only then that it actually becomes a problem.

The majority of 'lower' animals are considered to identify and give prefer-ential treatment to their relatives through chemical signals and similar means. Even 'higher' animals are sometimes thought to be able to directly or indirectly recognise their relatives through signs of genetic kinship. In most cases, however, scholars rely on the notion of *phenotype matching*. The term *phenotype* encapsulates the external expressions of an individual's entire genetic makeup, in the form of appearance, scent and behaviour as affected by environment and culture, if any. Phenotype matching means that an animal in some way uses its sense of itself as a frame of reference for recognising its relatives. In addition to this self-reflection, it is sometimes suggested that this frame of reference includes the animal's picture of the individuals it has grown up with or met in its immediate social sphere, and to which in both cases it is most normally related.

Since the phenotype is primarily an expression of an individual's genetic makeup, then social identification through self-reflection would essentially be identical with direct or indirect identification through genetic kinship.

All these ideas of self-reflection and group identification were created because of the need to explain how kin selection works in practice. They give a strong impression of theoretical artifice, and in fact prominent supporters of kin selection like Hamilton, Wilson and Dawkins had difficulty in finding empirical examples of the mechanisms that it requires.

Genetic self-reflection was a more credible idea when the theory of kin selection was new, and we still lacked systematic investigations of wild animals' social behaviour. It now gives off a distinct whiff of metaphysics. The picture emerging from modern zoological behavioural studies is very consistent: there is no secure evidence for positive social discrimination, based on the above criteria, among any larger mammals. The entire primate group, with human beings at the fore, seem to be completely lacking in such gifts. There is nothing to suggest that people can in any meaningful way identify unknown biological relatives, and even less sort them by degree of genetic closeness. Neither by self-reflection nor any other means is it possible to kin-determine scents, voices, external features or behaviour. Among other higher animals there are almost no examples at all. It is symptomatic that no one speaks of such qualities either. The problem is that this kind of reality is so suppressed that it does not appear either in the handbooks or research reports. When it does occasionally pop up, its theoretical implications are not appreciated.

All this should suffice to conclusively dismiss kin selection as a functioning evolutionary mechanism among higher animals and human beings.

In any case, the question we must ask is whether there is any secure evidence for phenotype matching among small mammals and among the social insects that are so often promoted as prime examples of kin selection.

The only small mammals for which data has been published, and which seem to display signs of phenotype matching, are certain rodents. Some experiments with litters of mice, ground squirrels, hamsters and beavers would seem to indicate a certain ability to distinguish their close relatives through scent. However, these observations and conclusions are not only contradictory but also coloured by preconceptions of what kinds of results kin selection will produce. The experimental environment is also somewhat different from conditions in the wild. If siblings or half-siblings who have been artificially hindered from growing up together show a degree of social preference for each other based on scent identification, this does not prove that they recognise their own scent in that of their siblings through phenotype matching. The scent to which they react is rather that of their mother and/or their siblings, as identified either from very early life or even from the womb. Certainly scent plays an important role for social preference among animals, but primarily as a marker for particular individuals.

It is also symptomatic that there is no general biological theory as to which mechanisms for kin identification and preference are active among different animals, and for how they might work in combination. At present it is simply taken as read that animals have some magic formula for identifying their own genetic kin, for sorting them by degree of closeness, for discriminating positively according to this scale of relations, and for estimating the total genetic profit and loss when helping several relatives at the same time. Contradictory facts are suppressed as uninteresting or irritating exceptions from the natural order, or are otherwise dismissed with the explanation that in any case kin selection functions 'in statistical terms'.

The fact that so many scholars continue to regard the world through the filter of kin selection theory may stem from the general impression that animals to a large extent really do behave as if Hamilton's rule of extended reproductive success was operating. I would argue that this is an illusion. The key lies in the way in which kin selection theory was so quickly adopted as a scientific axiom, which led researchers to ignore the lack of empirical support for its theoretical premise. Many attempts have been made to confirm the theory, but very few have tried to refute the notion that animals identify their relatives through phenotype matching or through direct genetic signal markers. If social behaviour in general had been based on such factors, then the proofs would be clear, secure and numerous. As it is, such proof is conspicuous by its absence.

It should be said that there are biologists who are more cautious about kin selection theory, worried about the contradictory data, the absence of good evidence for how animals identify and prioritise their relatives, and the lack of convincing examples of extended reproductive success or mutual assistance between non-kin. Nevertheless, still we see no general critique or decisive revision of the theory, and even fewer indications of an alternative general hypothesis.

The idea of reciprocal altruism was developed to overcome the theoretical objections against the kin selection theory, which are raised by the fact that even unrelated individuals among the higher animals also help one other. But not all positive social relations can be accounted for by reciprocal altruism. Outside the primates and a handful of other higher animals, the phenomenon is very rare indeed.

We are also dealing with something of a chicken and egg situation. Trivers' suggestion that reciprocal altruism between non-kin is simply disguised genetic egoism is, in my opinion, a circular argument. Reciprocal altruism could never have evolved if basic social behaviour had been evolutionarily founded on kin selection. The fact that it does occur points instead towards an evolutionary system that does not hinder unrelated animals from living peaceably together. It is also eloquent that reciprocal altruism between non-kin above all can be observed among the higher animals, whose notorious inability to discriminate through self-reflection or on other genetic grounds surely rules out kin selection as the explanation.

Hamilton's rules present us with a scenario where kin-altruism operates on a sliding scale according to the degree of close kinship. In practice, however, there are only limited possibilities for enhancing reproductive success in this way. The fact that at least one sex among the higher animals leaves the groups at puberty means that young as well as adult animals can only benefit from kin-altruism from *one* of their grandparents' lines, at the same time as the *other* line would surely regard them as a target of genetic selfishness. In the same way, outside the sphere of parents and children it is only possible for an individual to discriminate in favour of half their relatives at most. For many social animals the idea of kin-altruism would be purely theoretical beyond this inner circle. Monogamous mammals often have little or nothing in the way of extended kin contact, and would not therefore be able to benefit from extended reproductive success. Among many lower animals, we find that parents, children and siblings hardly even see one another. Against this background too the theory of kin selection appears as an unsupported construct with little basis in reality.

Despite the fact that the theoretical preconditions for extended kin selection are limited for the animal kingdom in general, we must admit that all animals without exception exhibit a self-interested behavioural pattern that is very deep-rooted. Egoism and self-centredness must therefore have other evolutionary explanations.

The theory of kin selection is not only weighed down by general contradictions like these, but also by constantly repeated exceptions to the principle of nepotism. As we shall see, these are not random but systematic. They indicate that it is primarily through forms of selection other than that based on kin that evolution ensures behaviour beneficial to one's own relatives.

Avoiding inbreeding

Evolution progresses primarily by natural selection, through adaptation to natural changes in the environment. This assumes genetic variation, which is best served by sexual relations that avoid inbreeding, and which in turn demand mechanisms and signal systems that hinder close kin from reproducing with each other. The fact of dynamic evolution among higher animals is therefore evidence enough for the existence of such inherited mechanisms.

To avoid inbreeding an animal must be able to identify its near relatives. We must therefore consider how this comes about among humans, higher animals and social insects. It would be surprising if evolution had wastefully produced several very different mechanisms for this purpose, among species that are closely related.

As we have seen, it is sometimes assumed that animals recognise their relatives as a consequence of growing up together. This is very different from using one's childhood associates as a frame for genetic self-reflection, which would presuppose a pattern of comparative behaviour based on an acquired general template. This question is rarely explored further. Nevertheless, for the higher animals everything suggests that closeness in early life functions in general as a hinder for inbreeding and as a model for positive discrimination.

In all human societies, with or without the support of formal restrictions, sexual congress within the nuclear family is avoided – that is between parents and children, sisters and brothers, grandparents and grandchildren, and between half-siblings. Many societies have also developed proscriptions against sex with more distant relatives, sometimes even with individuals who are not blood-kin but who are counted as relatives in social terms. There is thus great variation in the matter of what is and is not allowed in terms of choosing a sexual partner outside the nuclear family. The core of all human systems for avoiding incest is therefore exogamy: that young people of one or both sexes leave their family groups after puberty to marry and reproduce with other groups.

Exogamy was once considered unique to humans. Because it lies at the centre of almost all human familial and alliance systems, and because it militates against genetic damage, exogamy was understood as an expression of the civilised person's ability to apply social and moral principles for the good of the species. Essentially it was seen as a fundamental cultural acquisition of higher human societies.

Now by contrast, it is clear that not just our close relatives among the primates but in fact all higher animals have strong inherited barriers against inbreeding. In fact *all* animals with sexual reproduction have some kind of system for separating close kin in their mating periods. Mammals, birds, reptiles, amphibians, fish, spiders, insects and plants all apply more or less sophisticated systems that avoid long-term inbreeding. There is no doubt that the same must have been the case for our most recent primate ancestors. If the modern human was really forced to take personal responsibility for what all other animals receive naturally, then we must have lost this inherited ability at some time after our intelligence, morality and culture reached such heights as to enable us to fix this ourselves. In evolutionary terms this sounds like a fairytale.

Because the avoidance of inbreeding is a universal human phenomenon, many researchers assume that this must have some kind of biological basis. Some in fact refer directly to the idea of influence from growing up together. Despite this, however, we still have no generally accepted theory to explain the avoidance of incest among humans. As I understand it, this is because we have been more ready to interpret this behaviour in terms of cultural variation than in terms of its biological motor.

As Pat Bateson was the first to demonstrate, a significant mixing of genes is not always unproblematic because it can alter a successful adaptation to local conditions. On the other hand, the simple matter of physical distance and travel restraints usually send reproduction along a middle path.

That animals generally avoid inbreeding is a natural consequence of natural selection. If close relatives systematically mate with each other, then the risk increases that recessive genes will bring forth birth anomalies and illnesses, which in turn reduce vitality, fertility, competitive ability and the capacity for survival. Individuals with a tendency to avoid sexual congress with their close kin therefore produce stronger offspring. In this way their genes are more easily propagated and their avoidance of inbreeding is spread with them as a genetic quality of the population. In other words, the mechanisms that regulate the avoidance of incest have a strong evolutionary basis.

Among humans we find that a greater mortality rate, in-born sicknesses and mental abnormalities are well-documented consequences of inbreeding. At the first grade of incest, between parents and children or between siblings, the risks of these things increase between 17 and 25 times; between grandparents and grandchildren, and between cousins, the risks are 3 to 5 times increased. The damaging effects of inbreeding are also well known from cultivated plants and domesticated animals, from experiments with mice and fruit flies, as well as from zoological gardens and isolated populations in the wild. After only twenty generations, consistent inbreeding can lead to almost total genetic uniformity. With this disappear the most important requirements for evolutionary adaptation to natural changes in the environment.

The great dynamism of humanity's biological evolution, and our incomparable 'progress' as a species, indicate that the core of our social order is precisely the deep-rooted evolutionary barrier against systematic close in-breeding.

There are examples of animal populations that are so genetically uniform that at some point they must have successfully passed through a narrow genetic bottleneck – in other words that their population must at some time have been small and rather incestuous. Examples include Swedish beavers and wolves, African cheetahs and naked mole rats. Whether they prove to be genetically strong in the long term is a very different question. In the world of the lower animals there are also some examples of non-sexual reproduction, though mostly in connection with very special characteristics or with evolutionarily short-lived species. In general however, systematic inbreeding among animals in undisturbed environments is the exception that proves the rule. Examples of this have rarely been common in undisturbed environments. By far the most common and evolutionarily successful form of sexual reproduction is that which produces a certain degree of genetic diversity. The efficiency of evolution's tried and tested system for avoiding close inbreeding is demonstrated by the scale of genetic diversity within the majority of wild animal populations, for example among lowland gorillas, chimps and lions. Indirectly, it can be seen in the dynamism exhibited by all of biological evolution.

The fact that the outer borders of human beings' blocks against incest vary in different societies, and indeed are sometimes extended beyond biological relations, does not mean that the blocks are in themselves cultural. At the level of the nuclear family there is no cultural variation whatsoever. The animal avoidance of sexual congress between parents and children and between siblings is maintained as an absolute minimum in all human societies regardless of whether formal restrictions exist or not. Against the background of the infinite cultural diversity and complexity that characterises other aspects of human societies, this absolute uniformity removes any doubt that the avoidance of inbreeding within the nuclear family is fundamentally biological.

An old criticism of the inherited, biological avoidance of incest is that no social taboos against it would be required. However, Nancy Thornhill has shown that 56 per cent of 129 societies studied lacked any kind of formal proscriptions against incest within the nuclear family, whereas only 11 per cent lacked restrictions against sexual relations with more biologically distant or culturally constructed 'incest'. This is completely logical. The instinctive barrier against sexual congress between individuals is, for reasons that I shall explain below, strong within the nuclear family but weak outside it. It is only when the biological block against close inbreeding is extended to a broader cultural incest taboo that such restrictions become necessary. The taboo is focused on what is not self-evident.

As I will attempt to demonstrate below, the primary motor for the avoidance of inbreeding is the mental block that arises through physical proximity during childhood. In social terms, however, historical higher cultures and modern societies are too complex for there to be no variation in the strength of these inhibitions, with several consequent departures from the norm. We can also note that formal prohibitions against incest usually occur in more complex societies. The human block against incest within the nuclear family can be seen as fundamentally a social encoding of biologically inherited inhibitions. In this sense it is little different from several other formal expressions of human moral norms such as 'thou shalt not kill', 'thou shalt honour thy father and thy mother' and 'thou shalt not steal'.

Known historic examples of socially accepted incest are so few as to only prove the rule. There are instances from the Inka empire in Peru, ancient Egypt and Persia, and in later times, from Hawaii, Madagascar, Burma and several African kingdoms. Incest in these cases has usually been confined to specific ruling families as a means of ensuring hierarchic dynastic lines, and has had a ritual, formal character. For example, marriage might be allowed only between half-siblings on their father's side who have not grown up together. Above all the few exceptions from the rule have concerned a very tiny part of the population, and in evolutionary terms that are purely temporary. Only a few examples from larger populations are known, such as sibling incest among the scattered Greek peoples of late Hellenistic Egypt. In the latter example this was not so much a question of cultural tradition as a desperate attempt from an isolated and demographically threatened group to preserve their ethnic and cultural identity.

In modern societies incest appears very seldom in the nuclear family as a free choice between adults, and is usually an assault by a man on a younger, dependent female relative. In many cases it is due to psychosocial disturbance on the part of the aggressor or in the family as a whole, and a lack of togetherness during childhood. Statistically and demographically, the instance of incest among mentally and socially well-adjusted people is so low that its instinctive avoidance can be seen to function well even in modern cultures.

It can therefore be seen that human beings' avoidance of close inbreeding is just as fundamentally biologically programmed as it is among animals. It was built into our species' genes long before the time of mammals and its continuance since then has been carefully ensured by natural selection. The only evolutionary development has been that, through our capacity for abstraction and planning and through the spoken word, we have been able to convert this instinct into a social norm and to extend the concept of relationships beyond the nuclear family. This is how the extended, cultural taboo against incest came into being, which is the only thing specifically human in this context. Even though it may well have existed several hundred thousand years ago, it can hardly have been common before the last 10,000 years or so, when agricultural economies and permanent settlement brought with them greater social complexity.

Even now one still comes across explanations of the human incest taboo that rely on Freud's ideas about the Oedipus complex. He suggested that the deepest roots of the inhibition lay in an inherited tendency towards sexual congress between children and parents, and especially between mothers and sons. Freud based these ideas on the misplaced assumption that at an early stage in their evolution humans had lived in an 'animal' condition of incestuous promiscuity. It is hard to imagine a more preposterous starting point for a discussion of the incest problem. Animals are not incestuous, and neither were early humans.

Genetic diversity is maintained through various systems for keeping apart or in some other way preventing closely related individuals from systematically mating with one another. This is the background for the exogamous pattern of reproduction that we encounter in people, primates, other mammals, birds and various lower animals. It is not a problem that most animal males do not 'know' which young females are their daughters: they do not need to. Proximity during early life and exogamy together solve the problem.

The fact that exogamous reproduction is one of two basic evolutionary tools for creating biological diversity and genetic variation among higher animals is not contradicted by the fact that it can assume different forms and have different side effects.

Exogamous reproduction is expressed in the way that animals leave their birth-group at puberty – young males among most mammals and young females among most birds. In the case of monogamous and some polygamous species, both sexes move outside the family or the group.

For long-term biological vitality among wild animals a certain effective minimum population size is required, one in which everyone takes part in reproduction, of the order of at least 500 individuals. Unfortunately we know very little about the size of natural reproductive groups among wild primates in undisturbed environments. As far as humans are concerned, conditions in traditional societies point to 300–500 individuals as an absolute minimum to provide a stable long-term gene pool, and even here we are not speaking of efficient population size. Damaging effects of inbreeding have been observed to spread rapidly among humans in groups of 75–100 individuals.

The influence of early close contact

The question now must be posed as to which mechanisms regulate exogamous reproduction.

As early as 1891, the Finnish sociologist Edward Westermarck had claimed in his famous work *The History of Human Marriage* that the block against incest was based on inherited behaviour, an instinct. On the basis of a cross-cultural study of cultures at differing levels of development, he suggested that this instinct depended upon a mutual resistance to, and lack of interest in, sexual congress. This was activated when small children grew up together and adults lived alongside them, as is usually the case with children, their parents and their siblings in nuclear families. According to Westermarck, this was confirmed by the fact that no human society did not avoid incest, and that the extension of its inhibitions beyond the immediate family to a great extent followed a pattern of proximity in living circumstances.

Westermarck's perceptive analysis was for the most part rejected or toned down, by Freud among others, but at the same time it has never been completely forgotten. Today the idea is treated with considerable respect, and indeed this assumed human instinct to avoid incest is usually termed the 'Westermarck effect'. However, because the same phenomenon is encountered in all the higher animals I would prefer a more neutral and descriptive name, and to speak instead of *imprinting through early close contact*.

Studies of primates in the wild, other mammals and birds all point to the importance of this imprinting. In fact, immediately after birth the young of the higher animals seem to be socially imprinted on almost any individual that is physically present, regardless of their blood relationship, and this is often even extended to other species.

The fact that chimpanzee mothers live physically very close to their children from birth until puberty at 11–12 years lays the foundations for positive relations and a functioning incest barrier between mother and son for the rest of their lives. The strength of this inhibition becomes especially clear when we understand that chimps, to put it mildly, rarely set any limits to their sexual freedom. By contrast we find much less strong sexual inhibitions between fathers and daughters, because adult males do not live so close to their mates and children. This is the opposite of what is found among monogamous and harem-living animals, in which fathers live quite close to their daughters.

Chimpanzees solve the problem through systematic female exogamy. Under undisturbed ecological conditions young females move to another group when they reach puberty. If they do not, then they temporarily sneak away to a neighbouring group for reproduction when they come into oestrous.

When it comes to human beings, there are a great many examples of how proximity in upbringing brings with it unconscious inhibitions against sexual congress within this family unit. However, there are very few more large-scale studies. One well-known example is the work of Joseph Shepher with his study of 2,769 unrelated Israeli men and women, who from childhood had grown up together on different kibbutzes. Despite close friendships and the fact that people often encouraged marriages between them, these individuals avoided each other completely when it came to pair-bonding. No sexual relations were begun. This would all have been highly unlikely if these people had first begun to live together after puberty. The very small number of marriages or cases of mutual sexual interest concerned people who had not lived together before the age of six. Shepher concluded that among humans collective upbringing for a total period of four years, up to and including the age of six, was sufficient to instil an effective barrier against sexual relations.

Another much-discussed example concerns the arranged child weddings that earlier were common in Taiwan, the so-called *Sim-pua* marriages. A female baby was placed with a foster family that had a young boy of similar age, with the intention that the two children would later marry. They grew up together almost as twins. However, as the American anthropologist Arthur Wolf has shown, despite their close friendship the pair often made violent protest when the time for the wedding approached. The marriages were generally unhappy – above averagely so – and not least in sexual terms. A high frequency of infidelity and divorce was observed. A similar conclusion can be drawn from Justine McCabe's study of cousin marriages in a patrilineal society in the Lebanon, where the parents often took the initiative. The children grew up together almost as siblings, and from a very young age. Their marriages resulted in a four times greater rate of divorces and 23 per cent fewer children than normal.

How often do we hear of boys and girls who are inseparable friends from a very young age, matching their families' closeness, but who to everyone's disappointment go their separate ways as marriageable adults? For me the only surprising thing is that anyone is surprised.

A similar pattern can be seen with adopted children, where we see the enormous efficiency of imprinting through early close contact, regardless of the absence of blood kin relationships – but only if they were adopted at a very young age, and if the families function normally in other respects. The same applies to adoption and kidnapping in the animal world. Here, adoption often takes place between close relatives, but when it includes non-kin then its effects are still exactly the same.

An interesting example of inhibitions against sex arising through close contact can be found in the lesbian sexual behaviour of monkeys and apes. Among Japanese macaques, with their male exogamy, the whole group is dominated by the close contacts between kin females in the form of mothers, daughters, sisters, aunts and grandmothers. Despite their very strong social connections, no lesbian activities occur between them. These do occur, however, but exclusively between females with whom they have not been brought up. What makes this so telling is that homosexual behaviour between close relatives does not produce any damaging inbreeding effects, and in this case would not entail any decline in reproduction since the females are at the same time heterosexual.

A dramatic contrast is seen in the liberal lesbianism between all the females in a flock of bonobo chimpanzees. This has its basis in the species' consistent female exogamy, which means that the adult females in their new groups are not affected by the incest inhibitions acquired through upbringing in their original groups.

Just as remarkable is that human homosexual siblings avoid sexual contact with each other to just as great a degree as heterosexual siblings. This is especially true of twins, who tend to be closer than other siblings. They are in fact even more affected by imprinting through early close contact than ordinary siblings. The very few known examples of homosexual relations between twins all concern people who were separated at an early age and did not grow up together.

In combination, all these examples provide ample evidence of the power of these sexual inhibitions that are instilled through a close upbringing.

Another interesting study has been made of a group of American fathers who had committed incest. I was not surprised to read that the majority of them had been away from home for long periods during their daughters' first three years and that they had played little role in bringing them up. Just as unsurprising are the results of a control study of randomly chosen fathers who had not committed incest, which showed that they had lived close to their daughters at an equivalent age. What is especially telling in these instances is that the same results applied both to biological parents, stepfathers and adoptive fathers.

Incest in modern societies is thus primarily committed by stepfathers and fathers who have had little or superficial contact with their daughters when they were small, often in conjunction with mental problems, social disturbance and addiction. A related theme can be traced in the Oedipus myths found all over the world, of which the central motif is precisely the lack of influence from a close upbringing when a child is separated from its parent, with whom it much later commits incest. In my opinion the widespread distribution of the Oedipus story depends less on cultural dissemination than on a disruption of natural patterns of child rearing that occurs not uncommonly in complex societies.

It would be hard to find a more appropriate example of Carl Gustav Jung's idea of the collective unconscious and the archetype than the phenomenon of mental coding through close upbringing.

The avoidance of incest among humans statistically functions best between mothers and sons, next between sisters and brothers, and next between fathers and daughters, exactly following the average degree of close contacts within human child-rearing environments.

In many modern societies the situation is complicated by young girls' attainment of puberty in their early teens, at the same time as the school system keeps them in the home for six or seven more years. This can be compared with low technology societies and historic agrarian communities where girls left the home at puberty, which did not occur until they were 16 or 17 years old. In turn we can relate this to examples of monogamous animals, among which both young males and females leave their parents at puberty.

The instilling of inhibitions against inappropriate sexual relations is thus intimately related to the acquisition of the tools for social interaction and positive behaviour within the family. For obvious reasons this process in practice mostly concerns one's closest relatives, but most significantly it has the same effect on individuals who are not blood kin. This places proximity during childhood right at the centre of our attempts to understand basic social phenomena such as incest, infanticide, aggressive expression, familial altruism, mutual assistance between non-kin as well as true altruism.

Among both humans and mammals we find the 'teddy bear factor' making an important contribution to parental care, in the care of non-kin children and young, and in social codes acquired through close upbringing. Small children's appearance, movements and behaviour are instinctively viewed as 'cute' and awaken protective instincts in adults, older children and youths – primarily within a species but also between them.

The evolutionary expressions of kin selection are usually said to include infanticide, the care of non-kin children, reproductive altruism and warning cries, together with the self-sacrifice and sterility found among social insects. As I shall attempt to demonstrate below, it is possible to find a different explanation for all these things.

Infanticide

In general, male animals treat their offspring well. However, when serious violence occurs against young animals it is in contexts that emphasise the importance of close upbringing for the avoidance of such behaviour, regardless of kinship. The degree of closeness between males and young varies for different species, and sometimes even among different populations of the same species. But even when it is not especially visible it is usually enough to induce inhibitions against violence towards the very young, at least as long as a sense of social safety prevails in the group. It seems that special circumstances are required to unleash lethal force against the young.

Infanticide – the killing of the young – occurs in higher animals primarily but not exclusively among those who follow a flock instinct. Among the primates we find mountain gorillas, certain langurs and colobus monkeys, and some baboons and other monkeys in both the Old and New worlds; among the other mammals we can mention lions, hippos, prairie dogs, certain ground squirrels and many others. Infanticide is also found among certain birds. In many cases it appears in groups with a dominant harem-male who has more or less sole rights to the group's females. The act is usually committed by an outside male who has just joined a group of females with young and established himself as the new flock leader, occasionally in association with other changes in the group's hierarchy. Infanticide is sometimes also perpetrated by females, almost exclusively so among prairie dogs.

The most discussed examples are found among lions and certain Hanuman langurs in India. Groups of the latter are usually formed of a single dominant male who leads a number of females and is often father to their young. The other males are exiled to the periphery of the group, where in a state of unwilling celibacy they rove about in large, rowdy bands. Every third or fourth year such a band drives away the leading harem-male and one of its members takes his place. It is in connection with this, or shortly thereafter, that the new harem-leader tries to kill the young. Despite the females' collective attempts to prevent this, he usually succeeds in killing several. When a female loses an offspring in this way she ceases to produce milk, begins an immediate ovulatory cycle and is soon in heat. The new leader is at once on hand to mate with her.

Following Sarah Blaffer Hrdy's work, several researchers have seen an expression of evolutionary imperative in the behaviour of the new leader male, who according to the theory of kin selection tries to produce more offspring himself at the expense of the other males. The idea is that he kills the suckling young because they are not his kin and to make it possible to breed with their mothers. He is supposed to be so consumed by this evolutionary drive that he sometimes even kills babies born a short while after he has taken control of the flock, because he cannot be their father either. In this way the genes for male infanticidal behaviour would be spread through the population.

There are, however, those who suggest that the catalyst is instead provided by alterations in the surrounding environment, or other disturbances that create social tension or changes in the group structure. Infanticide does not occur in all species with male-controlled harems or even among all kinds of Hanuman langurs, and it is only committed by certain males in certain situations. Many other groups of the same langur species do not live in male-controlled harems with peripheral gangs of frustrated males, but instead in flocks with several males and females. The contrast is striking. The social and sexual atmosphere is more relaxed, the males are less aggressive and visibly more interested in the young, and there is no question of infanticide. The males' inhibitions against the latter have been activated by their close proximity to the mothers and their young.

These difference show that single-male harems with peripheral males in social disharmony are not evolutionarily anchored social orders, but rather a secondary adaptation to disturbances in the natural environment. This statement is supported by Paul Winkler's observation that Hanuman langurs in Rajasthan and southern Nepal apply harem polygamy when the terrain is sufficiently open for a male to easily keep his eye on a group of females. When the vegetation is denser and food resources more dispersed, then the males are not able to maintain and dominate a group of females, which then take the opportunity to mate with several different males.

The exiled langur males do not just live under chronic social stress but also in a state of long-term sexual need. With the females' scent right before them, their unfortunate lot is the spectator's view as they distantly watch the leader-male alone mate with his lovers as they come into heat. The peripheral males are socially disturbed, sexually frustrated and have long lived isolated from the young so that their inhibitions against violence have never been activated. When such a male has managed to establish himself as the new centre of the harem he understands that he is not getting it all handed to him on a plate. Often there are no females in heat, and therefore none that want to have sex with him. And as every male monkey knows, a suckling female is not interested in sex. In other words, the smallest babies become a direct signal to the frustrated male that he should not get up any hopes of sex.

The langur male thus fulfils a number of criteria for child-killers: he is socially frustrated, he is sexually starved, he has the motive, he has the opportunity and he lacks the mental blocks against infanticide that close upbringing would otherwise have given him.

We now understand a little better why it is only breast-feeding babies that are killed, while the slightly older, more independent young are usually spared. If it was only a question of favouring his own genes, then the new leader-male would remove even the older babies, still very dependent on their mothers, and in fact all the young monkeys that were not his. But he rarely does this. By contrast, as we have seen he sometimes kills a baby born soon after he takes over leadership. However, this does not mean that he 'understands' that he is not the father. There is nothing to suggest that primates or other mammals even instinctively understand the connection between copulation and childbirth. The only thing the male realises is that the suckling infant makes it impossible for him to have sex with its mother. Nor does the fact that he does not kill his own offspring when they eventually arrive mean that he 'understands' that he has become a father. Instead it depends on the damping of his social and sexual tensions as a result of living with the females, and because of proximity to his offspring that from birth onwards has instilled a block against harming them.

As I see it, the same primary cause lies behind the male's attempt to take over the leader role as his violence against the youngest infants, namely social stress and a suppressed sex drive in combination with a lack of positive attitudes towards babies acquired through a close upbringing.

A new evaluation of what we know of infanticide among chimpanzees indicates that this behaviour is very uncommon among them. Seen in the context of their extremely carefree sex life this is less surprising. Despite the fact that chimpanzees have been more intensively studied in the wild that any other mammal species, there are only 20 documented cases, of which only 11 were directly observed. In most cases a number of males had attacked a female with young, in one instance the aggressors were a male together with a female and a small baby, and in three cases the killer was the same individual female together with her daughter. There was only one single case where the perpetrator was a lone male. In 10 of the 11 observed cases the baby was also eaten. In at least one of the cases an attacking male was probably the father of the infant. Those who have compiled this data rightly argue that there is nothing to suggest that infanticide among chimpanzees should be evolutionarily steered by kin selection.

We should also ask why a harem-male does not maintain his grip on leadership longer than he usually does, as he is often dethroned before he is old and tired. Again, I believe that the answer lies with proximity during upbringing. After several years – a different number for different species depending on how quickly the young reach puberty – the male has too few mature females around him with whom he does not share blocks against sex due to being close to them while they grew up. Through this he has lost most of the drive that once compelled him to assert his sexual monopoly, and he more easily gives up when other males try to take over.

In the same way, the fact that monogamous males among gibbons and certain monkeys, as well as many polygamous males, behave like the fathers they are to the infants around them, rather than killing them instead, has nothing to do with any instinct that tells them this is the case. The explanation is that being around while babies grow up has an especially strong prohibiting effect on fathers.

Among North American black-tailed prairie dogs – a kind of herd-living squirrel that lives in deep tunnels – up to 40 per cent of infants die through infanticide. This occurs when the mother is away on some errand leaving the young behind in their underground home. The killers are most often females, and in fact usually close relatives in the form of aunts, grandmothers or elder sisters, often themselves breast-feeding mothers of small babies. But as soon as the young have made it up to ground level the previously murderous females are suddenly transformed into considerate proxy mothers, who whole-heartedly participate in a collective and tender nursing of all the infants in the group, even those they had recently tried to kill. Males too can commit infanticide, and can then also kill their own offspring.

As the great student of prairie dogs John Hoogland has noted, this killing of babies by their close relatives sits very poorly with the hypothesis of kin selection. It is hard to say what really triggers this behaviour, especially as it does not occur among Gunnison's prairie dogs that have roughly the same social order. The probable answer is some form of stress. But the fact that close kin do not restrain themselves from killing, as the kin selection theory would suppose, suggests that only the mothers are inhibited by their close relation-ship with the young during their first six weeks when they are isolated in their dark underground burrow. The fact that no infants are killed in daylight suggests in turn that these blocks in adult individuals are primarily triggered by visual impressions, probably with the care-related 'teddy bear' effect as an active element. The black-tailed prairie dog's infanticide behaviour is a striking example of higher animals' inability to distinguish biological relatives through genetic signals, and to positively discriminate in favour of relatives that they are not familiar with through early close contact.

The fact that most males of most species do not commit infanticide also shows that this is not evolutionarily deep-rooted behaviour. It should be self-evident that a reproductive strategy based on each male bearing an inherited tendency to kill other males' offspring would be evolutionary insanity. New studies of what we know about infanticide among lions, chimpanzees, Hanu-man langurs and other primates incidentally indicate that such behaviour is nowhere near as common as was once believed, and that its evolutionary foundation is doubtful. The idea that infanticide should reflect an evolution-ary drive to increase the success of one's own genes assumes first that males can identify their own offspring and assess the degree of relationship to others' infants, through the use of genetic markers or by genetic self-reflection. As we have seen there is no evidence for this.

There is much to say for the idea that infanticide primarily reflects social and sexual frustration in combination with weak blocking mechanisms against violence towards the young, caused by lack of early close contact. This behaviour is more an expression of an evolutionary system that normally mitigates against infanticide but that has now become unbalanced.

The connection between infanticide and weakened imprinting from early close contact is also suggested by the fact that this is more common among male harems than in groups where several males and females live together, or among monogamous animals. Similarly infanticide and incest in humans is more common among fathers who have frequently been absent from the home than among those who have stayed, more common among step- and adoptive fathers who have had contact with the child only after its youngest years than among those who have been there from birth, and so on. It is very clear in fact that infanticide among people is dominated by the same general categories as among primates and other animals: the socially frustrated, or step-parents newly arrived on the scene (especially stepfathers), and biological fathers who are seldom to hand.

This relationship has led some scholars to suggest, working from the theory of kin selection, that to some extent stepfathers might be genetically pre-destined to kill their stepchildren. Even though the kin selection thesis has inspired some pretty peculiar ideas in the past, it is truly astonishing to see the degree of respect with which this notion has been received. It is true that stepfathers – seen statistically and with all margins of social and economic error included – more often commit infanticide than blood-kin fathers. However, this does not depend on inherited behaviour through kin selection but rather on the fact that stepfathers on average have less early close contact with their stepchildren than biological fathers have with theirs.

Early close contact thus works at the level of the individual. A male who is inhibited from violence against a particular infant may still assault another with whom he has not had early close contact. As violence is a part of the nature of infanticide, and to some extent of incest too, it is not surprising to find that male sexuality and aggression both seem to be controlled by the same part of the brain.

When infants from an early age live close to each other and to adults, then this creates instinctive feelings of personal connection that improve social co-operation and provide blocks against incest and serious violence. Normally those involved are closely related, but the system functions just as well if they are not.

Caring for the young of others

For birds the nest often functions as a signal of blood relations. Among many species adult birds feed any young that happen to be in the nest. Parents can ignore one of their own chicks that has moved outside the edge of the nest and at the same time feed a foreign chick that has been placed inside it. A female herring gull will take care of any chick of the same species that happens to be in her nest, so long as it is not more than one or two days old. Immediately after birth chicks can attach themselves to any adult. At the same time a female can attack and eat a chick in a neighbouring nest, so long as it is older than one or two days. Social imprinting is here triggered solely by close contact and not by any biological signal of kinship.

DNA analysis has shown that many socially monogamous and harem animals can be fairly loose living, not least birds. Among magpies, sand martins, black and white flycatchers and coal tits up to a quarter of young in the nest can be fathered by a male other than the nest-parent, and for certain other birds the proportion is up to three quarters. In one group of North American tree swallows 70 per cent of all nests contained at least one chick fathered by a different male, at least half of all chicks were 'illegitimate', and almost 20 per cent of nests contained *only* such young. The observers noted with surprise that paternity questions did not seem to worry the fathers, who gave full parental care to all the chicks. They also noted that this went against the idea of kin selection.

Cuckoos and other parasitical birds lay eggs in nests that belong to other species. There are also species where the female either moves her egg to a nest that belongs to another pair of the same species, or secretly lays it there. A female starling can be so infernal as to even move another pair's egg onto the ground so as to deposit her own egg in their nest. For different groups of swallows and starlings it is calculated that respectively 3–31 per cent and 5–46 per cent of nests are visited in this way. Following the theory of kin selection this has been interpreted as the female favouring her genes by secretly mating with a more attractive male who can give her more attractive chicks. A common response is that examples like this do not shake the idea of kin selection because only a minority of the infants, litters or parental couples are affected on average. The majority are assumed to follow the dictates of kin selection. There is also an eloquent silence as to what could be the genetic profit for the male.

In fact the deviation from the principles of kin selection is systematic. Every male who happens to have a partner with young fathered by other males, and every couple who find their infants exchanged for those of others, continue to feed and care for the foreign young as if they were their own, unknowingly investing their own genetic capital in others' genes. As soon as an individual is tested, it reacts completely against the grain of kin selection. If the latter were real then the foreign chicks would be abandoned, thrown out, killed or left to starve. This does not happen. At most one can detect a marginally higher commitment from fathers to chicks that they have fathered themselves, but this can be explained by their interest in the mothers. The prime mover for infanticide of non-kin infants – non-existent or weak influence through early close contact in combination with social disturbance – is very rare among socially monogamous animals. Thus there is in these birds a total lack of ability to judge what is 'reproductively profitable' or not, and there is a telling absence of positive discrimination based on direct or indirect genetic signals of kinship.

The so-called reproductive care of non-kin young can only be understood in the light of proximity during upbringing and its ability to prompt positive discrimination independent of biological relations. This behaviour power-fully demonstrates that kin selection is not the fundamental evolutionary mechanism that it is usually assumed to be. But this does not just concern birds. The same picture is found throughout the higher animal world where secret mating occurs, not least among humans.

Reproductive altruism and warning cries

If they have failed to find a mate, young birds – usually males – often choose to help their parents with their new chicks. This is called reproductive altruism and is known from more than 300 species of birds, 120 mammals and some fishes. It is usually explained by saying that the helper is improving its own genetic success via its siblings, so that helping behaviour is spread in the group in accordance with the pattern of kin selection. However, some researchers do not see reproductive assistance as an expression of kin selection but more as a natural consequence of parental instincts, or as an attempt to increase the parents' social prestige in a way that helps their own chances of mating.

In line with the notion of imprinting through early close contact, I see the matter as follows. While the young female bird instinctively leaves the nest for good, the young male tries to establish himself close by his parents. If he fails due to a lack of potential partners or viable territory then he sticks to his parents. His parental tendencies will then naturally be directed towards his parents' newly hatched chicks, which are his full siblings in a second litter, or as a consequence of his mother's secret mating, his half-siblings.

In other words we do not have to assume some special selection of genes for kin-directed altruism in order to evolutionarily explain reproductive helping behaviour. It is sufficient with selection for social influence through early close contact, and with parental instincts.

Group-living animals' watching behaviour and warning cries against predators are also often cited as examples of kin selection. As kinship within the group is often great, the warning animal is seen as reaping a genetic profit even at the cost of its own life. This behaviour would thus be continued evolutionarily through kin selection. Now this interpretation is more and more being called into question. Following critical surveys of research in this field and new field studies, it seems more likely that there are more advant-ages than disadvantages in giving warning cries, and that this behaviour is, shortsightedly, simply selfish.

My own opinion is that the immediate mechanism behind warning cries in group-living animals is a combination of influence through early close contact and parental instincts. The overarching evolutionary mechanism is not then genetic selection for warning biological kin, but for warning those to whom the animal has been positively bonded through early close contact, and which are frequently also its relatives.

Colony insects

It is not easy to provide a collective overview of the maintenance of genetic variation among fishes, reptiles, spiders and insects, beyond what the chance distribution of other creatures, wind and water can achieve. The question is complex and insufficiently understood, and must remain unanswered here.

Let us therefore confine ourselves to the social insects, that is to say most bees and wasps, together with all ants and termites. These comprise a well-researched group with a fairly clear and uniform social pattern, and they are often put forward as such a good example of kin selection that they are actually recommended as an object of study for those who want to evolutionarily understand human behaviour.

Because social insects closely collaborate within the nest, researchers fixated with the theory of kin selection have long taken for granted that genetic uniformity within the colony must be almost total. We now know that this is not the case, and that it is not unusual to find several unrelated queens in the same nest, especially among ants. DNA analyses have also shown that queens of, for example, honey bees and dwarf honey bees, copulate with several males during their mating flights. The genetic uniformity within the nest is therefore not as great as was once thought; for dwarf honey bees it is as low as around 30 per cent.

The striking thing is that this genetic variation does not seem to lead to competition, aggression and nepotism within the nest, as the theory of kin selection would predict. But instead of sensibly questioning the theoretical starting point, the theory of kin selection, researchers have tried to explain the facts away. The absence of internal competition and aggression is said to improve the colony's reproduction, or to make it more collectively competitive, or to depend on the difficulty for the insects to detect such small genetic differences when there are so very many of them in the nest. That these explanations are inconsistent with the thesis of kin selection is ignored.

The fact that the helping behaviour of sterile workers and other positive discrimination among social insects does not vary according to the degree of kinship within the colony is a direct challenge to the theory of kin selection. However, it fits very well indeed with the idea that all the inhabitants of the nest have been imprinted on the same collective identity of scent that compels them to act as an indivisible social unit.

The collective scent that steers the social order of colony insects can take different forms. It can derive from the hive itself – from the childhood nest in the case of honeybees – from a collective diet in infancy, or from the queen. To the extent that genetic components are included, as with certain kinds of ants, it is nevertheless a collective scent.

Something similar seems to operate with the African naked mole rats, which in their underground colonies apply a social division of work that is unique among mammals and is reminiscent of the system practised by social insects. Reproduction is usually delegated to a dominant pair, while the sexuality of other females is hormonally suppressed. A collective scent in the burrow serves as a means of social identification. It is true that genetic variation within the colony is small, but just as with colony insects what little there is does not bring with it any positive discrimination. Even here it is clear that the collective scent of the burrow as experienced by all its inhabitants during infancy instils blocks against incest and for positive discrimination.

When a worker bee defends the group against an intruder, her barbed sting fastens in her adversary and she dies. With reference to the considerable genetic kinship in the nest, this 'unselfish' kamikaze behaviour has been seen as the ultimate proof of kin selection. In the same context are sometimes mentioned certain kinds of African worker ants who can literally blow themselves up to defend their communities. It is certainly true that the defender's kin are served if attackers are halted, and it does not really matter if a few individuals who in any case cannot reproduce die in the process, as long as they are not too numerous. Nevertheless, this has nothing to do with kin selection. Instead it concerns the selection of genes for helping behaviour towards all those who have come to share an identification scent with the helper through the influence of early close contact.

According to the kin selection theory, drones and helpers among ants, bees and wasps – who are most frequently female – are often sterile in order to wholeheartedly assist the queen in producing and raising their siblings with whom they are genetically identical. But their sterility and the fact that their sexuality is hormonally suppressed can have other evolutionary, functional or ecological causes, just as with non-dominant individuals among social mammals such as wolves, wild dogs, naked mole rats and small rodents. Their helping behaviour and group defence need not mean anything other than that they have instincts to protect and care for an offspring with whom they feel affinity through early close contact or a collective identification scent – regardless of kinship. That the latter is also true for social insects has been shown by experiment, when two newly hatched litters of ants from different colonies were mixed with each other. After a few months their different identification scents had been combined in a collective smell. The aggression that the two unrelated groups would otherwise have shown each other when they reached adulthood was thereby replaced by a mutual affinity, just as if they had been close kin.

All this indicates that helping behaviour among social insects is not an evolutionary expression for direct kin selection, but a combination of selection for parental care and for positive discrimination through early close contact, which is in turn primarily maintained through selection for genetic variation.

Collective imprinting among social insects therefore has the same basic function as individual imprinting among higher animals: to create blocks against inbreeding and to identify one's closest allies. The problem is that collective identification scents preclude alliances between the members of different colonies, and thereby between individuals who are not close kin. In order for out-breeding to function as the long-term continuance of the line demands, the females send out pheromones – chemical mating signals – that temporarily mask the collective scents that would normally block congress between non-kin. What makes them leave the colony to meet male sex partners is that the collective scent of the nest has also given them blocks against sex with the males in their own nest, with whom they are often, though not always, kin.

One can understand researchers' interest in colony insects. They are easy to observe, they reproduce rapidly and they have an advanced division of labour. But they mostly lack social life outside the immediate family, even though the latter may be very large. In this they stand far apart from the social complexity that we encounter in mammals and birds, with their permanent partnership between non-kin individuals. The value that social insects are often accorded as evolutionary models for higher animals and humans has therefore been exaggerated.

Among many non-social insects and spiders a complex social interaction is even more remote. Imagine that you are a praying mantis or a certain spider of the male sex. The only time you are not open-season prey for the ladies is the short moment when you fulfil your reproductive duties, if even then. You hardly finish your careful lovemaking to ensure the survival of the species before you are attacked and eaten by your Lady Macbeth, and at best stored up as nourishment for the children that you have just helped to conceive. There are times when one is glad to be a mammal!

Parenting

No doubt the evolution of parental care and instinct is connected with the fact that parents who tend to more actively assist their offspring in turn have children who are better able to fend for themselves. But this does not mean, as has sometimes been claimed, that the instinct for parental care is a result of kin selection. That this is not the case is demonstrated among higher animals by the consistent displays of parenting shown even to those infants fathered by others and to those who are not blood kin at all. Parental behaviour is instead primarily based upon an instinct for the care of small infants, strengthened by hormonal processes in connection with pregnancy, birth, weaning, egg-laying, living environment and similar factors, as well through imprinting received through early close contact.

Positive social behaviour among the siblings in a litter gives the infants a better chance of surviving and later reproducing than mutual aggression would provide. All this is instilled in them by their close contact at an early age. The system works just as well, however, if the infants are not related either with each other or their carers, which is quite often the case among higher animals, not least birds. Without mechanisms such as these then all kindergarten life in the animal world would be a nightmare – assuming there would even have been any higher animals at all. Individual influence through early close contact is also a core concept for the parental care that is a fundamental part of mammalian and bird reproduction.

Inbreeding is avoided and social discrimination is regulated primarily through the influence of early close contact, a mechanism under genetic control. Among mammals and birds this imprinting is individual, while among social insects and naked mole rats it is collective and functions through a uniform scent in the nest. In the latter case this creates blocks against sex and in favour of positive relations within the nest that is usually characterised by a high degree of internal kinship. The influence is nevertheless just as strong regardless of kinship. Blocks against sex within the collective force mating females to leave the nest in order to pair with males who possess a different scent – a temporary exogamy. The influence of this collective scent also leads to negative social relations between the inhabitants of different colonies, which are characterised by different scents and which are also not kin-related. The system often makes complex social life impossible between non-kin, at least in the form of permanent co-existence.

The fact that positive relations induced between individuals through early close contact do not primarily operate through scents means that there are no blocks against good relations between those who have *not* been subject to such influence. Among mammals and birds this leads to permanent exogamy and complex social life in the form of flocks and couples of individuals who are not close kin. The system assumes the ability to rapidly and confidently distinguish between many different individuals.

The different forms of exogamy do not therefore appear to be inherited in themselves, but instead to be functional expressions of an inherited barrier against inbreeding that is triggered by early close contact. The fact that this occurs among such evolutionarily distinct groups such as mammals, birds and social insects indicates that this mechanism is of great antiquity. Whether it emerged in one or several evolutionary contexts is, however, a different question. Among humans everything suggests that the earliest parts of the brain regulate imprinting through early close contact.

The active tool that steered the evolution of individual imprinting through early close contact was probably the positive selective potential inherent in social herd life. In human terms this concerns relations between non-kin individuals that we call sympathy, love friendship, empathy, true unselfishness, gratitude, a bad conscience, a sense of justice and so on. The primal evolutionary code for social complexity as it works outside our family circle – even between species – is thus not kin selection. It is individual imprinting through early close contact.

If genetic selfishness has not evolved through kin selection, how then can we explain the self-centred and selfish behaviour that is so common among animals and humans?

The theory of kin selection has so one-sidedly emphasised reproductive success as the basic motor for social life that other kinds of evolutionary selection have been overlooked. For reproductive success many different levels of selection are required: for sexual drive, for escape behaviour, for aggression, for appetite, for sleep, for genetic diversity and so on. Self-centred behaviour to satisfy hunger and sexual need, just like behaviour for flight, defence, watchfulness, caution, social assertion and submission, is naturally decisive for successful survival. No one can eat, mate, escape or hide through someone else's effort. Survival in an uncertain world assumes in other words a continuous selection for instinctive self-focus, that allows the individual to take responsibility for its own sustenance, its own protection, its own social assertion and its own reproduction.

Reproductive success demands, as Fisher showed, a strong focus on oneself, but not through kin selection. Instead it is achieved through evolution for successful survival and for the care of the young. The other side of the coin is the selfishness we encounter everywhere among animals and humans, both within and between species.

How then can we explain nepotism, 'genetic selfishness' through the preference of close kin, without kin selection?

The answer is that nepotism emerges when the evolutionarily deep-seated egocentricism – or self-preservation in a broad sense – is transferred to kin through the influence of early close contact. Human selfishness is therefore not of the evolutionarily unconditional nature that the theory of kin selection assumes. First, individual imprinting through early close contact also leaves room for behaviour that is not strictly genetically selfish – it can even be unselfish in the true sense of the word. Second, social group life among non-kin has also evolved mechanisms to keep self-interest within levels that the group can tolerate.

Despite this, evolution's need for selfishness is so strong that altruism does not function as a long-term evolutionary strategy – something sadly demonstrated by human affairs above all. Even if true altruism fortunately raises its head quite often, it has difficulties in establishing itself as a dominant human quality.

In the 1970s Wilson, Lumsden, Dawkins, Mayr and others tried to quieten those who would see human morality overshadowed by the evolutionarily unconditional selfishness that the theory of kin selection preached. They argued that human beings had somehow undergone a combined evolution of genes, intelligence and culture that placed us outside the pattern common for other animals, which has left some room for genuine social altruism. As I have shown, this argument is neither correct nor necessary. There *is* no overarching theoretical obstacle for the evolutionary emergence of social altruism among higher animals. The barrier lies in a lack of cognitive ability. It is only by coming to this conclusion that we can have a meaningful discussion about when and how human altruism and morality evolved. Some higher animals with considerable intelligence – such as apes, elephants and certain toothed whales – are also capable of an elementary empathy and selflessness. I assume that early humans possessed at least equal capacities in this respect as modern apes.

The key to understanding true human altruism is not that we were provided with special genes for it at some time during our evolution, but with a level of consciousness that includes a certain ability to contemplate other's needs and emotions. The ultimate precondition for this was the emergence of mechanisms for recognising individuals, perhaps several hundred million years ago. It is possible that even our last primate ancestors had reached a stage that permitted rudimentary empathy and altruism to come through, though balanced then by a measure of newly emerged reflective egoism. The next step may have coincided with the noticeable increase of intelligence in early *Homo* around two million years ago. Our present level ought to have been attained by modern humans approximately 200,000 years ago.

It is not our intelligence and culture that are in themselves the fundament of our morality, but rather our inheritance as group animals together with our ability to formulate moral codes and to make conscious decisions with moral consequences. Unfortunately, the same tools allow us to make consciously immoral choices. The ability for considered reflection is also the basis of genuine immorality, which in a rather embarrassing way separates us from most other creatures. Even if we can free ourselves from kin selection's intellectual straitjacket in which selfless behaviour is an evolutionary impossibility, this gives us no reason for moral rectitude. What we have gained on the swings we have partly lost on the roundabouts.

How did it come about that the theory of kin selection could have so greatly obscured the importance of individual imprinting through early close contact? As I see it, this is because the imagined social effects of kin selection are so similar to the actual effects of early close contact. Once the mistake was made the theory of kin selection was promoted in such eloquent terms that the centrality of imprinting through early close contact came to be overshadowed.

As the kin selection idea became accepted, so the notion of group selection was laid almost completely aside in favour of the evolutionary selection at the level of individual genes. Even Hamilton himself warned in 1975 of such a narrow viewpoint. Without questioning the theory of kin selection, some researchers such as David Sloan Wilson, Steven Rose and Christopher Boehm have suggested that selection more likely operates at a number of different levels in combination, from the individual's collected genetic make-up to large social groups, views that have gradually become more topical in the last decade. The insight that the theory of kin selection is essentially nothing but a construction could push this discussion much further.

The criticism of classic sociobiology for giving expression to a cynical and implacable genetic fundamentalism can thus be seen to be self-generated and at the same time unjustified. We do not need to assume kin selection in order to take a sociobiological perspective towards animals and humans.

Basic human social structure

Wilson and Dawkin's hypothesis, which argued that true altruism is a product of a unique combination of biological and cultural evolution, was mostly an attempt to divert critique of kin selection theory, according to which this kind of behaviour in principle ought not to exist. Today we find a more fruitful line of enquiry as to how basic human social behaviour can be understood in evolutionary terms: through comparative, often cross-cultural, empirical studies of social behaviour among humans and primates.

The seeds of human social morality were sown several tens of millions of years ago in connection with our primate ancestors' evolution of the social herd instinct. It is possible that this had certain evolutionary advantages, such as improved defence against enemies. Because herding behaviour cannot function without reasonable social stability, it demands a degree of ranking that is regulated through behaviour for dominance and submission. But herd life requires at the same time some functional norms for mutual assistance to balance the self-centredness necessary for successful evolutionary survival and reproduction. In this way the herd instinct appears central to the evolution of human social co-operation, solidarity, tolerance and altruism towards people outside one's immediate kin.

Fundamental social behaviour in humans thus ultimately rests on evolutionary mechanisms that simultaneously promote both egoism and altruism.

All human societies thus possess a basic social structure which, if not immediately biological, is nevertheless deeply biologically anchored. Notwithstanding cultural diversity in all its richness, there are limits to the variability of human behaviour. Our bodily, physiological and intellectual functions, our means of surviving, reproducing, communicating, reacting and organising ourselves, our behaviour as individuals and in groups – all of this shows repeating patterns and structures. They do not dictate what we do, think or feel in specific instances, but they make a very visible mark on the whole.

Finally, I can summarise some of evolution's basic components that contribute to the shaping of humans' daily environment and society both large and small. Through complex internal combination they also form the basis of human culture and for our social and cultural diversity.

Anatomy and physiology provide the prerequisites and the limits for our physical functions and needs, and therefore for all essential cultural evolution. Brain and psyche give all people a comparatively equal platform for reacting, thinking and functioning, both individually and collectively. This includes a certain variation between the sexes and a similar basic structure for all languages.

Our daily rhythm of mostly daytime activity and nighttime sleep sets a primary stamp on all human life. The bodily cycle and hunger prompt us to find food and hunt game. Even if people today are mostly wage-earners who buy their food, our daily schedule and social life is still regulated by a cycle that requires us to devote most of our time to financing, obtaining, preparing and consuming it.

The evolutionary need for self-preservation is the fixed evolutionary root of selfish behaviour and, in combination with imprinting through early close contact, for nepotism. It reaches deep into all aspects of life, from the daily round to politics. The sexual drive guarantees the continuance of the species, and has a direct and indirect effect on social relations between men, between women, and between the sexes, and through this it affects all social organisation. Our instinct for infant care ensures that reproduction is followed through. Together with weaning, the care of children, the early close contact factor and sexual drive, it is a vital steering mechanism for family structure and kinship ties, centring on mothers and parental couples. It is thereby central for basic social order. The 'teddy bear factor' also comes in here – the way in which appearance, movement and behaviour in infants triggers caring instincts in adults and adolescents, mainly within but also between species.

Individual imprinting through early close contact counteracts human inbreeding by instilling a block against incestuous sexual congress. It is also the primary tool in identifying biological close kin and for positive social interaction with them. Together with the herd instinct it is the basis of mutual cooperation and altruism towards non-kin. Via exogamous breeding, kin-based grouping and alliance systems it places kinship at the centre of human communal structure. At a micro level it steers aggression and violence away from close kin. At the same time it permits collective living outside the nuclear family between individuals and groups who are not kin, and it allows mutual social collaboration in the form of social and reproductive altruism.

The herd instinct's mechanisms for positive cooperation and competition through domination and submission, along with its suspicion of strangers, are fundamental for human group formation. This is true at a micro level but also, according to the capacity of available contact systems, at the macro level of society itself.

3

NEXT OF KIN

Present day apes

Even a few decades ago, the evolutionary line between humans and apes was drawn as far back as 20–25 million years. Since the 1970s, however, bio-molecular research has closed the gap to our chimpanzee cousins to between 5 and 7 million years. We stand between 7 and 10 million years from our second cousins the gorillas, and 10 to 13 million years from our third cousins the orang-utans, while some 20 million years separates us from the gibbons.

At the same time there has been critique of the methods by which biomolecular change is reckoned. For example, the Lund geneticist Ulfur Arnarsson has argued that these depend on far too limited comparative data with other animals. According to his data, humans and chimpanzees went their separate ways as long ago as 13 million years. For the moment, however, I shall follow the current oldest secure dating of probably bipedal early humans, to approximately 6 million years ago. It is still too early to say whether these really are the remains of our earliest bipedal ancestors.

Chimpanzees that once lived in a large part of the African rain forest belt exist today only in small areas of it, and in some places also in a wooded savannah environment. They belong to two main species, the ordinary chimpanzee *Pan troglodytes* and the bonobo or pygmy chimpanzee, *Pan paniscus*. The common chimp is the most widespread and is found in four sub-species: *Pan t. schweinfurtii* in Central Africa, *Pan t. troglodytes* in central West Africa, *Pan t. vellerosus* in Nigeria and *Pan t. verus* in western West Africa. The bonobo is found only in a limited area south of the Congo River in eastern Congo. Although DNA analyses show clear variation between the four sub-species of common chimpanzees, and despite the fact that *verus* has been isolated from the others for up to 1.5 million years, the differences in both their appearance and social behaviour are very small.

When I write in this book of 'common chimpanzees' I mean all the sub-species of *troglodytes*. By 'chimpanzees' in general, I mean both the common chimps and the bonobos.

The bonobos have apparently lived in isolation from the common chimps for 2.1 million years. They are only slightly smaller than the common chimpanzees, but they differ in terms of a slimmer body form, smaller head and ears, different hair growth, a darker colour, a small tuft of hair on their buttocks, a lighter voice, smaller teeth, more curving fingers, shorter lower legs and arms, and longer upper legs and arms. Their social, sexual and cultural behaviour also varies slightly from those of the common chimpanzee.

There are two main species of gorillas: the common lowland gorilla in two sub-species, *Gorilla gorilla gorilla* in western Central Africa and *Gorilla gorilla graueri* in mid-Central Africa, and the mountain gorilla, *Gorilla gorilla beringei* that lives in the forested mountain border country between Congo, Rwanda and Uganda in eastern Central Africa. The mountain gorilla is somewhat larger and has more close-knit, darker fur than its lowland cousin. As far as we know the different gorilla types have also been separated for a long time.

The orang-utan, *Pongo pygmaeus*, now only exists on Borneo and in a limited area of northwest Sumatra. DNA studies have shown that these groups have also lived apart from one another for several million years. Different species of gibbon such as the siamang, lar and holok, all from the family of *Hylobates* which was once common all over Southeast Asia, are now very much reduced in distribution.

The four species of great apes – common chimpanzees, bonobos, gorillas and orang-utans – each exhibit their special similarities with human beings. But among them, the two chimpanzees are without doubt closest to us in terms of their collective anatomical, physiological, biomolecular, genetic and behavioural likeness.

When it comes to their form and skeleton, humans and apes can seem very different – but appearances can be deceptive. Even if we humans have an extra chromosome and a slightly different chromosome packaging in our genes, the similarities are considerable, in genetic terms very considerable indeed. It is especially striking what close correspondences can be seen at the biomolecular level in terms of DNA structures, amino acid sequences, haemoglobin, blood groups, chromosomes and similar. The amino acid sequences for six proteins are identical for humans and chimpanzees, and for 44 other proteins the differences are not above 0.8 per cent. Of 1,271 amino acids we share 1,266 with the chimpanzees. The immune system and blood groups A and O are sufficiently similar to at least theoretically carry out organ transplants and blood transfusions between the two species. The genetic correspondence between humans and chimps as expressed through DNA hybridisation has long since been estimated to be 98.4 per cent, between humans and gorillas 97.7 per cent and between humans and orang-utans 95 per cent. However, revised calculations have recently arrived at a rather lower level of genetic correspondence between humans and chimpanzees, at around 95per cent. If this is correct then the figures for the other apes should also be adjusted downwards.

On the other hand we know very little about the small portion of DNA that accounts for the great differences that actually make us human. There is much still to be done before we can answer all the questions about genetic comparisons between ourselves and the apes. Few systematic studies have been carried out so far, but some exciting surprises are almost certainly in store in the coming years.

It would be a serious mistake to view the apes as comical shadows from a distant past that no longer concerns us. The molecular links between humans and chimpanzees are so close that some researchers have followed Jared Diamond in suggesting that they should be counted as part of the same species. In which case it is not the gorilla who is the chimpanzee's closest relative, but you, dear reader. It is not too much of an exaggeration to see human beings as de-furred, upright apes on the loose, albeit heftily upgraded in the brain department and spruced up with a bit of anatomical cosmetics.

Because we have no fossil remains of chimpanzees' ancestors, we know very little of their evolution as a species after we went our separate ways. But since they seem to have lived in essentially the same environment all the time, they have probably not been subjected to any particular evolutionary pressure. This is also supported by the fact that the anatomical and behavioural differences between West and East African chimpanzees are so small despite their long separation. The bonobos have on the other hand evolved more specific characteristics.

All common chimpanzees, regardless of small variations in environment and cultural traits, exhibit very similar social behaviour, even in the details. This suggests that it is of great age and probably biologically inherited at least in its essentials. When we add the great biomolecular, physiological, anatomical and to some extent behavioural similarities between chimpanzees and humans – and the even greater anatomical correspondence between chimps and early humans – then there are good grounds for suggesting that our last quadruped ancestors were apes of a kind very close to modern chimpanzees.

Chimpanzees and bonobos therefore appear to be the animal kingdom's best objects of comparison for the study of human evolution and universal human behaviour. Apes are not people by any means, but to look into their world is like peering at our own reflections in the ruffled surface of a pool.

Our last quadruped ancestors

We do not know exactly what the environment was like just before the earliest humans' family tree branched off from that of the great apes at the end of the Miocene. But we know that there were enormous primeval forests in eastern, northern and southern Africa that were perfect for apes. The same is true of southern Europe. There is no doubt, however, as to where the cradle of humanity lay. Only in Africa have finds been made that are more than three times older than in Asia and Europe. In addition, our closest relatives the chimpanzees and gorillas are known only from Africa. Its north-eastern regions and the Horn of Africa have in particular been seen as the home of the human race.

If the split from the apes' family tree occurred about 6 million years ago, then more than two thirds of our bipedal ancestors have lived in Africa. But there is more. As modern humans seem to have migrated out of Africa as late as 100,000 years ago, then 98 per cent of the ancestors of all modern humans north of the Sahara were Africans – regardless of whether we today are brown, black, yellow, red or white.

The oldest known monkeys have at least 60 million years on the clock; the Old World monkeys are 40–50 million years old, and those of the New World around 25 million years. The family of apes can be traced at least 20 million years into the past. The Miocene was their time, with over 30 different species in existence. Between 15 and 10 million years ago there were also several species of apes in southern Europe and Asia, among them *Oreopithecus*, the probable ancestor of orang-utans and gibbons. Because we have so few fossil finds from the late Miocene it is hard to put forward a definite candidate for the last collective ancestor of chimpanzees and humans. A possible nominee is *Morotopithecus* in East Africa about 20 million years ago, well suited to a life in the trees. More recent finds have also revived the claims of the 14 million-year-old *Kenyapithecus* as a possible younger ancestor of chimps and gorillas, and by extension of humans too.

A different picture has been painted by Caro-Beth Stewart and Todd Disotell. Having combined the results of DNA studies on modern apes with data from the fossils of Miocene apes in Africa, Europe and Asia, they claim that *Oreopithecus* has more in common with chimpanzees and gorillas than the known African Miocene apes do. They therefore suggest that at least one ape left Africa 18–20 million years ago, from which the European and Asian apes descend. They go on to argue that one of these, a branch of *Oreopithecus* or one of its relatives, returned to Africa 10 million years ago to become the ancestor of gorillas, chimpanzees and humans. But to really answer the question of our last quadruped ancestors we quite simply need more and better fossil discoveries from this period.

Between 1872 and 1958 near Monte Bamboli in central Italian Tuscany, hundreds of fragments and an almost complete skeleton of *Oreopithecus bamboli* were discovered. In their analyses of the finds, Meike Köhler and Salvador Moyà-Solà from Barcelona have reached the surprising conclusion that it walked completely upright. It was a 110 centimetres tall, 30-kilo bipedal ape that lived 8.5 to 6.5 million years ago. Its S-form curved spine, long thigh-bones and straight knees are very typical for a bipedal posture. On the basis of the hipbones other researchers have reached the same conclusion. Even *bamboli*'s pelvis, knees and feet look more like those of early bipedal humans in East Africa than those of an ape.

The big toe is very strange, sticking out at right angles from the others rather like a bird's. It must have given this bipedal ape excellent stability so long as it kept still, but at the same time a slow and strutting walk. According to Köhler and Moyà-Solà this was not initially a problem since *bamboli* lived on a great island that was left when the Mediterranean rose dramatically 8.5 million years ago, an island that was too small to long sustain larger predators. But as soon as the island rejoined the mainland 2 million years later, it was invaded by new ones. With its slow walk and its deselected escape instincts, *bamboli* was easy prey for creatures such as the sabre-toothed tiger and bear, and it was soon extinct. The same fate also befell other animals that evolution had specially adapted for this particular environment.

There are thus no indications that *Oreopithecus bamboli* had any descendents or that it had any evolutionary connection with the bipedal hominids that were emerging in East Africa at about the same time. Everything suggests that *bamboli* was a dead-end variant of the ancestors of modern east Asiatic apes. This makes it no less remarkable that two different apes in utterly separate places, independent of each other and with partly different results, simultaneously evolved into bipedal ape-people.

Based on what we currently know of modern African apes and fossil finds of earlier ones, we can draw a few conclusions about human beings' last quadruped ancestors. They were apes of roughly the same size as the bonobo and the earliest known hominids. They probably weighed between 30 and 50 kilos, and stood about 1.1 to 1.5 metres high. They lived in dense or semi-dense woodland, mostly in the trees but also on the ground. They were generally four-footed but raised themselves up on two legs occasionally, just like modern apes. Because it seems that gorillas and chimpanzees evolved their knuckle-walking independently of each other, and because the known early hominid skeletons show no signs of this, it is likely that our last quadruped ancestors did not really move like this. They had quite long arms, short legs, long curved fingers, flexible thumbs and big toes that were good for climbing in trees. Their bodies were covered in fur. They supported themselves mostly by eating ripe fruit, delicate plants and plant fibres, insects and some small animals.

In social terms they probably lived in flexible, somewhat male-dominated flocks without fixed mating partners. Their settlement pattern was most likely patrilocal in the sense that young females moved to another group when they reached puberty. A less plausible alternative would be harem groups consisting of a dominant male together with several females, and both male and female exogamy. Apart from close relatives, in principle everyone had sex with everyone else.

The connections between mother and young, between mother and adult sons and between adult brothers were very close. Apart from this, group structure was rather loose with shifting alliances between non-kin individuals. This social pattern could also vary according to changes in the environment. At night they slept in individual beds in the trees – infants together with their mother. They reached puberty at about the age of 9 or 10 years, when the young females moved to other groups. Pregnancy lasted about 8 months and the female gave birth every third to fifth year, while the young were breast-fed for about the same length of time. They lived about 30 or 40 years.

With a brain volume of barely 400 cubic centimetres, not much less than that of a modern chimpanzee, our ancestors' ancestors were relatively intelligent apes, very social with a strong emotional life and a well-developed communication system.

4

TRACES OF THE EARLY
HUMANS

As a background to my attempt to put flesh on the bones of the early humans, I give here a short orientation in the finds that illuminate the origins and earliest evolution of the human race in Africa, up to about 2 million years ago. But because this subject also raises questions as to our biological and cultural heritage, I follow this evolutionary thread all the way to the appearance of modern humans on the same continent. The different side branches of the family tree, those who populated Europe and Asia before the modern humans, are also given a little corner to themselves despite falling outside my main theme.

Terminology

The enormous corpus of bones from early humans would be quite chaotic and could tell us nothing if it was not first sorted by similarity and dissimilarity in named groups. Apart from the names of individual finds, in the literature we also encounter several names for species, and some for families. This terminology is far from self-evident and may require some comment. Families and species are named in accordance with Linnaeus' system of biological classification. The names are usually in Latin, sometimes Greek, sometimes both at once, and often garnished with something from the language of the find spot or a local place name. Sometimes it is like staring vacantly into a linguistic abyss, which can make pidgin pale by comparison.

In 1924 at Taung in South Africa, the anatomist Raymond Dart discovered the skull of a young individual, whom he understood to have been a bipedal ape. It was given the Latin-Greek family name *Australopithecus* and the Latin species name *africanus*, in English 'African southern ape'. Since then *Australopithecus* has been used as the common family name for early humans.

Some of the terms have aged. For example, the 'southern' part of *Australopithecus* has latterly become an irrelevance. Most find spots are now north of the equator and it is not at all certain that the creatures with this name should be seen as apes. Nor is the species name *africanus* particularly illuminating, because *all* australopithecines are from Africa.

Homo habilis, the 'handy human', received that name because at the time she was thought to be the first to make and use stone tools. We found out long ago that other humans got there first. It is not clear any longer that we should connect the *habilis* to the *Homo* family, but she is allowed to keep her honourable name. In the same way *Homo erectus*, the 'upright human', has kept her noble title, despite the fact that we have long known that the upright posture is several million years older.

Thus in many cases it is not possible from the terms' linguistic content to work out what they mean; one must learn from case to case. Researchers have no problem with this, because most of the terms are so well used and defined that they can still function as scientific tools. For this reason they cannot be ignored, and I do not do so here, albeit with a few exceptions.

Hominid, roughly 'humanlike creature', has often been used as a synonym for the clumsier *Australopithecus*, and now also for the older *Ardipithecus*. It would have been an excellent term were it not for some researchers who have begun to use it for gorillas and chimpanzees as well, referring to their close genetic kinship with humans. In reply there were many who started to call an early bipedal creature a *hominin*. But it did not take long before still other scholars welcomed the gorillas and chimps into the *hominin* club, and it was back to square one.

To this we can add *hominoid*, a collective term for humans and apes. These indistinctions, and the fact that hominid, hominin and hominoid sound so alike, have prompted me to abandon them altogether.

Although the earliest known humans had some degree of apelike characteristics in terms of skull form and size, facial features, jaw and other skeletal affinities, I feel it is inappropriate to speak of two-legged apes. If we wish to emphasise these simian relics then perhaps the term 'ape-man' is better. Because bipedalism is the quality in focus when defining the hominids as something different from the apes, and because it can be repeatedly seen as the key to understanding human evolution, I find the term 'early human' to be well motivated. I use it in this book as a synonym for hominid.

The oldest creatures to have so far been honoured with the name *Homo*, Latin for 'man', are *Homo rudolfensis* and *Homo sp.* (= *Homo* without a closer species identification). They emerged almost 2.5 million years ago as the first to acquire a slightly larger brain and the suggestion of human qualities in their faces, jaws and skulls. At present the finds are too few to be sure whether we are here speaking of one, two or more species. For the moment I will therefore do as others have done before, and collect them all in the single group of early *Homo*.

I actually think it would be best to use the well-known Latin *Homo* as the family name for all bipedal creatures, from the separation of the family tree until today. This is why I here employ the Latin familial series *Prehomo*, *Homo* and *Subhomo*. These terms are rooted in the core concept of the human, they are specifically comparable, and relevant in their meaning. They are also in the same language, easy to understand and simple to pronounce.

Prehomo, which roughly means 'prehuman', is used here as the family name for all early humans who had a brain that was not much bigger than an ape's, and who in most cases lacked obvious human traits in their skulls and faces.

Homo, 'human', can consequently stand for the first early humans with brains somewhat bigger than the apes' and with certain tendencies to human physiognomic features, as well as standing for all subsequent human types.

Subhomo ('collateral human', 'pseudo-human', 'demi-human') refers to the later, more robust australopithecines. They had somewhat bigger brains than *Prehomo* but much heavier teeth, jaws and skulls than both *Prehomo* and *Homo*. The term *Subhomo* means approximately the same as the Greek *Paranthropos*, which they are sometimes also called, showing how they are viewed as a side branch of our family tree that later died out.

Evaluating the sources

The arguments that break out between researchers are often seen as expressions of competition and the desire to see their own fossil discoveries used as the basis of classification. A big part of the problem, however, is that it is also difficult to tell the species apart when one has only fragments of bone to study instead of living beings and populations. Well-preserved and articulated skeletal parts are rare, and it is often difficult to tell whether bones found together are from one or several individuals. Similarly it is hard to know if the differences in form and size reflect different sexes, ages, species or just natural variation within the same species.

It is therefore a good idea to exercise some caution about the 'families' and 'species', and about the connections between them. There is also a self-evident difficulty in determining from individual bone fragments and teeth whether one is dealing with an early bipedal human or a closely related contemporary ape – the nearer to the divergence of species, the closer the similarity. The whole thing is complicated by the fact that we do not really know what kind of skeletons our last four-footed ancestors, or those of chimpanzees, possessed. In the first instance we concentrate upon details indicative of an upright gait, together with the thickness of the skull and tooth enamel, the form of the jaw and the nature of the teeth. On average, humans have thinner crania, thicker tooth enamel, smaller canines and front teeth, heavier and flatter molars, and a greater curvature in their tooth alignment than modern and many Miocene apes. However, some of the latter nevertheless seem to have had thin tooth enamel, and it becomes steadily clearer that skeletal remains in fact provide a rather uncertain basis for distinguishing species and determining kinship between them.

It has been a long time since anyone believed in a simple, straight line of evolution for the human race. There seems little doubt that during the age of early humans and afterwards there were several species of humans living at the same time, sometimes even in the same area. In evolutionary terms there is nothing strange about that. If anything, it is more unusual that for the last 25,000 years there has only been one, very uniform, species of human beings on the planet.

There are many publications on the history of research that show how from the 1920s onwards discoveries of human fossils have built up our knowledge of early humans. Therefore I prefer to give only a summarised presentation of the situation as it looks today, beginning with the earliest finds.

For the species and important find groups of *Prehomo*, early *Homo* and *Subhomo*, I give below approximate datings, and where we can say anything about it, an assessment of their average body mass, height, brain size and EQ. The latter is an abbreviation for *encephalisation quotient*, the calculated average measurement of brain size in relation to body size, compared with what can be expected for mammals in general. A chimpanzee's EQ has been determined to be 2.0, and that of the modern human to be 5.8. In general, I have not listed the various scientific methods that have produced the datings.

Prehomo: from 6 to 2 million years ago

Until very recently there were no secure traces of the earliest humans from the point at or around the split from the apes. For a long time we had little choice but to accept a gap of several million years from which we had very few finds at all. It has therefore been difficult to say much about how our species and our oldest two-legged ancestors actually came into being.

In July 2001 a team of researchers from France and Chad under the direction of Michel Brunet discovered a relatively well-preserved skull at Toros-Menalla in the Djurab area of western Chad in the southern Sahara. The find was published in preliminary form a year later. In this part of Africa radiometric dating does not work, but thanks to associated finds of a number of different animal bones the cranium has been dated to the period between 7 and 6 million years ago, and probably to the earlier part of that range. The skull has some contradictory features. Although the brain volume is no bigger than that of a modern chimpanzee, the face is less sloping, the canines are small in size and the tooth enamel is comparatively thick – all characteristics that we otherwise meet first in early Homo several million years later. The huge brow ridges are also striking. Brunet has argued that the skull is that of a very early human, one of the ancestors to the later species that we already know from East Africa. He has christened the skull *Sahelanthropus tchadensis*, but the media has begun to call it simply Toumai.

Unfortunately no other parts of the skeleton have been found that could tell us if this really is the remains of a biped human. Several other researchers are sceptical of Brunet's interpretation. Some have suggested that the skull belongs to an extinct ape, while others have opted for an early human that itself died out in an evolutionary dead end. Still others argue that we simply cannot be sure about this contradictory skull with nothing surviving below the neck and found in a place so distant from other early finds. Future discoveries will hopefully solve the problem. For my part, I feel that the location of the skull in water lain sediments does not support the idea that this was an ape.

In December 2000 it was announced that a Franco-Kenyan expedition with Brigitte Senut and Martin Pickford had found the remains of several early bipedal humans in the Tugen area of Lake Baringo in northern Kenya. There seems little doubt of the date of around 6 million years, as the finds were made in well-researched geological layers that have already been dated by two independent studies. The official name of this creature is *Orrorin tugenensis*. Referring to the year of the discovery, the mass media have called it 'Millennium Man'.

What little data that has been released mentions finds of thirteen bones, including two jaw fragments, a number of canines and molars, three heavy thighbones and the remains of an upper arm. The excavators argue that the strong thighbones, small canines and crude molars point to a biped. Small teeth with thick enamel suggest a diet dominated by thick-skinned fruit. The hand and finger bones, together with the heavy upper arm indicate that it was still able to climb trees. Altogether the bones represent at least five individuals of both sexes, including one infant. It is interesting that the discoveries were made in fossilised sediments that had been deposited in water. This environment close to water is also confirmed by nearby finds of the bones of hippo-like animals and shells of aquatic molluscs. The early human from Tugen obviously lived near water. The terrain by the lake seems to have been rich in vegetation, which is also shown by the fact that their primary food was fruit, even if the tree savannah was within reach. To judge from the bite marks on the bones, at least one of the individuals had fallen victim to a predator, probably a big cat.

In July 2001 an international team of scholars including Yohannes Haile-Selassie from Berkeley made public the remains of a biped human between 5.8 and 5.2 million years old. Found in central Awash in northeast Ethiopia, it has been called *Ardipithecus ramidus kadabba*. A total of eleven finds were made, with parts of a jaw, hand, arm, toe and collar bones, and teeth from at least five different individuals of about the same size as a chimpanzee. One of the toe bones has been interpreted as very characteristic of bipedalism. The finds were made in volcanic soil that has been securely dated. One problem, however, is that while most of the discoveries came from deposits that were 5.8 to 5.6 million years old, the vital toe bone was found 16 kilometres away in sediments only 5.2 million years old.

Clearly the finds from Chad, Tugen and Ethiopia need to be more carefully studied before definite conclusions can be drawn. Hopefully more discoveries will be made in these areas.

As long as secure evidence was lacking for early humans older than around 4 million years, many researchers were reluctant to see the beginnings of bipedalism any earlier than that. For those who argue that bipedalism evolved in conjunction with the split from the apes, the finds described above were less surprising.

As a result of these discoveries, earlier finds of individual bones from possible early humans have been cast in a new light. As early as 1967 part of a right mandible and a few teeth fragments were found at Lake Baringo in a layer that suggested an age of at least 5.6 million years. This find was once interpreted very differently, but even before the Tugen discoveries the rather strong jaw, large molars and thick enamel had begun to be seen as proof of an early human. Again, I feel that the location of the finds near water points in the same direction, as a consistent feature of early human habitats.

At Tabarin not far from Baringo, a 5 million-year-old fragment of right mandible and part of an upper arm were found that may stem from a bipedal creature, but this is not certain. The discovery has rather unnecessarily been given its own species name, *Australopithecus praegens*.

From 4.4 million years ago and later, the finds are more numerous. We meet a number of different familial and species names, but in fact they do not differ very much from each other. They seem to have lived on relatively unchanged until around 3 million years ago.

These early and clearly bipedal humans still retained certain apelike features in their extremities, skulls, faces and jaws. They were no bigger than bonobos and their brains were the same size or only slightly larger than those of apes.

In the course of a few years from 1992 onwards, Tim White and his colleagues discovered a number of hand and arm bones together with a few skull fragments at Aramis in northeast Ethiopia. These were preliminarily interpreted as the remains of a gracile, completely bipedal early human who had lived about 4.4 million years ago. At first it was thought to be an *Australopithecus* and a possible ancestor to the slightly later *afarensis*. However, when up to 40 per cent of the skeleton had later come to light, White decided that the teeth and bones were more apelike and changed the family name to *Ardipithecus* with the species name *ramidus*, roughly 'ground ape'. After the new finds of *Ardipithecus ramidus kadabba*, White modified his find again to *Ardipithecus ramidus ramidus*. Even though the latter has some primitive features and her kinship with *Australopithecus* is unclear, her status as a biped is beyond doubt.

At Kanapoi, Allia Bay and other localities by Lake Turkana in northwest Kenya, since 1988 Meave Leakey and her team have been finding parts of a cranium, an almost complete set of teeth and individual teeth from different individuals, complete upper and lower jaws and the so far oldest known find of a clavicle, that all point to a completely upright walking creature. This early human has been named *Australopithecus anamensis* and is usually seen as a transitional form from *ramidus ramidus* and the later *afarensis*. The finds are dated to the period from 3.9 to 4.2 million years ago. *Anamensis'* body mass has been calculated to have been 46–55 kilograms.

Another piece of an upper arm bone has been found at Lake Baringo in Kenya that also bears a resemblance to *afarensis*, as do a number of teeth from Fejej in southern Ethiopia. These have been dated to around 4.2 million years.

In Hadar in northeast Ethiopia in 1974, Donald Johansson found the *ca.* 3.2 million-year-old skeleton of a young human female, the famous Lucy. About 40 per cent of her bones survived, but it has been possible to reconstruct the skeleton almost in its entirety. Nearby, as also at Laetoli in Tanzania, the bones of many other individuals have been discovered: women, men and children, albeit not so well preserved. Lucy and her kin bear the name *Australopithecus afarensis*, a species that covers essentially the entire period from 3 to 3.9 million years ago.

During the 1990s Johansson's team and other international expeditions have made a number of similar finds at Hadar and nearby sites in northeast Ethiopia.

We know pretty much how the afarenes looked. They had rather gracile body forms, they were only 100–50 centimetres tall and weighed between 30 and 45 kilograms. They were thus somewhat smaller than a modern chimpanzee. The resemblance to modern humans is considerable in terms of the larger parts of the skeleton like the pelvis, spine, feet, legs, arms and the angle of the head to the backbone. The likeness with chimps is closest when it comes to the skull and smaller bones such as hands, fingers and toes. The toe bones were slightly bent and the big toe was still separate from the others. Even though the afarenes were fully bipedal, they did not walk with the straight stride of a modern human but with a somewhat swaying gait at a side angle. They probably could not run as well as a modern human.

Height for women has been calculated to have been about 105 centimetres with a weight of 29 kilograms, while men could reach 151 centimetres and a mass of 45 kilograms. Their average brain volume seems to have been 413 cubic centimetres and their EQ around 2.4.

After much argument the majority of researchers have now agreed that we are dealing here not with separate species but with different sizes within a single, fairly uniform species, *afarensis*. There seems to have been considerable variation in body size between the sexes, so-called sexual dimorphism. The men seem to have been on average 30 per cent taller than the women, a much greater difference than in both modern chimpanzees and humans. 'Normal' size relations would reappear first with *Homo ergaster*. In one sense there is something forced about the attempts to explain the afarenes' great sexual dimorphism, and my own account here is no exception. It is therefore to be welcomed that the idea of the afarenes as several species of different sizes is now beginning to return.

In 1995 Ron Clarke and Philip Tobias presented their analyses of four bones from a left foot and two inner bones of a big toe from what was thought to be an afarene. These bones had been found much earlier, in 1981, in a cave at Sterkfontein in northern South Africa. The angle between the big toe and the others indicated a mobility almost equal to that of an ape. Three years later Clarke found a complete skeleton that matched exactly the break where the toes found earlier had joined. Surprisingly enough the arms proved to be proportionally as long as an ape's. This early human has been preliminarily classified as an early *africanus*, and dated to around 3.5 million years. The work of preparing the skeleton continues and a final interpretation and dating must wait. The discovery of these early humans at Sterkfontein, with their mobile big toes and long arms, has refuelled the discussion as to whether they were still primarily adapted for living in trees. Not least, the area around Sterkfontein at that time was covered in thick forest. This idea finds support in Fred Spoor's earlier observation that the inner ear, which governs balance, appears in all members of the *Prehomo* and *Subhomo* far more like that of a chimpanzee than a modern human. Not until early *Homo* does an inner ear of modern type appear. Spoor argues that the afarenes therefore must have had a rather unusual way of moving, which a number of apelike features in their skeletons also suggests.

In my opinion the early humans could never have evolved such an adapted upright body posture if they had not been primarily ground based. This understanding is not contradicted by the 3.7 million year old footprints in fossilised volcanic ash that Mary Leakey's team discovered in 1976 at Laetoli in northern Tanzania. They show typical human feet in the position of the big toe and they have a clear arch. The latter is also seen without a doubt in the Sterkfontein foot bones.

It would be natural if both *afarensis* in the east and early *africanus* in southern Africa retained a certain anatomical adaptation for a life in the trees, or even if they became readapted to this under localised conditions. However, since the skeletons of both species and the Laetoli footprints all indicate a clear adaptation for an upright gait, then bipedalism must in evolutionary terms have been clearly prioritised before the need to climb trees. A more mobile big toe, perhaps more so in some populations and individuals than others, should instead be seen as an anatomical relic that was slowly disappearing. A primarily ground based, bipedal life may very well have been combined with tree climbing if it proved necessary, as a protection from enemies and to provide better access to the fruit that was still an important part of their diet. Because *afarensis* and *africanus* both lived in forests, it is likely that they still slept in the trees. But as early *Homo* completely lacks the mobile big toe there seems to no longer have been any strong selection pressure in this direction.

In 1995 at Koro Toro, Bahr-el-Ghazal in Chad in the southern central Sahara, a French research team under Michel Brunet found several fossil bones, including a lower jaw with seven teeth. In association with other faunal finds their age has been estimated at 3.5 to 3 million years. The interpretation of the bones is still unclear, as there are similarities with *afarensis*, early *Homo* and *Subhomo*. This early human has been dubbed *Australopithecus bahrelghazali*.

Between 1996 and 1998 within a relatively confined area in central Awash, north-east Ethiopia, a research team that included Berhane Asfaw and Tim White found bones, cranial pieces and jaw fragments together with teeth belonging to several individuals. The skull fragments suggest a brain capacity of around 450 cubic centimetres, while the bones point to a height of about 140 centimetres. In total the bones of nine individuals have been found. This early human has been called *Australopithecus garhi* and is dated to 2.5 million years. The powerful molars and their size in proportion to the canines, together with the length of the thighbone in relation to that of the upper arm, are the same as in modern humans. This has led the excavators to speculate that *garhi* was a direct ancestor of early *Homo*. This is possible, of course. On the other hand *garhi*'s molars are even more powerful than those of *Homo*, and even than those of *Subhomo*. *Garhi* also has the suggestion of a comb on top of the cranial vault. At the same time its forward-jutting lower face and long underarms are reminiscent of the afarenes. There are therefore many doubts as to just where *garhi* belongs, or even if she is a species in her own right. It seems a matter of taste as to whether she should be classified as *Australopithecus* or early *Homo*.

In the same sediments, only a few metres from the skull fragments and immediately adjacent to a collection of bones from a single individual, were also found the bones of antelope, horse and other animals bearing clear marks of cutting with stone tools, indicating where the flesh had been sliced away. There were also crosscuts of the same kind that prove that the marrow was also eaten. At some of the find-spots of bones, the tools themselves were also discovered. This makes *garhi* a strong candidate for the role of the first maker and user of stone tools. The oldest find of stone objects that were without a doubt fashioned by human hand comes from Gona in Ethiopia, barely 100 kilometres north. They are insignificantly older than the *garhi* finds, at 2.6 million years.

During the period from 3 to 2 million years ago, there is only one human type that diverges strongly from the others, *Kenyanthropus platyops*. The find was made public at the beginning of 2001 and had been made by an inter-national research team under Meave Leakey on the west bank of Lake Turkana in northern Kenya. It consisted among other things of skull fragments that could be assembled into an almost complete cranium, and a cranial fragment from another individual. The brain was no bigger than that of other early humans of this time. What distinguishes *platyops*' skull is its relatively flat face with a markedly straighter profile, long before these features appear in other finds. Despite this, it seems a little hasty to declare *platyops* to be a family in its own right, set her up as the mother of the entire line of *Homo*, and thereby relegate the afarenes to the sidelines. Until we are sure that the reconstruction of the skull is accurate or that the flat face is not just an individual exception from the rule, then we need more finds. In other respects neither the rest of the cranium nor the teeth deviate from those of the afarenes.

Early humans kept mostly to forested ground near water. It was therefore natural that they spread along the Rift Valley, the broad and water rich system that stretches from the Horn of Africa in the northeast right down to northern South Africa. However, one must also acknowledge that one reason why most finds of early humans have been made there may not only be due to the good preconditions for life but also because of especially favourable preservation in that area.

The find from Koro Toro in Chad is important because it proves that early humans appeared relatively early outside the African rift valley system. It is not really surprising at all. The faunal fossils show that the contemporary environment around the site was nothing like today's desert landscape, but was in fact made up of lakes, waterways and forests – in other words the same milieu as the majority of early human finds in eastern and southern Africa. It would have been just as natural for these people to spread west along what was then a belt of forests and lakes, between the line of rain forest in the south and the then smaller desert in the north. The discoveries from Sterkfontein show that the equivalent border zone in southern Africa had already been colonised at this time. There is thus much to suggest that large regions of Africa in the area between rain forest and savannah had been settled by early humans before Lucy was even on the horizon.

The finds become more complex in the period between 3 and 2 million years ago. At least half a dozen types of early human 'suddenly' appear more or less at the same time. The lack of well-preserved bones makes any assessment of human evolution during this period difficult. It is tempting to link the increasing pace of human evolution, which has its equivalent among mammals, to the major climatic changes in eastern and southern Africa that led to a drier environment and a spread of savannah. What appears before this as an essentially uniform human family tree now branches out in all directions, through adaptation to different ecological niches with partly different resources. Several different species therefore emerge, that vary not so much in terms of size and skeleton than in relation to the form and musculature of the jaw, the shape of the skull and the size, form and wear patterns of the teeth. In the middle of this period the human brain first began to noticeably increase in size. The oldest known stone tools are also from this time.

One variant of early human is the above-mentioned *Australopithecus africanus*, which is only securely known from South Africa. In size and anatomy she differed very little from *afarensis*, of whom she is sometimes considered a direct descendent. She is dated to between 3 (or 3.6) and 2.4 million years ago. The *africanus* women were on average 115 centimetres high and weighed 30 kilograms, while the men stood 138 centimetres and weighed 41 kilograms. Brain capacity was around 440 cubic centimetres, and EQ 2.6 – a little greater than that of the afarenes. There has been disagreement as to whether *africanus* was an ancestor of ours or not. Because they are only known from southern Africa, and because they had a slightly more robust skull and teeth than both *afarensis* and *Homo*, many see *africanus* as the specifically southern ancestor of

Subhomo. They are noted for their rather ape-like body proportions with longer arms, shorter legs and more mobile big toes than are found among both the afarenes, early *Homo* and other *Subhomo*. This could suggest that they reverted to a somewhat more tree-based way of life.

We know very little of what happened when the family of early humans divided into different species between 3 and 2 million years ago. It is quite clear, however, that adaptation to the great environmental changes of the time was fundamental to this. When the forests shrank and competition for food increased accordingly, we can assume that some groups of early humans began to venture out into more open terrain. Some incorporated animals more into their diet and evolved into early *Homo*, while others specialised in hardy, ground-growing vegetable fodder and evolved into *Subhomo*.

The fact that the family of early humans underwent such massive evolutionary change at this time is generally seen as indicative of equally dramatic alterations in their manner of existence. In that case, the slow rate of change during the much longer preceding period ought to reflect a correspondingly stable environment.

Subhomo: from 3 to 1.1 million years ago

Subhomo, which is understood to have been a side-branch of our family tree, is known from East Africa under the names *aethiopicus* and *boisei*, and in southern Africa as *robustus*. No finds have been made outside Africa. *Subhomo* was completely bipedal and as gracile as *Prehomo*, but with a slightly more modern skeleton. Special for the species are the heavy jaw, molars, jaw muscle platforms and upstanding cranial comb for the attachment of the massive muscles for chewing. It is the heaviness of this apparatus for chewing that has given rise to the term 'robust' australopithecine as opposed to other more gracile types. It should be noted that this applies only to the skull, not to the rest of the body.

The particular feature of *Subhomo* is commonly understood to be an anatomical adaptation to heavier, more fibre-rich plant food that included roots, nuts and other fibre that is hard to chew. Their crude appearance, and the fact that *Subhomo* did not evolve any further during its long existence and at last died out, has promoted an impression of an ape-like, almost retarded unfortunate. But their brains were actually 15 to 20 per cent bigger than those of *Prehomo*, and in spite of everything they managed to live for 1.5 million years, so they can't have been completely hopeless. They were fated to share the stage with more advanced relatives. It is likely that this competition was in the end too much for them, living alongside the ever more intelligent and culturally advanced *Homo erectus*.

In 1967 a 2.5 million-year-old, toothless lower jaw was found at Omo in southern Ethiopia. The bowed form of the jaw was different to that of other contemporary early humans, and its owner was named *Australopithecus aethiopicus*. The species was first taken seriously when a skull with intact upper jaw was discovered in 1985 west of Lake Turkana in Kenya. This early human had massive platforms for the attachment of chewing muscles, an unusually heavy skull comb and very crude molars. With reference to similarities with both the older *afarensis* and the younger *boisei/robustus*, many have seen *aethiopicus* as a link between these two and the oldest known representative of the *Subhomo* family. We do not know how big *aethiopicus* was. The brain capacity of the Turkana skull is around 410 cubic centimetres.

The finds of *Australopithecus boisei*, which is securely known only from East Africa, belong to the period between 2.5 and 1.2 million years ago. The women stood up to 124 centimetres high and weighed up to 34 kilograms, while the men could grow to 137 centimetres and weigh 49 kilograms. Their brain capacity was around 465 cubic centimetres, with an EQ of 2.7.

Definite finds of *Australopithecus robustus* have only been made in southern Africa. They are sometimes divided into two subspecies: *robustus* after the find from Swartkrans, and *crassidens* after the find from Kromdrai. *Robustus* is dated to between 1.9 and 1.1 million years. Among the discoveries is the skull of a woman, perhaps the best preserved of all early human fossils. The women were up to 110 centimetres tall with a mass of about 32 kilograms, and the men stood 132 centimetres high and weighed up to 40 kilograms. Brain capacity was approximately 530 cubic centimetres, with an EQ of 3.1.

It is possible that *aethiopicus* evolved into *boisei* in East Africa, and that *africanus* became *robustus* in the south. But others have suggested that *boisei* and *robustus* should be seen as a single primary species of *Subhomo* with regional, temporal and individual variations.

From early *Homo* to *Homo sapiens* in Africa: 2.4 million years ago to the present

Early *Homo* had a more modern skeleton that late *Prehomo*, although some individuals seem still to have resembled their ancestors to a high degree. They were the first people who not only had more human features in their skulls, faces and jaws but also slightly larger brains – after a time some 30 to 50 per cent larger than *Prehomo*'s. They lived between 2.4 and 1.6 million years ago. As we have seen, *Prehomo* in the form of *garhi* had already begun to make stone tools. Similarly primitive examples have also been found in association with discoveries of early *Homo*. They too seem to have made and used simple stone tools.

There are also a few finds that are usually connected to early *Homo* in general, without closer species determination. One of them is a 2.4 million-year-old side section of a skull from Chemeron at Lake Baringo in central Kenya. Another example is the 2.3 million year old upper jaw with a clearly human curve to its teeth alignment, recovered from Makaamitalu in the Hadar region of Ethiopia. Some 34 worked stone flakes and cores were found in association with it.

Homo rudolfensis can be dated to the period between 2.4 and 1.8 million years ago. The type find is a relatively well-preserved cranium from Koobi Fora in northern Kenya, 1.8 to 1.9 million years old. A 2.5 to 2.3 million-year-old molar from Uraha in northern Malawi has been dated through its association with faunal finds. We know very little of its appearance from the neck down, and even the definition of *rudolfensis* as a distinct species is controversial.

Homo habilis is represented by finds from eastern and southern Africa, with an age of between 2.3 and 1.6 million years. They retained some earlier features such as long upper arms and a compact body, and they were smaller than the contemporary *ergaster*. The women could reach 100–25 centimetres in height, while the men could grow to 130–57 centimetres. Women could weigh 32 kilograms, and the men 52. Brain capacity was 600–800 cubic centimetres, with an EQ of 3.1.

At Nariokotomo in northern Kenya, Kamoya Kimeu, Richard Leakey and Alan Walker have discovered a 1.5 million-year-old almost complete skeleton of a 12–15-year-old boy, belonging to the species *Homo ergaster*. As an adult he might have grown to as much as 180 centimetres, and weighed 68 kilograms; the women could reach 155 centimetres and a mass of 52 kilograms. The arms, legs and torso are completely modern in their proportions, and there are no remaining signs of adaptations suited to tree climbing. They are quite simply the first known humans who had a modern skeleton in every respect, and who were as tall as we are today. Finds of *ergaster* have also been made in Tanzania and South Africa. A recent find of an *erectus* skull from Ileret east of Lake Turkana demonstrates that they could also be of very small size.

Ergaster is dated to between 1.8 and 1.5 million years. They had a brain capacity of 700–900 cubic centimetres, and an EQ of 3.3. On the basis of the teething of their molars, *ergaster*'s average life span has been calculated at around 52 years. About 2 million years ago it was probably early *ergasters* who were the first humans to leave Africa, and in the form of early *erectus* quickly spread themselves out through southern Eurasia.

In Africa, Europe and Asia the period between 1.5 and 1 million years ago is even more impoverished in terms of finds, which makes it difficult to paint a picture of the people of that time. It is here that archaeological material can be of some help. The simple methods of early stoneworking (defined as Olduvai technology after the classic find spot for early stone artefacts in northern Kenya) continued for up to 1 million years, but about 1.5 million years ago in Africa we see the start of a new and more advanced technique, typical for *erectus* and known as the Acheulean tradition. Among several well-made stone tools we can especially note the double-sided, symmetrical hand axes and the flaked scrapers.

From around a million years ago and onwards there are secure finds of quite advanced *erectus* in Africa. Then their brain capacity was about 1,000 cubic centimetres; 500,000 years later it had evolved to around 1,200. The border between advanced *erectus* and archaic *Homo sapiens* is blurred. The elements we can point to as definitive for the latter are not so much the size of the brain as the degree of neotene qualities in the cranium and face. Several skulls like this have been found in eastern and southern Africa. From Buia in the eastern Danaqil region of Eritrea comes an almost complete cranium together with two hip fragments and two front teeth. These are approximately a million years old (in the range 1.4–0.6 million) with an estimated brain capacity of about 800 cubic centimetres. It is reminiscent of both *ergaster* and early *erectus*, but also of *sapiens* in the sense that the cranium's greatest width is high up.

A cranium of archaic *sapiens* about 600,000 years old has been discovered at Bodo in Ethiopia, and an equally well-preserved skull has been found at Kabwe in Zambia, though this has not been securely dated. The Bodo cranium is seen as the oldest definite example of *Homo Heidelbergensis*, who appeared in Europe around 500,000 years ago. In the light of DNA analysis that places the split between modern humans and Neanderthals at about half a million years ago, it would seem that *Heidelbergensis* left Africa at about this time or earlier.

It therefore appears that *erectus* in Africa began to develop more visible *sapiens* traits about a million years ago, in a continuing process until its skull, teeth and face took on more modern forms some 200,000 to 300,000 years ago, and its brain grew to its present day size. Finds of anatomically modern skulls have been made in South Africa and Ethiopia spanning the period from 100,000 to 250,000 years ago. Nevertheless, we still have too few examples of good quality to be sure of how advanced *erectus* became archaic *sapiens*, and ultimately *Homo sapiens sapiens*. But the find of, *inter alia*, a more or less complete and well preserved modern human skull dated to 154,000–160,000 years from Herto in the Afar region in Ethiopia, recently announced by Tim White and colleagues, leaves no doubt about an early African origin for modern humans.

Thus, an important conclusion must be that the complete evolution of the present human race took place from beginning to end in Africa against the background of a tropical environment.

The finds of fossil bones thus agree with the molecular biological studies that point to Africa as the cradle of modern humanity. This is supported by the fact that the genetic variation among the indigenous peoples of sub-Saharan Africa is greater than among any other population groups anywhere else in the world.

The oldest examples of *Homo sapiens sapiens* outside Africa are several finds from Israel, with an age of about 90,000 years. In southern Asia the earliest finds are around 60,000 years old. From a grave in New South Wales in southern Australia the remains of a modern human may be 60,000 years old have been recovered. The earliest discoveries from eastern Asia date to perhaps 40,000 years, while the oldest finds from Japan go back at least 30,000 years. America seems to have been populated either 30,000 or 15,000 years ago – there is still no agreement as to which figure is more correct. In central Europe the earliest finds of modern humans are 35,000 years old, and Scandinavia was reached as late as the end of the Ice Age, around 12,000 years ago.

Advanced *Homo* outside Africa: 1.9 million to 30,000 years ago

A series of finds of human bones and stone tools has now been made that suggests that people spread out from Africa into southern Eurasia 2 million years ago. These first emigrants were probably *erectus/ergaster*.

The finds from Venta Micena in Spain with a supposed date of 1.85 million years are, however, controversial. The best evidence comes from the well-dated finds at Dmanisi in the Caucasus, where German and Georgian researchers initially recovered a lower jaw and a number of stone tools of the Oldowan type. Later two human skulls were found, one of an adult that lacked a lower jaw, and a smaller example belonging to a youth. These people have been interpreted as early *erectus*. In the larger cranium were two holes made by the teeth of a powerful predator. At the same site were found bones from rhino, giraffe, elephant and sabre-toothed cat, all of which suggest a savannah landscape. The dating of the Dmanisi finds is considered secure.

At Riwat in Pakistan stone tools of Oldowan type have been found that date back 1.8 million years. Similar artefacts have been discovered in a cave at Longgupo in Sichuan, central China, in layers dating to 1.9 to 1.7 million years, and also at Yanmou in southwestern China, up to 1.7 million years old. From Longgupo also come a few teeth and mandible fragments that appear to more resemble early *habilis* and *ergaster* than the Asiatic *erectus*.

In recent years thousands of animal bones have been retrieved from a limestone quarry at Renzidong in central eastern China, with an age of between 2.5 and 2 million years. Some of the bones were found together with what have been interpreted as worked cutting and scraping tools of stone and bone. Furthermore some of the bones from larger animals seem to have been sorted by human hand. The discoveries have prompted a hasty discussion as to the presence of a very early *Homo erectus* in China that could have evolved from a 10 million-year-older local ape. The value of these finds is still uncertain, and it must be said that they do not include any human bones.

In the 1930s on Java in Indonesia were found skull fragments of the so-called 'Java Man', with an age reckoned at 200,000 years. Its brain capacity was around 800 cubic centimetres. However, some years ago a few of the finds were re-dated using argon-argon methods with very different results. A child's skull from Modjokerto turned out to be 1.8 million years old, and a cranial fragment from Sangiran was dated to 1.65 million years. At Ubeidiya in Israel have been found a skull fragment and some stone tools of Acheulean type from about 1.4 million years ago.

Just as in Africa, this first phase of settlement in southern Europe and Asia is typified by a long period from which we have few finds. There are few known human bones from the period between 1.5 and 1 million years ago. On the other hand, and again as in Africa, we have stone tools.

At Lantian in central China has been found a 1 million-year-old skull of an *erectus*. From different sites on Java have come cranial fragments of up to 40 individuals, including an 800,000-year-old well-preserved skull of a man with an estimated cranial capacity of 1,000 cubic centimetres. Several finds of stone tools from Flores Island in eastern Indonesia have been dated to between 900,000 and 800,000 years.

In northern China at Zhoukoudian finds have been made of a large number of fossil human bones from the period 200,000–500,000 years, representing at least 40 individuals and large quantities of stone tools. Here too the brain capacity of a number of skulls from the earliest phases has been calculated at around 1,000 cubic centimetres. The latest find of an advanced *erectus* in Indonesia is about 100,000 years old.

The oldest secure evidence of advanced *erectus* outside Africa comes from a large number of fragmentary bones found at Gran Dolina in Spain and dated to around 800,000 years. They exhibit a unique mix of both early *ergaster* and later *sapiens*, and have been given their own species name, *Homo antecessor*. Part of a 700,000-year-old skull has also been found at Ceprano in Italy.

From about 500,000 years ago all of Europe as far as the northern central region, and including southern England, seems to have been populated by *archaic sapiens* (*Homo Heidelbergensis*). At a number of sites in England, Germany, the former Czechoslovakia, Hungary, France, Italy and Greece there have been found remains of both humans and archaeological material. Among the famous find-spots are Boxgrove in England, Tautavel and Terra Amata in southern France, Maurer in Germany and Sima Atapuerca in Spain.

As early as 1.4 million years ago the African Acheulean tradition of stone working had reached Israel (Ubeidiya) and spread from there to western Asia. In eastern Asia by contrast there continued a modified variant of the original Oldowan tradition, which came there with early *erectus*. Among the sites where the new technology has been found in Europe are Isernia in Italy, from about 700,000 years ago, and Boxgrove in southern England, from about 500,000 years ago. In Africa the Acheulean tradition last until 200,000 years ago, while continuing slightly longer in Europe.

This means that the rapid increase in brain capacity in early *Homo* and *ergaster* in Africa was not followed by any noticeable refinement in the simple tool culture that had emerged as long as 2.4 million years ago. We have also seen how the simple Oldowan technology continued in eastern Asia long after human brain capacity had exceeded 1,000 cubic centimetres. Even the Acheulean tradition remained in principle unchanged for more than a million years, if one does not count the slow process whereby the hand axes became small masterpieces of harmonic perfection, struck from ever more carefully prepared cores.

The Neanderthals are represented by a rich archaeological find material and skeletal remains from large parts of central and southern Europe, but also from the Near East and the western parts of central Asia. Their average brain capacity of 1,450 cubic centimetres was a little larger than that of modern humans. The Neanderthals lived during the period from 200,000 (perhaps 300,000) to 25,000 years ago. The youngest finds of them come from southwest Europe. Discoveries of stone tools in southwest Denmark and central western Finland suggest the presence of Neanderthals and their immediate ancestors even in Scandinavia. The Neanderthals are seen as a special regionally evolved form of *Homo Heidelbergensis*. They were short, stocky, powerfully built and very muscular – an anatomy that to all appearances was evolved as a biological adaptation to a colder climate. The fact that this particular character of the skeleton and skull can be seen even in their babies indicates its deep genetic roots.

Two DNA analyses of a male skeleton from western Germany and one of a child's skeleton from the Caucasus suggest that the ancestors of the Neanderthals split from the line of modern humans about 500,000 years ago. This suggests a migration of *Homo Heidelbergensis* out of Africa at about this time.

Proponents of the multi-regional model argued on the basis of bones and archaeological material that modern humans essentially evolved in parallel in separate parts of the Old World, with a limited mutual exchange of genes. Proponents of the alternative explanation argued on the basis of genetic studies that we evolved wholly and completely in Africa. The long drawn out debate between these two positions is now generally understood to have been resolved in the latter's favour. Nevertheless we have barely begun to understand how modern humans came to replace the different regional groups. Did these become gradually marginalized until they disappeared? Were they wholly or partly exterminated with violence? The former alternative is not only more appealing but is also seen today as the more likely primary explanation.

5

BECOMING HUMAN

On two legs

The steady stream of new finds of fossil human bones can give an impression that we have a good idea of how the human race began. Unfortunately this is not the case. We know quite a lot about early humans, but almost nothing about the actual transition from a four-footed ape to a bipedal human being. Some interpretations of this event are in fact no more enlightening than any other creation myth.

Of all the many species of quadruped apes that once existed, why did more of them not raise themselves up on two legs? If it really had been evolutionarily advantageous in general for an ape to become bipedal, then of course many more of them would have been. But as far as we know this step has only been taken twice and only in one of these cases – our own – with any lasting success. This shows that a bipedal gait is not a self-evidently functional evolutionary adaptation for an ape. It therefore seems that our ancestors became bipedal because of a very particular evolutionary situation. The question is simply: which one?

Until the mid-1970s we thought that we had a pretty firm notion of how early humans had evolved from their ape ancestors. Part of this rested on the notion that the brain had begun to grow as a direct consequence of bipedalism. And then in 1974 Donald Johansson found 'Lucy' in Ethiopia, a discovery from which it took researchers a long time to recover. This female had a relatively modern skeleton that demonstrated a long history of bipedalism. But her skull was ape-like and her brain was no bigger than that of an ape's. There was a shocking contrast between the body and the head. Against our will we were forced to conclude that at some point Lucy's ancestors had been subject to a strong selective pressure directed only towards bipedalism, not towards intelligence. Lucy quickly became the media's favourite fossil and for a long time was treated like the missing link in person – this despite the knowledge that the gap between Lucy and the split from the apes was almost as great as the distance from her to us.

The question of human origins and the appearance of the early humans is not made any easier by the fact that we know next to nothing about the

64

ancestors of modern chimpanzees and gorillas during the entire period from the division of the species until the present. The beginnings of the human race can still only be estimated from circumstantial evidence and comparisons. Nevertheless, because it is so decisive for our potential to understand human qualities, I shall make an attempt to discuss it here.

The savannah hypothesis

The traditional view of human origins, which we can call the savannah hypothesis, went as follows. During the Miocene, the period in which it was once believed that humanity evolved, a great drought turned large parts of the East African forests into savannah. Suddenly our forest-dwelling primate ancestors found themselves out there on the grasslands without any trees to climb. In order to survive they began to hunt, and in order to follow their prey and escape predators they raised themselves up on two legs and began to run. In this way their arms and hands were freed up so that they could begin to make and use tools. This in turn stimulated the brain, which made further cultural achievements possible, leading in their turn to an even greater rate of intellectual development.

But the savannah hypothesis attempted to explain not only human beings' bipedalism but also their smooth skin, subcutaneous fat and sweat glands. In concise form, the argument ran like this. So as not to get over-heated while running around in the sun, early humans lost their fur. But this meant that they got cold at night, which can be quite cool on the savannah. This led to the evolution of a thick layer of fat under the skin. But when dawn came and with it the heat of the day, this layer of fat proved to be a hindrance for the process of cooling down. To avoid over-heating, humans therefore quickly evolved large quantities of extra sweat glands. An abbreviated version of the same idea skips the subcutaneous fat and is satisfied instead with losing fur and sweating to keep the temperature down.

This all sounds reasonable enough. However, on closer inspection cracks start to appear in the argument. The first objection comes, of course, with the finds that show beyond any doubt that we became bipedal not on the savannah but in the forests. It is a very different matter that many of these sites are located in what is *now* savannah or semi-desert: in the past these places were not as they are today. Studies of the flora and fauna, and other analyses of the environment around these find-spots, in fact show that early humans primarily lived in forested areas. Furthermore, almost all discoveries of early human remains have been made by or near contemporary lakes and water-courses – in some cases, as with Lucy, even in water lain sediments. To this we can add the solid front teeth and thick tooth enamel that suggest fruit and certain seeds and roots as the main food of early humans; this too indicates a richness of vegetation in the environment. The type of wear on the teeth of early humans also supports this view of their diet.

All the data thus indicate that, several million years after the split from the apes, early humans were still living largely in a vegetation-rich environment, often close to water. This does not mean that they never ventured onto the savannah beyond, but this was not their normal habitat and they did not have meat as their main food.

The idea that bipedalism evolved because the rain forests dried out arose when it was still thought that the origins of the human race lay as far back as 20 or 15 million years ago, in the early Miocene. For several decades now we have known that we should instead be looking at the later Miocene, a period when the climate actually began to be cooler. Certainly the rain forests shrank in East Africa even then, but for other reasons and not to the extent that was once believed. Not least, what business would our primate ancestors have had on the savannah? For more than 50 million years they had been specially adapted to a woodland environment. What usually happens when rainforests increase or decrease in size is that their populations do the same. The idea that a group of apes should have moved out onto the savannah just because the forest began to recede is not particularly convincing.

All of this is more than sufficient to dismiss the savannah hypothesis. Today it is as good as dead as a general theory. Well, perhaps not quite. Because no other convincing alternative has been seen, the savannah hypothesis still lurks beneath the surface in several ideas that have arisen from it. I shall therefore examine these a little more closely.

It was long thought that the revolutionary achievement of bipedalism was that it freed the arms and hands for the manufacture and use of tools. The problem with this is simply that early humans walked around on two legs for several million years before they began to make stone tools. Nor is it easy to see any other direct connection between bipedalism and stone technology. When they need to, almost all apes can raise themselves up on two legs and sit with a straight upper body posture that frees their hands. Sure enough, both apes and monkeys use their hands and fingers for all sorts of things, with superb hand to eye co-ordination. This ability is not therefore something that we acquired with bipedalism, but instead a part of our primate heritage. In some ways apes even have advantages over people, because when seated they also have their prehensile feet to work with.

So, the idea that the bipedal revolution freed up the hands for work is a myth. In reality the hands were freed long before. When people got up on two legs, the result was if anything that they thereby *lost* two useful gripping feet. An ape actually has hands that are almost as free to do other tasks as those of a human. When a chimpanzee wants to use its hands it behaves just like a human, leaning forward or sitting down. Nut-cracking chimps in West Africa often work seated so as to use their hands and feet at the same time. Recent Stone Age people also generally work stone in a seated position, in order to achieve stability and balance. If the problem had depended solely on free arms, then apes would have had the same potential to create tool cultures as people had.

So, what made early *Homo* a toolmaker was not bipedalism in itself but a combination of higher intelligence, more mobile wrists, and a better opposable grip than their ancestors possessed.

In 1979 Owen Lovejoy suggested that bipedalism originated to make it easier for the first human males to carry home food and essentials to their woman and children in a home base. In this way there was no need for daily movement, and people could instead begin to cultivate characteristically human social institutions such as monogamous partnership, the division of labour between the sexes, collective responsibility for subsistence, and the systematic sharing of food.

However, in the first place evolution's goal has never been to promote the kinds of social conventions that we now see as typically human. Second, there is nothing in the archaeological record to even remotely suggest that at the period of human origins there existed fixed settlements or a division of labour more advanced than that of the apes. And even if that had been the case, then such habits would not have been sufficiently advantageous in evolutionary terms as to occasion an anatomical innovation like bipedalism. It is also clear that apes as well as many monkeys are quite good at transporting things by cradling them in their arms – over shorter distances on two legs and over longer ones on three legs. Chimpanzees can do this with an impressive speed and over quite long distances. Thus in purely anatomical terms it would not be any problem for a male chimp to bring home food to a settled partner with children. Nevertheless chimpanzees persist in obtaining all their own food as individuals, as well as moving around on a daily basis and living in large polygamous groups. We can add that a number of primates are monogamous without being bipedal in the slightest.

The transition to an upright gait can therefore be explained neither by the freeing up of the hands, a need for home bases nor through some obscure evolutionary need to establish the human nuclear family.

Another idea that one still encounters today is that our ancestors evolved an upright walk in order to see over the high grass of the savannah. This would not be convincing even if we had become bipedal on the savannah, which we did not. A person walking around at full height in open terrain with the idea of spotting dangerous predators will soon discover that the predators can see them as well. If our four-footed ancestors had had a problem with visibility on the savannah, they would have been much better advised to do the same as apes, monkeys, bears, prairie dogs and many other animals, namely to raise themselves up on their back legs for a moment and then drop down on all fours again.

Scarcely any more sensible is the idea that we became bipedal so as to move more quickly between the dispersed food resources on the savannah. This is based on the misconception that one can move especially fast on two legs. On average, people actually run more slowly and with a worse balance than four-footed animals of a comparable size, something that must have applied even more acutely to the first humans. The fact that a modern human has a slightly more energy-efficient walk and a faster run than a chimpanzee does not mean that this was true for the first bipedal humans. Even the much later afarenes seem to have moved with a rather swaying walk and cannot possibly have run as fast as a skeletally modern human from *erectus* onwards. Early humans could hardly have run down large prey, and if they had a large predator on their heels out on the savannah then it was time to say goodbye. In short then, if our primate ancestors had really needed to run faster then evolution would have invested in improvements to their existing four-footed gait. If against all the odds a group of four-footed apes *had* left the forests to wander about on the savannah, then they would hardly have lived long enough to become our ancestors.

Another argument that regularly pops up is that bipedalism would have made it easier to reach up to food hanging high in the bushes on the savannah. But a four-footed chimp is better at that than any human ever could be.

Another unconvincing argument is that people became bipedal so that early human mothers could free their hands to take care of their helpless children. If the last common ancestors shared by both humans and chimpanzees really had such helpless young that they were forced to get up on two legs, then why are there still any four-footed apes at all? In any case there is nothing to suggest that the children of early humans were any more helpless and parent-dependent than the infants of apes. In fact bipedalism probably had the opposite effect. So long as a mother was four-footed, then her offspring could ride on her back and hold on to her fur, even when she was racing around in the trees. But with a mother who walked upright, with or without fur, this became impossible. And as early humans were hardly capable of making or arranging any kind of carrying device for small children, their only option was to carry the child in their arms. In other words the bipedal mother's arms and hands were actually permanently taken up with children. Thus bipedalism did not arise to make it easier to carry small infants; it instead arose despite the fact that it made it *harder* to do so.

So, neither the need to run fast on the savannah, nor to see long distances over ground vegetation, nor to carry food home to the family settlement, nor to bear children, can have created a selective pressure towards bipedalism.

As Elaine Morgan has pointed out, the savannah was a very bad place to lose one's fur. The purpose of such a covering is to provide protection against thickets, bugs, rain, cold nights, sunshine and ultraviolet radiation. Out on the savannah the rain pelts down harder, the heat is more painful, the sun more merciless and the nocturnal chill more biting than in the tropical forests. In other words the savannah in fact demands more dense fur, not a thinner coat. Savannah animals that do not have much fur, such as elephants, rhinos, hippos and warthogs instead have thicker skins. The human hide is strikingly thin.

The savannah hypothesis thus explains our thick subcutaneous fat and abundance of sweat glands in the following way. To prevent the newly bipedal humans from suffering heat stroke when running about on the savannah, they lost their fur and gained an extra layer of fat under the skin as a protection against the cold nights. But because this fat layer hampered heat loss this had to be compensated for by a few million extra sweat glands. So, the savannah hypothesis proposes in all seriousness that evolution provided early humans with extra sweat glands to cope with temperature regulation, that had been hindered by the subcutaneous fat, that had been built up against the nocturnal chill, painfully cold on the skin, that had lost its fur in order to provide – temperature regulation. It would have been simpler to have kept the fur!

Morgan has also emphasised how unsuitable it would be to regulate body temperature through sweating specifically on the savannah, since there it would be particularly hard to replace the loss of moisture and salt that are necessary to survive. In that case selection should have provided the hunting man, who ran most, with less fur, and the woman, who moved about less, with more fur. But precisely the opposite is true. We should also remember that no other known African quadruped mammal has taken a permanent step up on its back legs in order to adapt to a life on the savannah.

The savannah hypothesis has also been kept alive by Peter Wheeler's calculations, which suggest that a two-legged creature on a sparsely wooded savannah would receive up to 30 per cent less solar radiation that a quadruped of the same size. Because the wind higher off the ground also lowers temperatures by around two degrees, Wheeler argued that an upright walk would bring evolutionary advantages on the savannah. It is strange how this idea could receive so much attention long after we began to realise that humans did *not* become bipedal on the savannah. Nor does Wheeler's hypothesis solve the problems of fur loss and sweat glands. It may possibly be of interest in relation to the question of how later on early *Homo* was also able to adapt itself to a life on the half open grasslands, though early humans had by then been bipedal for several million years.

The knowledge that our human ancestors did not become bipedal on the savannah has sometimes shifted the focus to the border zone between savannah and forest. But studies of common chimpanzees that live in such environments have shown that they do not behave much differently from other chimps, nor do they show the slightest tendencies towards bipedalism. To reveal possible anatomical structures from which bipedalism could have evolved, there have also been analyses of the different ways of walking and climbing that our last primate ancestors may have had. These have not been able to produce a single credible example that would produce the degree of selective pressure for bipedalism that we must assume to be required.

Thus there is nothing to suggest that a savannah environment could have unleashed selective forces strong enough to produce in primates such unique qualities as a two-legged gait, an absence of fur, subcutaneous fat or an abundance of sweat glands. And, as we have seen, bipedalism did not evolve on the savannah. On the other hand it is not easy to see how the forest environment where our last quadruped ancestors lived could have given rise to a strong selective pressure for either bipedalism or the other qualities mentioned above. No one has ever really tried to argue for this either.

The theoretical strength of the savannah hypothesis was that it tried to explain bipedalism in the light of an evolutionarily imperative situation, and it viewed bipedalism, an absence of fur, subcutaneous fat and sweat glands as interlinked problems. Of all this only fragments remain, vague and contradictory ideas that these factors might have had some kind of general evolutionary advantages.

But bipedalism is not the only mystery, as the same applies to all the other qualities named here. It is true that we do not know that they all have the same evolutionary background, but we can make a good guess that this is the case. As it stands there is no single, general theory of human origins, and even less one that is generally accepted. Even the many researchers who are not openly critical to the savannah hypothesis are cautious about this. Phillip Tobias, a Nestor among palaeo-anthropologists, has on several occasions declared that in all honesty we have no choice but to start again from the beginning. Research on human origins has gone down a one-way street.

One thing that most agree upon, however, is that bipedalism is the key factor that defines the early humans. Regardless of what primitive traits they had, the upright walk marks the point of transition from ape to human. From a primate perspective bipedalism is absolutely extraordinary, and this suggests that the evolutionary situation that set the ball rolling must also have been exceptional. It is highly likely, though not certain, that bipedalism evolved in connection with the circumstances that made the last common ancestors of humans and chimpanzees go their separate ways.

The aquatic hypothesis

Neither savannah, woodland savannah nor forest can either together or separately have created the selective pressure necessary to make our ancestors bipedal, furless and well provided with subcutaneous fat and sweat glands. We therefore have to direct our thoughts towards another feasible evolutionary situation. It is no longer possible to ignore the so-called aquatic hypothesis, or perhaps more accurately, the shallow water hypothesis. This was launched in 1960 in a short essay by the English marine biologist Alistair Hardy, who had then been mulling over the idea for almost 30 years. Unknown to him, the German biologist Max Westenhöfer had been thinking along similar lines in 1942.

Hardy had noticed that humans share a number of anatomical and physiological qualities with mammals that live permanently in water. Because apes lack these qualities, Hardy suggested that our ancestors must at some point have lived half in water and half on land. The qualities that he saw as signals of an earlier aquatic life were on the first hand bipedalism, thick subcutaneous fat, regressive fur and a natural diving and swimming ability. With reference to the many other land mammals who could be proved to have either completely or partly adapted to life in the water, and in some cases then returned to a life on the land, Hardy argued that his aquatic hypothesis was not as evolutionarily odd as it might seem.

Hardy's ideas were subsequently taken up by the English cultural journalist and playwright Elaine Morgan. In a series of books that included *The Descent of Woman* (1972), *The Aquatic Ape* (1982), *The Scars of Evolution* (1990) and *The Aquatic Ape Theory* (1997), Morgan has energetically developed Hardy's aquatic hypothesis and strongly criticised its savannah counterpart. The fact that Morgan was not a professional scholar, and in her first book poked ruthless fun at the male-fixated research on human origins that was common at the time, contributed to researchers' general dismissal not only of her enthusiastic arguments in favour of the aquatic hypothesis but also of her well-founded rejection of the savannah hypothesis. Her contributions have therefore made their impact primarily outside professional palaeo-anthropology. In Sweden her work has been taken up by the physiologists Karl-Erik Fichtelius and Erika Schagatay, and the zoologist Jan Lindblad.

I shall now present a summary of the aquatic hypothesis as I understand it from Hardy and Morgan, with a few additions and adjustments suggested by others, and a few comments of my own.

The upright gait: Hardy saw humans' upright walk as a natural evolutionary effect of a long period spent wading in shallow water by the shore. He also noted that human beings' extended skeletons, forward-facing genitals and tendency towards face-to-face sexual intercourse are all found in many aquatic mammals.

The absence of fur: this is typical for aquatic mammals in tropical waters, because fur does not afford any protection against cold water and only serves to slow down movement. The short, dense fur of arctic aquatic mammals is related to the cold on the ice and on land. The only tropical land mammals that are essentially hairless are hippos, elephants, rhinos, tapirs and to some extent wild pigs, all of which have a definite affinity with water and seem to have some kind of evolutionary past there. In evolutionary terms it is not unreasonable to suggest that our ancestors' fur was lost during a period of life in the water.

Subcutaneous fat: the fat that humans, and especially women, have beneath their skin is much thicker and more evenly distributed than it is in apes, other primates and most tropical land animals. It has an equivalent only in certain whales, seals, manatees and other mammals in cooler waters. Subcutaneous fat protects against cold both in water and on land. Because the body temperature of mammals is higher than that of the tropical sea, a lengthy period spent even in these kinds of waters necessitates a degree of cold protection. On the other hand humans' subcutaneous fat is thin by comparison with that of proper aquatic mammals, as if we were only partly adapted to a life in the water.

Hardy also emphasised that the 'aquatic ape', to use Morgan's phrase, probably did not spend more than 5 or 6 hours a day in the water, and must have spent the night and part of the day on land and by the beach.

If the loss of fur was a result of biological adaptation to a daily turn in relatively lukewarm water, then subcutaneous fat could have evolved to cope with the chill of the water and the nocturnal cold on land. The aquatic hypothesis also presupposes that the soft contours of our bodies were present from the beginning.

Other fatty glands: we still possess all the fatty glands that were designed to make rain slide off the fur of primates. We also have more of those glands that are connected with the hair follicles than the furry apes have, albeit in rudimentary form. In a possible life in the shallows these could have served the same function as subcutaneous fat.

Back hair: Hardy argued that men's back hair has a clear growth pattern of having been formed in flowing water. Morgan also pointed out that human embryos in the fifth to seventh month of pregnancy are covered by a fine down called the *lanugo*, with a swirling growth pattern that is strongly reminiscent of how water flows over a body in motion. This down has usually disappeared before birth.

Swimming and diving abilities; the dive reflex: for a land mammal, the human being is a remarkably good diver and has excellent physiological mechanisms for deep diving. We also have a marked affinity for water. Babies have spontaneous swimming skills and adults learn easily. Newborn babies and infants under the age of 4 months have a breath-holding reflex that is triggered as soon as their faces touch water. Different studies have shown that human babies can be born in water without problem, and immediately make spontaneous swimming motions under the surface. Erika Schagatay has also shown that the decline in pulse rate that occurs when a human dives is much greater than in land-dwelling animals, and is almost equal to that of semi-aquatic animals such as otters and beavers. These aquatic adaptations cannot have evolved in a tropical forest or savannah. Most common chimpanzees have a well-known respect for water, not to say fear of it: they are unable to swim, and they have a tendency to quickly drown if they happen to fall in.

Nose: while the noses of the great apes mostly resemble an electric socket – two holes in their faces – the human nose is large, projecting and downward facing in a manner that allows us to swim and dive without getting water in our breathing organs. As Morgan has noted, there is only one other primate that can boast of something similar – the proboscis monkey of Borneo with its impressive hooter. It lives very near water and amuses itself with long swimming trips, something quite unique among apes and monkeys. It is true that early humans seem to have had rather flat nasal bones, but on the other hand nasal cartilage is not preserved. A projecting cartilaginous tip to the nose with downward pointing nostrils would have been quite enough to prevent the water from streaming in.

Genitals: just as in many aquatic mammals, the human female genitals are embedded deeper in the body than is the case among the apes. The vagina and womb are constructed so that water and water-borne particles have difficulty in getting past the hymen, due to a curve in the vaginal profile and large outer labia. This arrangement is found in numerous aquatic mammals but is lacking among the great apes.

Blood: as Karl-Erik Fichtelius has observed, humans share with sea-dwelling mammals a low count of red blood corpuscles and a higher level of haemoglobin in each blood cell, in contrast to our close relatives the chimpanzees and gorillas, and other land mammals.

Hardy suggested that humans separated from the apes during the long heat and drought of the Miocene, when they lived in shallow water by the shore. He proposed that they sustained themselves there with a diet of crayfish, crabs, mussels, oysters and other shellfish, as well as worms, small animals and fishes. At first they kept to the beach and the tidal mud flats, then later ventured out into the shallows and deeper water. After a time they could even have caught helpless young seals on the beach.

Morgan added to Hardy's argument in several ways. She suggested that the chubbiness of newborn babies, which is very obvious by comparison with skinny newborn apes, has an obvious survival value in an aquatic animal. She also argues that a woman's comparatively large, fatty breasts evolved to prevent their milk from being chilled by water. She further proposed that humans' long head hair might have served the same purpose as a mother ape's body hair, namely in giving a child something to hold on to in the water. Morgan has also pointed out that women's head hair thickens markedly during pregnancy. One could add that a newborn child's body weight is made up of 10–15 per cent fatty tissues, which during the first 10 weeks increases to a massive 20–25 per cent. This is more reminiscent of arctic mammals than of African land animals.

Morgan also argued that humans' tear glands secrete salt to an extent that is unique among apes and most land animals, but typical for animals and birds in saltwater environments. She has later admitted that the proof for this is uncertain.

Because the oldest skeletal finds are so few and unclear, it is not possible to formulate a theory of human origins on the basis of fossil discoveries alone. These also tell us nothing about physiological functions, or about such things as hair, skin colour, sweat glands and subcutaneous fat.

I have earlier mentioned the importance of the great similarities between humans and apes. But when it comes to the question of the origins of our species, it is mostly the dissimilarities that are interesting. Any hypothesis concerning how we came into existence must in the first instance address anatomical and physiological differences between our closest relatives and us. In summary, the qualities that most clearly distinguish us from the apes are those that suggest a background of temporary activity in an aquatic environment:

- upright walk
- absence of fur
- thick subcutaneous fat
- fatty female breasts
- streamlined body contours
- a large number of sweat glands
- fatty glands in the rudimentary hair follicles of the body
- thick hair on the head
- a nose tip with downward pointing nostrils
- a closed vagina
- the streamlined pattern of embryonic down
- a marked physiological diving ability
- the dive reflex in babies
- a marked swimming ability
- a mental affinity for water.

There are other qualities that separate us from the apes that may – though not necessarily – have a connection with a life in the water. These include the ability to speak, the lack of a clear mating season, and a front-facing vagina. I will return to them all later on.

Just like the savannah hypothesis, its aquatic counterpart is based on dramatic environmental changes that took place in Africa. Some time during the Miocene the great low-lying area in the Horn of Africa was underwater, as seen in the enormous deposits of salt still found there today. Deep arms of the sea penetrated the land and created several islands, including one that is now the Danaqil mountain range in northeast Ethiopia. This seems to have been the situation about 6.8 and 5.4 million years ago.

Morgan imagined that a group of early human ancestors were cut off on this or another similarly large island in the area. To avoid predators on the island as its tree cover declined, to cool themselves in the heat, and quite simply to feed themselves, they fled to the shallow coastal waters, perhaps near the mouth of a half dried-up river with fresh water. Here they could live on water plants and shellfish, smaller fish and other protein-rich food, and on the nearby shore there was fruit, fresh plants and insects. Shelter for the night and a place to rest in the day were provided by cliffs or vegetation near the shore. If one ventured even a little way out in the water on all fours then it quickly reached one's face, and to move farther out it was necessary to straighten the back and walk on two legs. The wobbly primates found that the water even helped to keep them upright. Later they also learned to swim and dive, and at last the four-footed ape had evolved into a two-legged aquatic ape, that evolved first into early humans and finally into us.

The key question is what could have made a creature biologically adapted to life in the forest, and that had an instinctive respect for water, want to wade out into the shallows and establish itself there for a long period of time. Why didn't they just die out if living on the land became impossible?

Common chimpanzees are usually afraid of water, but among bonobos it is less obvious, and it varies among gorillas. Even the occasional common chimp, like many lowland gorillas, can voluntarily wade out in smaller watercourses and pools. The respect for water thus varies between species and individuals. The aquatic hypothesis merely requires that a sufficiently large number of individuals, those least afraid of water, took the first footsteps out into the blue. The others died out or continued to live on the land as apes.

A critical point for the aquatic hypothesis is obviously the question of the natural geographic changes that it presupposes. It is nevertheless clear that during the middle and later Miocene and the Pliocene there really were major shifts in the earth's crust and volcanic eruptions in east and northeast Africa. Part of the Afar area was submerged again and again, and islands of varying size were created only to later join the land once more. Another problem is that we lack especially diagnostic fossil finds from the period of the split from the apes that can definitely be linked to this scenario.

When Hardy set out his idea that the ancestors of the early humans were forced out into the water by increasing heat and drought, it was still thought that humankind evolved in the early or middle Miocene. In fact this seems to have occurred towards the end of the period, which if anything was rather less warm and a little more humid. If our ancestors really did experience an adaptation to water about 6 million years ago at the latest, this was hardly caused by climatic change in itself, but instead primarily through a volcanic–tectonic realignment of the earth's crust.

It is well known that islands that are created through isolation from the mainland often play host to rapid changes in the species that live there. Among other things this is caused by the fact that large predators, with a low population density, die out through inbreeding. Animals that were earlier held in check by the predators suddenly increase in numbers, with the result that intra-species competition begins to expand. In situations like these parts of the population establish themselves in previously unexploited niches, and this gives rise to a rapid change in the species. If there is no selective pressure for defensive qualities against predators, then rather peculiar species can result.

Strangely, a group of apes of the *Oreopithecus* family living in central Italy between 8.5 and 6.5 million years ago seem to have evolved complete bipedalism. This happened at the same time, or shortly before, our human ancestors in Africa became bipedal. It is perhaps more than coincidence that this occurred in exactly the kind of evolutionary geographic environment that Hardy theoretically predicted as the reason for humankind's emergence: a rapidly created, isolated island.

The triggering factor for the evolution of bipedalism cannot in this case have been drought, because the island was richly forested. Köhler and Moyà-Solà suggest instead that when the predators died out – as the fossil finds prove that they did – and the population pressure among the island's apes increased, then a group of *Oreopithecus* climbed out of the trees and established themselves on the forest floor. In order to more easily reach food in the trees and bushes, they raised themselves up permanently on two legs.

This interpretation of bipedalism is clearly influenced by parts of the savannah hypothesis. It quite simply cannot have happened like that. First, both the trees and the ground must already have been within the range of a large ape like *Oreopithecus*. Second, and as mentioned above, the need to reach high up to food cannot possibly create a strong selective pressure for bipedalism in an ape of this kind. This is no problem for such an animal. Not least, the most ground dwelling of all apes, the gorilla, shows no sign at all of bipedalism.

But Köhler has also pointed to the island's broad stretches of beaches and inland marshes as a possible habitat for *Oreopithecus bamboli* after they became bipedal. In actual fact, these seem to have been the only biotopes that were not already occupied by *Oreopithecus*. The most likely explanation is that it was there a group of quadruped *Oreopithecus* came to evolve the completely bipedal body posture that would define the 'ape-man' *bamboli*.

The case of *bamboli* lends strong empirical support to the notion that our ancestors became bipedal in connection with long-term residence in a beach environment on a large island, roughly as Hardy had proposed for humankind. It is worth noting, however, that in contrast to *bamboli* the early humans show no anatomical features that suggest an evolutionary adaptation to a life without predators.

No doubt the aquatic hypothesis has its problems. But what the example of *bamboli* shows is that two million years is a sufficiently long time to achieve full bipedalism on a temporarily isolated island.

The oldest known early humans had shorter upper arms than one might expect if the upright walk had emerged at a slow pace under weak selective pressure. Nor do the spines of both early and modern humans show any signs of a gradual evolutionary process of straightening up, with different stages along the way. Robin Crompton and Yu Li have studied Lucy's skeleton through three dimensional computer simulation, and according to them she did not in any way walk with a curved back and slightly bent knees as we often think, but instead fully upright. They claim that a spinally curved, knee-focused gait uses twice as much energy as full bipedalism or four-footedness, and is a clear handicap in relation to predators. Natural selection therefore saw to it that the transition from four to two feet went rather quickly in evolutionary terms. There is thus much to suggest that bipedalism evolved during a short and intensive period under very strong selective pressure for it. This is exactly what the aquatic hypothesis presupposes.

In the next chapter I suggest that early humans lost their fur through so-called neotene processes for bipedalism. If this is correct, then we have not had fur since the division of the species some 6 million years ago. In that case, this fur could naturally also have disappeared even on land, if we only had a good explanation for how bipedalism could have evolved there. But as yet we do not.

The aquatic hypothesis' explanations of subcutaneous fat, the absence of fur, pigmentation and the lack of a clear mating season must also show themselves to be tenable in the light of a subsequent life on land.

Subcutaneous fat has hardly protected the skin against ultraviolet solar radiation, which in a possible aquatic or similar life is if anything increased by the reflections from the water. Since our last four-footed ancestors' skin ought to have been rather light, roughly like that of a chimpanzee with little pigment except for in the face, then the loss of fur could have led to a synthesis of D vitamins in damagingly high doses, a serious deficiency of folic acids, and even skin cancer. But regardless of whether the 'creation' was played out on dry land or in tidal shallows, it still demanded a new form of sun shield that evolved at the same rate as fur disappeared.

In fact, we never really lost our primate fur – it just regressed. It would therefore have been simple for natural selection to give our ancestors back their fur if this had proved to be really necessary. That this did not happen indicates that the level of melanin in the skin increased as the fur receded, and that early humans were brown-skinned from the very beginning.

The aquatic hypothesis therefore presupposes that early humans were already hairless, brown coloured, sweaty and endowed with the gentle curves that come with a generous layer of fat under the skin.

We can think what we like about the aquatic hypothesis. But as long as we cannot point to any other evolutionary situation on land that can more convincingly shed light on our bipedal gait, our subcutaneous fat, our sweat glands and a great many other things, then it should be treated with respect.

The problem of over-heating caused by fat cannot have been very serious in a possible watery environment, but it might have become so later, on the land. If evolution solved this problem with lots of new sweat glands, then these probably evolved as the last physical features that separate us from the apes. It is relevant here that for several million years after the split from the last ape ancestors, early humans lived in a rather shady milieu that perhaps only demanded slightly more pigment in the skin than was there from the beginning. I would therefore assume that the earliest furless humans evolved a rather brown skin. The first people with really dark skins could have been found among groups of *Subhomo* and early *Homo* who much later, 3 or 2 million years ago, moved out more permanently into open terrain.

With her rather broad, balanced pelvis, much wider than that of a female chimpanzee, early woman might already have had typical feminine proportions and subcutaneous fat.

For a long while early humans were depicted in reconstruction drawings as fair skinned and lightly furred. But this white early human never existed. Pale skin evolved first when people began to live in the more sunless regions of the northern hemisphere, where the combination of less ultraviolet radiation and too much pigment could be a problem, in that it prevented the synthesis of vitamin-D from the weak solar rays. It was first in the sub-arctic and arctic areas that the strong reflections of the sun off snow necessitated a greater pigment protection, as modern arctic peoples' appearance clearly demonstrates. White people often have more body hair and more beard growth than those with darker skins. This hints of a degree of re-furring as an adaptation to a colder climate. In recent years it has become common to reconstruct early humans as relatively dark and hairless, though never accompanied by an explanation of how this should have come about. It is as if the aquatic hypothesis is gradually becoming accepted, but without any open discussion.

The aquatic hypothesis must also be able to tell us how this life in the water was abandoned. Why did we come back to the land and become early humans, instead of evolving further into a completely marine mammal? It is not enough to say they got tired of their beach holiday. This too must have been a sufficiently drastic change of environment that it can only be understood in the light of strongly compulsive circumstances.

If the aquatic hypothesis holds up, then the return to the land might have happened approximately like this. When the Afar basin emerged from the sea and the Danaqil and other similar islands once more rejoined the continent, then the bipedal early humans found themselves standing there on dry ground through no fault of their own, deep inland and a long way from the coast. In this case one cannot speak of returning to the land. The only alternative was to adapt again to life there, or to die out.

An evolutionary scenario of this kind could also have claimed its victims. But because they had never really cut their links to the land, and had most of their old anatomy and physiology intact, then these casualties would have been far fewer than when they took those first steps down into the water.

Almost all important finds of early human bones have been made by contemporary lakes and watercourses. That this attraction did not apply to our last quadruped ancestors is clear from the fact that the same find spots, otherwise full of bones from many other animals, are completely lacking in remains of chimpanzees' and gorillas' ancestors. This is a striking contrast. It is strange that it should be only very recently that we have begun to even discuss the odd way in which our early ancestors seem to have lost their fear of water and gained an affinity for it. The fact that early humans were drawn to watery environments reflects a fundamental change in their mentality. It would prove to be of decisive importance for our whole species' history and cultural development.

Elephants and hippos are also excellent swimmers, they love the water and have strongly regressed fur. It has long been suggested that the elephant's skeleton shows that its ancestors 40 to 30 million years ago lived partly in water. Finds of 50 million-year-old elephant ancestors in Africa and Asia point in the same direction, and can be linked to contemporary shallow water environments. At the same time the similarities that have long been observed between elephants and sea cows in terms of skeleton, embryonic development, the construction of the inner ear, and biochemical structure have been confirmed through DNA analysis, which shows that the two animals are each other's closest living relatives. The zoologist Ann Gaeth has also shown that, unlike those of other land mammals, an elephant embryo's testicles remain inside the abdomen and do not sink down into a pouch outside the body. That the trunk emerges early in the embryonic cycle may also point to an original snorkel function. Gaeth has proved too that young elephant embryos have kidney structures that can only be paralleled among freshwater vertebrates. She suggests that the elephants' ancestors once underwent a partial adaptation to a life in the water. New DNA studies have similarly shown that the hippo's nearest genetic relative is not to be found among land mammals, but instead among marine whales.

In evolutionary terms Hardy's aquatic hypothesis appears less fantastic with every year that passes.

The state of research

The aquatic hypothesis is rarely mentioned. When somebody does so, it is usually dismissed as a fantasy or as having insufficient support from the fossil record. And then in the next breath some part of the old savannah hypothesis is brought up that suffers from exactly the same lack of fossil support, that is evolutionarily much more unlikely and that offers only a partial solution to a large complex of problems. The savannah hypothesis and other land-based hypotheses have come nowhere near a logically cohesive and empirically credible explanation of human origins, and of all the anatomical and physio-logical qualities that separate us from our closest relatives. If even the loss of fur could be a side effect of neotene processes on land, with the primary pur-pose of creating bipedalism, they still lack every convincing form of collective explanation for the beginnings of humankind.

The greatest weakness of the aquatic hypothesis is the uncertainty as to which environmental conditions it is based upon. But its inner logic is good and its evolutionary credibility is considerable. For the moment it is the only logically cohesive and evolutionarily reasonable total explanation of human origins that includes the upright gait, the absence of fur, subcutaneous fat, sweat glands and a mass of other anatomical and physiological features.

The aquatic hypothesis has still not been subjected to a thorough and unprejudiced test. If it should prove to be untenable then we have no choice but to conclude that generations of research has not produced a single reason-able hypothesis about our origins. Our only hope would be that new and richer fossil discoveries would allow the missing link to walk onstage and say hello.

Six million years ago our creation was complete. On two legs and probably furless, brown-skinned and sweating, Eve and Adam stepped forth without fig leaves into a veritable Eden full of lakes and watercourses surrounded by gallery and closed woodlands and a rich world of plants and animals. In the distance lay thinly wooded and bushy grass savannahs with an even greater variety of animal life.

For a long time in that world the early humans could maintain a diet that did not depart too much from what their last primate ancestors had eaten. Because water was always close, their eating habits did not differ dramatically from what they would have been during a possible aquatic period. Free from their original fear of water, they could spice their diet with all kinds of aquatic plants, molluscs and fishes. It was probably unavoidable that quite a number of early humans ended their days as crocodile food. Fossil finds have long made us aware that many fell victim to the big predator cats.

It is hard to know whether the bipedal early humans who now began to wander out across Africa could have produced a viable offspring with their closest quadruped relatives. Obstacles had probably been placed in the way of this early on by distinct anatomical, social and sexual differences. But one way or another, a sufficiently large population was able to survive in genetic isolation for the line of the human species to be established. The split from the apes was definitive.

6

EVOLUTIONARY TOOLS AND THE PATH TO HUMANITY

The process of evolution from single cells to complex creatures such as mammals, people, and the whole rich spectrum of species, could hardly have occurred solely through random mutations, sexual selection, genetic drift and other evolutionary self-sustenance. Its primary mechanism has been adaptation through natural selection in a dynamic environment.

Behind global changes in climate and environment we can trace astronomical factors and geophysical events such as continental drift, alterations in the earth's crust and so on. And the climate has always fluctuated, sometimes rhythmically, sometimes irregularly, by greater or lesser degrees, globally, regionally and locally – most clearly during the last few million years in the form of switches between ice ages and warm periods. Climate zones have consequently moved back and forth from north to south and up and down in altitude, albeit with a consistent internal structure. Major climatic changes have either directly or indirectly affected the entire planet and all living things. Because all life has its special environmental needs and tolerances, environmental change has been a powerful force for evolution. So when we today complain about the climate's inconsistency, we should remember that if it had not always been this way then you and I would perhaps have still been bobbing about on the world-ocean as aimless little creatures, simple minded and single celled.

From this perspective it is no accident that the human race emerged and underwent its oldest evolution in connection with major changes in the global climate. The two most decisive events – first the split from the apes and bipedalism, and second the division into many different species with a faster evolution of the brain – both coincided with dramatic convulsions in Africa's geography, climate and environment, and with periods when the arctic ice caps started to expand on a large scale. While the sea drowned some parts of northeast Africa, other areas rose by up to 1,000 metres and increasingly moved out of the rain belt. The climate became drier, the rain forests receded, and the savannah and steppe slowly began to spread.

An unusual geographic event close in time to the origins of humankind was the drying out of the Mediterranean. This was caused by the trapping of large amounts of seawater at the poles in the form of ice, so that global sea levels fell and a land bridge formed between Africa and the Iberian peninsular. Completely isolated from the world-ocean, the Mediterranean at last dried out. This happened around 6.4 million years ago, and the situation lasted for nearly 2 million years.

Not only human beings but many other species also underwent rapid evolutionary changes towards the end of the Miocene, during the Pliocene and the early Pleistocene, between 6 and 1 million years ago. Through evolutionary adaptation to a world in the process of dramatic change, the number of animal species increased considerably and laid the foundations for much of the present day fauna on the African savannah. The origins of humankind and our early evolution is just one of many examples.

New species are often created through changes in their environment and living conditions, whereby competition for food and space increases so that distinct populations specialise in different niches, and ultimately isolate themselves to evolve in separate directions. This seems to have been the case with the early human family during the period from 3 to 2.5 million years ago, when a number of new species 'suddenly' branched off in different directions.

Evolution is not just emergence and change, but also extinction. In the same way as many animal species died out at this time, so too did species of humans both then and later. At last only one was left: our own. When one considers that 99 per cent of all animal species that once lived on earth are now extinct, then one can appreciate that our own species will probably not last forever.

Even though it sometimes appears that way, evolution cannot conjure up new species from nowhere. It operates through step-by-step changes in existing qualities. But this does not mean that it progresses at a steady pace, and in fact the opposite often seems to be the case. There are also good reasons for believing that it was a rather fast process whereby our last quadruped ancestors became bipedal early humans. We must therefore ask ourselves which evolutionary selective mechanisms can then have been in play.

Permanent neoteny, *pedomorphosis*, is the evolutionary process whereby characteristics typical for embryos and newborn infants are retained later and later, to at last become a permanent part of the adult condition. Neoteny is often used as a collective term for a number of similar but nonetheless distinct mechanisms. It is clear that neoteny has contributed to the evolution of many species, both vertebrates and insects. Many researchers also claim that neoteny has also played a crucial role in human evolution, whereas others are more sceptical. My own opinion is that neoteny has been of decisive importance for the evolution of humankind and its further evolution.

This especially relates to certain anatomical features in humans that are lacking in adult apes, but which are present in their embryos and newborn infants. These include an upright skeleton, forward-facing vagina, a high round cranium, a flat facial profile and large quantities of hair on the head, under the arms and in the genital region.

It is usually noted with approval that during our evolution we humans have become less and less like our ape ancestors. This is a qualified truth. When it comes to newborn apes the situation is paradoxical, in that the more modern the human in question so the closer are the links to the apes, and the more ancient the human, the fewer the links.

A special explanation is now presented for the immaturity of human babies at birth by comparison with ape infants, for the fact that our brains continue growing after birth, and for our more prolonged childhood. Because the time taken for the brain to grow and develop is usually related to the different phases of early life, intelligence and consciousness are thought to have evolved through a progressive extension of infancy and childhood, so-called *peramorphosis*. Another important observation is that the human embryo's brain takes 25 per cent longer to develop than that of other primates, and that many of the neurons that make up the brain cortex with its complex thinking functions are built up precisely during this extra stage of growth. Thus the evolution of the human brain should in the first instance have been concerned with the extension of the period spent in the womb and in childhood.

Bipedalism

In order for infants to pass through the birth canal without being hindered by four arms and legs that stick out from the body, the skeletons of four-footed mammals are stretched out and straight at birth. This does not prevent the youngster from very soon raising itself up on four legs.

The late-stage embryos and newborn infants of apes are like a mirror image of an adult human and the opposite of an adult ape: a straight skeleton, forward-facing vagina, the pelvis in line with the body's centre of gravity, head and neck following straight up from the spine. In a newborn chimp the hole through which the spinal marrow enters the head (the *foramen magnum*) is placed almost centrally under the skull, before it slowly moves back to the rear underside of the cranium. It is no surprise that this hole is much farther forwards in bipedal early humans than it is in quadruped apes.

As in most four-footed mammals, the vaginas of apes are generally backward facing. This applies even to those who temporarily raise themselves up on two legs, because this does not alter the angle of the pelvis to the skeleton. Their embryos and newborn by contrast have vaginas facing forwards. There is therefore much to suggest that the transition to bipedalism was made possible by a neotene process for the adult retention of the embryonic straight skeleton and forward-facing vagina. Even the earliest humans that we can reconstruct had a relatively straight skeleton and pelvis, and therefore almost certainly a forward-facing vagina.

Some water-dwelling mammals such as seals and whales have sex face-to-face in classic human fashion. This can be explained by these animals' evolution of a straight skeleton with forward-facing vagina, acquired through neotene selection in order to facilitate movement through water.

Although we humans see ourselves as smooth-skinned and the apes as furry, we in fact have *more* hair on our heads, under our arms and in our crotches than an adult chimpanzee. In this respect we are the image of a newborn chimp or an embryo, which has very little hair on its body but a great deal in these areas.

There is thus considerable support for the idea that our straight skeletons, pelvises in line with our bodies, forward-facing vagina, smooth skins, hair on our heads, in our armpits and in the genital region was evolved through a powerful neotene selection in connection with our transition to bipedalism.

The aquatic hypothesis proceeds from the notion that we became bipedal and smooth-skinned in an adaptation to one and the same evolutionary situation, just as the hypothesis of neoteny presupposes. Hair on our heads, under our arms and in our groins could thus be seen as something secondary that was included in the neotene bipedal package. But naturally water is not needed for this, and it could also have happened on dry land.

The crown of a human head is unusually thin, and lacks both fat and muscles as protection from a glaring sun. Hair on the head can therefore have possessed a positive selection value in connection with a possible aquatic life after the division of the species, and much later when early *Homo* began to expand onto the sun-drenched savannah.

Elaine Morgan suggested that a woman's long head hair evolved so that children could hold fast to their smooth-skinned aquatic ape-mothers. But men have hair just as long as women, and because ape males sometimes also carry children then the same explanation ought to work for the hair of early human men. Long hair could also have been practical for a life on dry land, with or without a distant past in the water.

In any case I would propose that humans have had a neotene tuft on their heads since the split from the apes, and that this grew denser when early *Homo* took to the savannah.

When in heat the female primate's backward-facing genitals send out inviting scents to the male's nose that he presses up close. But with bipedalism the distance from the source became too great for a weak scent organ. It has therefore been suggested that the functions of the vaginal scent were to some extent assumed by the glands in the armpit, which produced erotic scents that the hair growing there helped to spread to the man's nose.

Pubic hair may have afforded a degree of protection to the female genitals, even though the chimpanzees seem to happily do without. For the male organ this hair cannot have provided much defence. Perhaps the neotene pubic hair was simply retained because it was not actually disadvantageous.

According to this scenario, a whole package of typically human anatomical features may have evolved simultaneously through a neotene process based on the embryonic anatomy of our last primate ancestors: a straight frame, a head directly above the spine, a pelvis in line with the body, forward-facing vagina, smooth skin and hair on the head, under the arms and covering the genitals.

Early *Homo*

The next great neotene process seems to have begun 2.5 million years ago, and concerns the skull and face of early *Homo* and its successors *ergaster* and early *erectus* (I do not count here the flat face of *Kenyanthropus platyops* almost a million years earlier). It may have been triggered by an external selective pressure for intelligence that gave impetus to the expansion of the brain, which in turn demanded a bigger skull to house it. A somewhat higher, broader and rounder head also comes in here, together with slightly thinner bones in the cranial vault, smaller brow ridges, jaws and teeth, a different angle of the jaw and tooth alignment, and a rather straighter forehead and face. In other words, these concern a number of details that together make up a more 'human' skull and facial form.

If the brain of early *Homo* grew in size through the extension of infancy and early childhood in a peramorphic selection process, then the skull grew bigger through the adult retention of the embryo's relatively large head and small jaws, a process of pedomorphosis or permanent neoteny. None of this rules out the reduction of jaws and teeth as a result of early *Homo*'s diet additionally becoming less vegetarian and more carnivorous.

At the same time we find brain size increasing also in many other East African animals, which according to the palaeontologist Elisabeth Vrba is clearly an evolutionary adaptation to the great environmental changes of the time in that area.

Already by the period of the early afarenes, the canine teeth had been dramatically reduced in size, apparently without any other traces of neoteny. I have interpreted this to mean that the canines lost their original function early on.

The Japanese primatologist Takayoshi Kano has made the important observation that the adult bonobo exhibits almost all the features that I have listed here as neotene in humans, albeit not so pronounced. Compared to the common chimp, the bonobo has a tad more upright body posture, a slightly greater tendency to walk on two legs, a somewhat less backward-facing vagina, denser hair on the head, a rounder skull and a straighter facial profile, together with smaller jaws, teeth and brow ridges. The bonobo, which is no more closely related to humans than the common chimpanzee, thus seems to have undergone a degree of neotene evolution of the skull and body. It is tempting to place this event at the time around 2.1 million years ago when the bonobo and the common chimp went their separate ways in evolutionary terms, when early *Homo* also evolved its first neotene features of the skull.

Early humans therefore seem to have experienced at least two neotene processes and one peramorphosis. The first of these was triggered by a strong selective pressure for bipedalism and concerned the skeleton below the head. The second began with early *Homo* and affected the whole head apart from the canine teeth. The catalyst was a brain that was increasing in size through a prolonged period of growth. I would imagine that both these neotene processes led to our ancestors passing through narrow genetic bottlenecks that came to noticeably limit the genetic variation of humankind.

Research on the genetic similarities and differences between humans and chimpanzees is still in its infancy. It would nevertheless be surprising if certain fundamental differences in our genetic heritage were not found to be connected with mechanisms for peramorphic brain expansion and for pedomorphic selection of the skeleton from the temples to the toes.

Modern humans

Increased intelligence and a prolonged childhood with extended learning times are important ingredients in the story of human evolution. But it is also possible that the neotene processes that seem to have given our anatomy and physiognomy their typically human forms have also left some juvenile patterns in our behaviour and mentality.

This idea is strengthened by Kano's observation that the adult bonobo's neotene anatomy is matched by similarly neotene characteristics in its behaviour. For example, he notes how young individuals are dependent on their parents a little longer than among common chimpanzees, and that the sexual behaviour of the adult bonobo is reminiscent of the common chimp's as a 'teenager'. I see this as strong support for the notion that the much more juvenile behavioural traits in humans are a side effect of a neotene anatomical process.

Curiosity is often seen as humanity's most typical trait, as the seed of our eagerness to explore the world and to try something new, of our attempts to understand the unknown and to ask the eternal questions. As the core of all creativity, curiosity may have been a decisive quality for all our subsequent cultural and social evolution.

Curiosity is particularly found in mammals and not least among apes and humans. Infants and children are in their turn more curious than adults, probably because curiosity and play are so important for the acquisition of social and cultural skills. For this reason Konrad Lorenz suggested that human curiosity was an evolutionary consequence of neoteny. Few creatures are as playful, curious and keen to learn as the intelligent dolphin, once a four-footed mammal that evolved into a streamlined water animal with a straight skeleton, probably through neotene selection. Several studies also point to the close link between neoteny and the degree of domestication in the domestic dog. The more distant a canine race is in genetic terms from its wolf ancestors, the more juvenile characteristics are found in its anatomy and behaviour, and the stronger they will be.

I therefore suggest that the neotene processes affecting the human anatomy during our evolution have simultaneously given us a large dose of curiosity and playfulness, qualities with a tangible value in terms of competition and survival. In this case it may not be an accident that the two main phases in our evolution, those that left clearly neotene marks on our skulls, coincided with periods of increased cultural creativity that can be traced in the archaeological record. The first occurred with the emergence of early *Homo/ergaster*, and the second with *sapiens sapiens*.

For this reason I propose that it was just such an addition of neotene curiosity and creativity that contributed to early *Homo* being the first human to begin to work and use stone tools, to systematically exploit an environment like the savannah that was foreign to its species, and to shortly thereafter begin to colonise Asia and Europe.

With their record-breakingly large brains the Neanderthals may very well have possessed logical and analytical, maybe even linguistic, thought on a par with *sapiens sapiens*. But at the same time their clearly more rudimentary neotene features in the skull and face point to a reduced capacity for the playfulness and inquisition that are important for the ability to change one's own way of life and material culture. Exactly this kind of palpable tendency towards cultural and social conservatism has long been noted on archaeological grounds as being typical for archaic *sapiens* – including the Neanderthals – both in Europe and Asia, by comparison with early *sapiens sapiens*, especially in Europe.

Recent studies of a large number of Neanderthal teeth, undertaken by Bermudez de Castro and Rozzi, demonstrate that these people reached maturity 15 per cent earlier in life than modern humans, corresponding to an age of around 15 years (instead of 18 for us). This indicates that early modern humans had passed through a final phase of neoteny resulting in a distinctly slower developmental growth rate compared to Neanderthals.

If my assertions are correct, in that these two groups differ in terms of neotene cranial evolution, then archaic *sapiens* throughout all of Eurasia may have had more a limited potential for cultural adaptation to their natural environment, and a lower population density than the modern humans when they stepped onto the same stage. We suddenly understand more clearly why archaic *sapiens* in Europe and Asia could not ultimately assert themselves genetically, and in the long run were pushed aside by modern humans.

But this also has consequences for the cherished idea that it was precisely with the modern human in Western Europe around 30,000 years ago that 'modern' creative thinking emerged. Instead this must be pushed back to a couple of hundred thousand years ago and moved to Africa, to the time when the modern, neotene human cranium was formed. The lack of extensive archaeological evidence for creativity in Africa may be a result of the relative lack of excavations. In passing we can note that modern thinking can easily go together with an absence of 'creative' expressions of material and artistic culture (see Chapter 8, Intellect and language). An alternative explanation could be that the hard Ice Age environment in Europe allowed human creative potential to express itself more clearly than in the environment of Africa.

In any way, to better understand the emergence of modern human creativity, it seems me to be more fruitful to start regarding it as a possible result of a neotenic evolutionary process than simply of the sudden appearance of a special new gene for creativity.

The genetic variation in the entire modern human race is many times less than is found even within a single small group of chimpanzees, lowland gorillas or lions in the wild. This indicates that our ancestors on at least one occasion were so few in number that they nearly died out.

Because most of this uniformity also applies to indigenous peoples south of the Sahara, then the explanation for it must basically be sought before the time 100,000 years ago when modern humans left Africa. The new knowledge that the Neanderthals' genetic variation was just as small as our own also raises the possibility that we passed through a genetic bottleneck together while we were still part of the same evolutionary process, which would have been at least 500,000 years in the past.

There is nevertheless reason to believe that our species has passed through several such narrow genetic passageways during the course of evolution. I am thinking here of exactly the kinds of special evolutionary situations discussed above, which with the help of neotene processes led to bipedalism perhaps 6 million years ago, and to increased intelligence 3.5 million years later.

7

A NEW SEXUAL PATTERN

When oestrus was lost

The sex life of early humans is usually either ignored completely or else treated with some degree of delicacy. But in order to understand their lives we must lift the veil of discretion, and I do this here in the knowledge that it would not have embarrassed them in the slightest.

A key question here is to ask how our last four-footed foremothers' reproductive system could disappear, and what consequences this loss of a mating season could have had. By being 'in heat' I mean the primate female's strong, hormone-steered sexual engagement in connection with, and immediately before and after, ovulation. When in heat the female herself often takes the initiative for sex and she is especially open to sexual invitations. The male is often only interested in sex when the female is in heat.

During this period the female's genitals send out a hormonally charged scent and perhaps other chemical signals that prove very attractive to the male. Among chimpanzees, baboons and certain other species this state in the female is additionally signalled by the swelling of the outer genital organs and the fact that they take on a reddish colour. The mating signals of gorillas and orang-utans are not so clear to us humans, but they are obvious enough for them. Their sex life is also controlled by the female's mating cycle.

According to several investigations there are echoes of this phenomenon in many women today, in that their sex drive increases in connection with ovulation. But this is still but a shadow of the mating frenzy that we find in most primate females, not least the chimpanzee. Because human women do not come into heat in this way, do not send out obvious aromatic and visual mating signals when they ovulate, and do not confine their sexual activity to this period, then it is right to say that humans have lost the mating system of the primates.

The male mammal is always in a state of sexual readiness. His latent sex drive is activated by that of the female with its accompanying erotic signals, which are in turn triggered by ovulation. So, ultimately it is the female's ovulation that guarantees that both partners will do their duty when reproduction calls. Because the mating cycle fulfils such a basic function in mammalian reproduction and social life, human beings' loss of it appears just as contradictory as bipedalism and our lack of fur.

We do not know whether our last four-footed ancestral mother had as obvious erotic attractors as a modern chimpanzee female. But she did have a mating cycle based on a period of coming into heat. In other words this must have disappeared at some point after the split from the apes. I would hazard a wager that it had something to do with bipedalism. According to the traditional interpretation, the mating cycle was lost when people had established themselves as two-legged hunters or gatherers on the savannah. Despite a lack of factual support and an absence of internal logic, not to mention evolutionary credibility and social understanding, this explanation for the disappearance of the mating cycle has been well received.

The argument runs roughly like this. Because gathering and hunting required long periods of travel, women and children were compelled to wait decently at a base camp to which the men would bring what was needed for collective consumption. But when these early human females were in heat, they could not help themselves from playing around with other men. When our early 'husband' found out, he was consumed with rage. This was not helped by the fact that he could not be certain whether he was actually the father to his woman's children. All this led to aggressive male competition for the attentions of the women, which disturbed the harmony of the whole group. But evolution did not sit idly by. The root of the problem, the mating rhythm of the women, was quickly disposed of, and instead they became permanently sexual available in suitable moderation. In this way a woman could force a man into a fixed partner relationship, and acquire a provider, helper and protector that she certainly had need of as a child-carer out on the savannah. Because ovulation was no longer signalled, the man was compelled to stay close to and control his woman, and to make sure that his efforts were being invested in children who were actually his own. He thereby avoided sexual competition, and could calmly devote himself to promoting the furtherance of his genes in proper accordance with the dictates of kin selection.

According to this idea, the disappearance of the mating cycle was evolution's canny method for ensuring 'positive' human social institutions such as an established home base, a traditional hunter-gatherer lifestyle, monogamy, marital fidelity, altruism and traditional Western sex roles. One would really have to search to find a more graphic example of evolutionary rationalisation.

The notion of early human males aggressively guarding their exclusive sexual rights to a particular woman has links to the traditional Christian view of the masculine role in marriage, but also to the patriarchal baboons of the savannah with which comparisons were eagerly made so long as it was still thought that we became bipedal there. But as we have seen, early humans did not settle on the savannah until several million years after the division of the species. For that matter the baboon is also a rather remote ancestor of ours in evolutionary terms. As an interpretational model the aggressive harem behaviour of the male baboon has no relevance at all for the sexual and social life of early humans. For this we should in the first instance work from the sex life of the chimpanzees, which is notably free from male aggression and strong competition. As Jared Diamond has pointed out with reference to gorillas, gibbons and many other animals, permanent sex is not at all necessary for males and females to stay together in fixed social relationships.

There is nothing to suggest that the early human male regularly went hunting. Even if this had been the case, he hardly travelled alone but instead in the company of the other gentlemen in the flock, just like male chimps and men in traditional hunting communities today. And why should the jealous early man be so stupid as to leave his woman just at the moment when after years of waiting she finally came into heat? In passing we can note that there is no known archaic hunting society in which the man brings home supplies only to his own family. He always does this for a larger group.

Evolution does not usually mess about with reproduction in such a way purely because of a little natural male sexual competition for females in heat. However aggressive such competition becomes among some polygamous primates, it does not lead to the disappearance of the mating cycle. Different social strategies instead keep the aggression at a manageable level. Sexual competition does not seem to be a big problem for chimpanzees. Even though high-ranking males may have certain advantages, the matter is handled with considerable generosity and tolerance between the males. And in a stable flock of gorillas the silverbacked male's exclusive right to the group's females is often calmly accepted by the other males, despite the fact that they thereby cannot mate at all, or at least only occasionally on the sly.

Before *Homo* there were hardly such great changes in the environment of early humans that the women had more reason than chimpanzees to acquire private providers. Furthermore the finds of bones suggest that it was first with *Homo* that early childhood began to stretch over an extended period, and children perhaps became dependent on their parents' shelter and nourishment a little longer. In my opinion, the only thing supporting the idea that the early human woman became dependent on others at an earlier date is that as a bipedal mother she was forced to carry her offspring who could no longer just hang on to her body.

Another suggested explanation for the loss of oestrus is that the woman ceased to openly signal her ovulation, and became permanently sexually available in order to stop male strangers from killing her children according to kin selection's principle of promoting one's own genetic success. Because it was no longer possible to know when the woman's ovulatory cycle had commenced, and because she copulated with several different men, then all of the latter would refrain from infanticide because they could not know which children were theirs.

First, this assumes that oestrus did not disappear before the connection between sex and childbirth was understood. The capability to do this can only have come with *erectus* at the earliest. Second, this hypothesis starts with the fashionable assumption of male infanticide based on the myth of kin selection. Third, the whole idea is contradicted by our cousins the chimpanzees, who despite their clearly signalled mating cycle have only limited male sexual competition and a lower degree of infanticide perpetrated by males than is the case with most other primates. Finally, there is nothing to suggest that a traditional settled hunting lifestyle was established before *Homo* or early *erectus*.

Although high-ranking male chimpanzees often have slightly greater access to females when these are most lovesick at the height of their ovulatory cycles, and therefore perhaps become fathers more frequently, all chimps usually behave in a friendly way towards the young. In a gorilla flock all the males show great consideration for the group's infants despite the fact that they are mostly fathered by the silverback. The treatment of young by primate males is not primarily steered by an instinctive concern for their own genes. If such an instinct had existed and was the cause of monogamy, then monogamy would be the most common family pattern among mammals. But only 3 per cent of mammals and 10 per cent of primates are monogamous. By far the most common social relationship between the sexes is male polygamy, so-called polygyny. Thus biological population theory gives no support to the idea that early humans lost their oestrus in order to make monogamy possible.

In latterday traditional cultures we find that people's social and sexual systems have much more in common with those of chimpanzees than those of other apes. This must have been even truer for the earliest humans. No male chimp usually has any great difficulty in satisfying his sexual needs when a female in the flock is in heat. By comparison, what then would an early man gain in terms of sexual advantage if oestrus disappeared and led to the promotion of fixed pair relationships? In fact reproductive monogamy would have limited the man's sexual possibilities, as he would have been neatly compelled to keep his paws away from other women while at the same time enduring long periods of abstinence when his own woman had given birth.

While we are on the subject, what a strange thought that the disappearance of oestrus would make early women stop having sexual relations with other men. The female chimpanzee can choose sexual partners only during the short periods when she is in heat every third or fourth year, while the early woman who no longer had a mating cycle had the same year-round possibilities as men for having sex with whoever she chose and whenever she liked. She also became just as sexually interesting for other men as for her would-be mate. So if an early man thought to obtain a private sex-partner for himself when oestrus was lost, then he was on a losing wicket. Not least, oestrus could very well have been combined with monogamy, so long as the man – like the monogamous gibbon – kept a watchful eye on his partner and envious companions on the rare occasions when the female was in heat.

The disappearance of oestrus therefore occurred not so much because of increased male sexual competition and social tensions in the flock, as in spite of them. This suggests that strong selective mechanisms were in operation.

Among monogamous animals the males usually aggressively guard their territory and access to females. There is nothing in the behaviour of our nearest relatives or in present-day people to suggest that this was the case for early humans. If monogamy appeared early, then it more likely took the form of a social monogamy with strong elements of sexual polygamy.

This is where testicle size comes into the picture. As Roger Short first noted, among many primates, for example the apes, there is an approximate correlation between testicle size and reproductive pattern. The greater the competition for the fertilisation of females, and the greater the number of males with whom the female copulates while she is in heat, then the larger the testicles. The males that produce more sperm have an increased chance of fertilising females by comparison with those who produce less sperm. The gorilla has small testicles because the dominant male has almost exclusive sexual rights to the females. Chimpanzees have large testicles because in practice every male has sex with every female in heat. In size, human testicles are somewhere between those of the gorilla and those of the chimpanzee. This fits with the notion that pair relationships in most human societies are socially rather than sexually permanent. The size of male testicles thus reflects a real pattern of human reproduction over a long period of time, and contradicts the idea of an early establishment of sexually faithful monogamy.

One also encounters other explanations for the disappearance of oestrus, which through a similar process of retroactive reasoning suppose that one sex or the other had something to gain from the loss of the mating cycle. What most of these models have in common is that they ought to be just as applicable to many other primates, and yet almost all of them still have oestrus. It is also hard to see what evolutionary advantages the loss of oestrus would have under normal conditions.

It can be seen that the traditional explanation for the disappearance of the mating cycle differs very little from the models put forward to explain bipedalism. They start at the wrong end. Instead of formulating a hypothesis on the basis of a specific evolutionary situation, they begin by peeking at the answer. It is there they believe themselves to have found the key signs of true humanity in such things as bipedalism, a lack of fur, monogamy, marital fidelity, the nuclear family, division of labour, settlement strategies, hunter-gatherer economies, a spoken language, the sharing of food, altruism and I don't know what else. In an anthropocentric frenzy people then assign these things an evolutionary value in their own right, as if they were predetermined objectives for evolution.

Many hypotheses on why humans left the broad path of oestrus therefore begin from false assumptions, are self-contradictory or else go round in circles. They also assume selective processes so universal that they could never have had the evolutionary strength that must have been necessary to make the drastic departure from natural order that the loss of oestrus implies. In my opinion, such a unique event as the disappearance of the mating cycle can only be understood in the light of an evolutionary situation that was also unique. If monogamy, the nuclear family, the hunting life, systematic food-sharing, settlements and similar phenomena had anything at all to do with oestrus, the relationship was if anything the reverse of what has been proposed.

Mammals living in areas with large seasonal variation and uneven access to food resources often give birth to their young during the time of the year that gives them the best chance of survival. By extension their mating period and sexual activity occurs in an earlier season, according to the length of pregnancy. A different situation arises with mammals living in stable tropical environments with limited seasonal variation (I do not include here group-living female monkeys and women whose oestrus and menstruation respectively can sometimes become synchronised through social or hormonal stimuli). Such species often lack a special oestrus season and both mate and give birth irregularly throughout the year in line with the females' individual rhythm for ovulation and coming into heat. This is the case with many primates even though a mild annual fluctuation can be seen among, for example, gorillas and chimpanzees. Even humans mate and have children more or less anytime of the year regardless of external environment, apart from the most marginal of seasonal variations. This can thus be an evolutionary inheritance from an original life in a relatively stable tropical environment.

It is therefore interesting that this sexual pattern could be retained through thousands of generations in temperate and cold climates, where most of the other mammals, including the primates, have seasonal reproduction. One might therefore imagine that it would have been easy for evolution to give people back their oestrus cycle and to allow it to become co-ordinated with an appropriate season. That this did not happen suggests that reproduction without oestrus had become a biologically deep-rooted mechanism long before we came to an environment where seasonal mating would have been natural.

The fact that people all over the world copulate and successfully rear their babies without any special regard for the seasons indicates that it was at an early stage that we acquired intelligence, experience, knowledge, social organisation, cultural capacity and the ability to communicate. This critical point may have been reached as long ago as 2.5 million years, when humans began to settle clearly seasonally variable, half-open terrain, and shortly thereafter began their colonial journey out of Africa.

I have proposed that the unique loss of oestrus can only be understood in relation to an equally unique situation. It is hard to point to any such event more likely than that which gave rise to our bipedalism, and thus we are led back once again to the time of the last common ancestor.

Menstruation and ovulation

First we have to look a little closer at our nearest relatives' reproduction. In chimpanzees oestrus occurs around the same time as ovulation, menstruation in turn between the two. This happens roughly once every 36 days, or about every 42 days in the case of the bonobo that has a somewhat more drawn out and irregular oestrous cycle. Both species have the same short ovulation as humans, just a day or so. For common chimps oestrus lasts between 10 to 12 days, while for the bonobo it continues for up to 20 days. In practice, however, this cycle looks a little different. Common chimpanzee females in the wild do not come into heat, ovulate and menstruate more often than once every fourth or fifth year, which corresponds to the total time for pregnancy and breast-feeding, or if one prefers, roughly the gap between one child and the next.

We find exactly the same pattern among traditional peoples of more recent times. For mobile hunter-gatherers, pregnancy and breast-feeding as a rule place three to four years between each period of ovulation and menstruation. The same pattern must have existed generally before adequate replacements were found for mothers' milk and before economic factors mitigated against a natural weaning period on the child's own terms – in other words during most of our evolution and the greater part of the time that modern humans have been in existence.

This means that the majority of all women before the advent of permanent settlement – in many places even down to the most recent generations – had only a limited number of menstruations and ovulations during their lifetimes. This is a massive contrast to modern women who with only shorter inter-ruptions ovulate and menstruate every month for their entire reproductive lives. What is today usually seen as natural is thus a biological anachronism of huge proportions. Connected with this is the fact that the number of children per child-bearing woman is low nowadays, that many children are breast fed for only a short time and with low intensity, and that many women quite simply never become pregnant. As an effect of modern food and lifestyles the point of first menstruation has in just a few generations sunk to the early teenage years. Instead of the 10 to 15 occasions as nature intended, a modern woman ovulates and menstruates about 400 times during her reproductive life. We can encounter the same phenomenon sometimes among apes. Sterile females in the wild, like females in captivity who are prevented from mating, have monthly ovulations and menstruations just like present-day women. Female apes in captivity also tend to menstruate earlier than females in the wild.

It is surprising that this self-evident evolutionary perspective has not been employed more often to illuminate the question of physical and mental prob-lems that are so common in conjunction with ovulation and menstruation in modern society. A biological mechanism as fundamental and ancient as ovulation should not bring with it such difficulties. Continually repeated ovulations and menstruations are an expression of permanent cultural disturbance that evolution has not yet had a chance to deal with. Nature has quite simply not equipped us for meeting the physiological stresses that are caused by monthly ovulation and menstruation from the early teenage years.

As we have seen, among chimpanzees oestrus lasts 10 to 12 days, and 20 days among bonobos. The period of ovulation among all primates and mammals is by contrast short, one or two days, probably because it is so physiologically demanding. In order for a female to really become pregnant during the short period of ovulation, oestrus begins some time before and continues throughout. During this period the female chimpanzee mates with great enthusiasm, often with many males, even if she occasionally contents herself with only a few or even one. The female common chimp is sexually active only when she is in heat, and it is usually only then that the males are interested in intercourse. While the female's oestrus is controlled by her individual rhythm of ovulation, the male's sexual interest is normally triggered by the female's coming into heat. Between periods of oestrus both sexes are usually uninterested in copulation. Because ovulation occurs in the middle of oestrus, mating is guaranteed to always occur when the chance of fertilisation is greatest.

Humans are almost alone among the higher mammals in having abandoned this evolutionarily tailor-made method for the continuance of life. It therefore cannot be explained by reference to conditions that are evolutionarily advantageous only in general terms, such as normal changes in environment caused by normal climatic fluctuations. The loss of oestrus must be seen in connection with a unique evolutionary situation that created a strong selective pressure for precisely the disappearance of the mating cycle or that made it superfluous. I have difficulty in seeing any other situation than that which led to bipedalism.

I must now take the liberty of opening the door to the chimpanzees' bedroom a little wider.

The mass media is in the habit of portraying the life of the bonobo as one long sexual orgy, in which lustful females fling themselves between heterosexual encounters and lesbian diversions, and the males get erections through sheer excitement if they are merely served some extra bananas. It is certainly true that the bonobo is one of the animal world's sexual athletes, and they certainly have a sexual over-consumption in relation to the demands of reproduction. But the picture is still exaggerated. What would the bonobo have to say about the sex life of humans if it, like theirs, unfolded in broad daylight on the open street? In fact the erotic tone in the bonobo's environment fills roughly the same social function as the common chimpanzee's frenetic but more platonic kissing, cuddling and physical contact. The colourful sex life of the bonobo has a clear effect in diminishing aggression and promoting social calm, that makes their environment less prone to conflict and violence than is the case among common chimps and other primates. That the bonobos' sexual activities beyond the range of ovulation have social and not reproductive functions is clear from the fact that their ovulation period is just as short as that of the common chimps and humans.

The male chimpanzee is similar to a human man in that in principle he is always physically prepared for mating. No male chimp will fail to notice when a female is in heat. Her genitals swell up, take on a red colouring and emit a stimulating scent. As if that were not enough, the female often approaches her chosen lover backwards with her genitals exposed. The male chimp that can withstand such temptation has not been born. On the other hand, the act of love is usually over in a few hectic moments: sex takes on average 7 seconds for the common chimpanzee, and 12 for the bonobo. Then again, it is more often repeated. The gorilla devotes a marginally greater time to the same task.

The end of oestrus signals

When the effects of bipedalism are discussed, they are usually confined to the ability to walk and run, and do things with the arms and hands. The consequences for reproduction and childcare are often bypassed.

The sexual behaviour described here during oestrus can be found in its essentials among all apes and many other higher primates. It must therefore also have been the case for our closest primate ancestors. But on the day that they raised themselves up on two legs, then the female's aromatic and visual mating signals largely lost their effect and the whole traditional pairing system fell to pieces.

Because apes and monkeys are basically quadrupedal, their female genitals face backwards even when they occasionally stand up. The same must have been true for our last four-footed female ancestors. But then came bipedalism and made the almost level backbone vertical. The angle between the pelvis and thighbones levelled out at the same time as the upper part of the pelvis moved backwards. Simultaneously the lower part of the pelvis moved forwards, and with it the whole genital region, womb, vagina and all. Seen superficially, it was as if the backward-facing genitals were pushed down and in between the thighs, to at last pop up round the front.

As I have earlier discussed, the transition to bipedalism should in evolutionary terms have taken place through the extension of the primate embryo's straight skeleton and forward-facing vagina to the adult stage, via a neotene selection process. This gains further support when we note how the skeletons of both early and modern humans indicate that bipedalism came quickly without an extended evolutionary period in between.

The process of becoming human is defined in the first instance by the switch to bipedalism. It is therefore important to note that early humans very soon adopted a fully upright body posture, even if some elements of it were still reminiscent of a tree-dwelling ape. The basic skeletal components in the form of spine, pelvis, legs and feet are all adapted to an upright gait. Finds of bones from early humans with an obviously upright walk now date to 6 million years ago, which supports the idea that bipedalism arrived in connection with the division of species. From this it follows that the forward-facing vagina is also at least as old.

In order to ensure that the primate male is on the alert during the short time that ovulation lasts, the female signals its onset in ways irresistible to him. Because both apes and monkeys have a rather weak sense of smell; however, reproduction demands close contact between the male's nose and female's sexual organs. Their four-footed world is also so ingeniously arranged that the male moves around with his nose at the same height as the female's genitals. He simply cannot avoid these seductive scents when the female is in heat. Quadrupedalism is thus in itself a guarantee that the primate male's sexual urges will be awakened in good time before ovulation. It is an inextricable part of the primates' reproductive system.

So what happened when our ancestors raised themselves up on two legs? Well, the female's erotically inviting posture on all fours was the first to go. The distance from the early woman's genitals to the early man's nose and eyes grew a thousand fold, from a few millimetres to more than a metre. Having been previously laid out on display, the female's genitals were suddenly remote and inaccessible. The male could no longer, in true primate fashion, make a close inspection of the sexual organs with the help of his sense of smell. The primordial erotic nosing of the backside no longer worked, and early man's brain was not reached by the magical oestral scent triggers. The whole primate oestrus system was disturbed. This is not contradicted by the fact that people today send out and to some extent are unconsciously affected by pheromones and other chemical signals from, for example, the armpits. The effect is negligible.

We do not know whether our last quadruped female ancestors signalled their oestrus by a swelling of the genitals in the same way as common chimpanzees and bonobos, or with a more discrete signal like the gorilla. Szalay and Costello have argued that a possible swelling must have been so uncomfortable when the early female's genitals were pressed in between the thighs by the new two-footed posture that it must have soon been selected away. This is possible. In any event, the swelling and red colouring of the genitals disappeared through selection principally because they became useless as mating signals when the distance from the early male nose grew so great, and the female genitals were hidden by a fresh bush of neotene hair.

If bipedalism arose in connection with an aquatic environment, the problem was even greater. In water the primates' aromatic and visual pairing signals would have been definitively disrupted. A vagina opened through oestrus would also have been susceptible to water-borne infections. The effect would have been a reduction in fertility and a loss of sexual interest for the early human woman. Watery surroundings would have further contributed to the vanishing of oestrus.

The fact that the mating cycle came to be replaced by permanent female sexuality may quite simply indicate that oestrus became evolutionarily disadvantageous as a result of bipedalism.

The strong aromatic signals emitted from the primate female's genitals came into being because her lustfulness could not alone guarantee that the male was properly prepared during the short period of ovulation. When the genital signals no longer found their mark, they needed to be replaced by others. As we all know, a woman's most important erotic signals are now of a more permanent nature. They include the gently rounded body contours connected with subcutaneous fat, that only the aquatic hypothesis has so far been able to adequately explain. For both sexes, we must also consider a whole battery of conscious and unconscious movements, postures, gestures, facial expressions, glances and tones of voice. The lack of fur should not be forgotten, as the smoothly naked skin of humans became a new erotic signal with new erogenous surfaces. These permanent erotic triggers can be seen as a replacement for the reduced intensity of the female's original oestrus behaviour. With permanent sexuality, permanent mating signals and perhaps still a slightly increased sexual urge around the time for ovulation, the fertilisation of early human women was only a matter of time.

The survival of the newly bipedal creatures now depended on enough individuals being inclined to mate with each other despite the fact that the men were no longer stimulated by traditional pairing signals. The early man whose sexual impulses were less dependent on the scent and appearance of the female genitals in oestrus, but instead egged on by the attractions of a woman's ever-increasing permanent sexual signals, thereby obtained a considerable reproductive advantage. The same applied to the early woman who retained her erotic attraction without recourse to the traditional primate methods. The females who were interested in sex without regular oestrus were more easily fertilised than those who only assented to intercourse during the short period of ovulation that the early human men now hardly even noticed. This gave them a reproductive edge that in turn spread their tendency for sexual interest outside periods of ovulation. In this way the original visual and aromatic oestrus signals lost their function and disappeared step by step.

By contrast with most other mammals, all female apes and monkeys can physically have sex even when they are not in heat. This ability must therefore have also applied to our ancestral primate mothers at the time of the division of the species.

It now seems that females of certain primates, for example bonobos, macaques and vervets, are sexually active outside their mating periods. In the wild, sometimes a few common chimpanzee males will try to force themselves sexually on females who are only slightly or not at all in heat, occasionally with some success. The bonobo female has a considerably greater sexual appetite than the female among common chimps. Not only is her oestrus longer, but she is sometimes sexually active both before and after it. The human female's permanent sexuality is thus more like that of the bonobo than the common chimpanzee. In passing we can note that the female bonobo's genitals, in line with her slightly straighter skeleton, are somewhat less backward facing than those of the common chimp. Bonobos also have sex face-to-face about a third of the time.

The early human woman had no anatomical or physiological barriers that would prevent sexual intercourse during her menstrual cycle. Natural selection therefore had all the tools necessary for spreading genetic tendencies in both sexes for sexual interest without the stimulation of traditional oestrus signals. Finally a new mating pattern evolved, typical for humans, in which the woman's ovulation was not signalled openly and fertilisation was ensured in the first instance through women's permanent pairing signals, and by the fact that they maintained the same permanent sexual readiness as the males.

I have made a connection here between human beings' loss of oestrus and the origins of the bipedal gait, but it also fits well with the idea of an aquatic environment as the cradle of humankind.

The female orgasm

Ejaculation in men and animal males does not require any great evolutionary investigation. Not much would get fertilised here on earth without a gradually increasing enjoyment followed by release. Without such a thing, when a female was in heat it would lead to a pointless copulation in a manner directly disadvantageous in evolutionary terms. The same would apply if the first early human women had practised their new permanently sexual lifestyle with the same energy that the females had earlier invested in the short and infrequent period of their oestrus. Permanent female sexuality is quite simply incompatible with permanent sexual arousal of the kind that briefly characterises being in heat.

There is no doubt that primate females enjoy sex when in heat. They take the initiative to intercourse at least as often as males, and even though most of them do not show any recognisable signs of relaxing climactic orgasm, there is much to suggest that they do in fact experience it. Female bonobos often cry out during the short sexual act and in connection with lesbian encounters. Common chimpanzee females and other primates also seem to achieve orgasm during lesbian sex and through masturbation. It is not clear to what extent this is a question of true orgasm in human terms or just strong feelings of pleasure, but the former seems more likely. There is no doubt at all that females among Rhesus macaques and short-tailed macaques can achieve orgasm during sex. Experiments with the sexual stimulation of Rhesus females has even shown that they undergo roughly the same copulation and climax phases that Masters and Johnson have demonstrated as typical for modern women.

When one considers that sex among the primates is often over in a few brief seconds, it is easy to wonder how the female's orgasm mechanisms – not to say a human observer of them – can keep up. Maybe it is as Sarah Blaffer Hrdy has suggested, that the primate female achieves orgasm not so much through individual short sexual acts as through the accumulated effect of many such in succession, and the male's intensive attentions. A chimpanzee female in heat and in good form can find time for 50 copulations in a single day.

The female genitals

I apologise now to women everywhere, but someone has to say it: your sexual organs are upside down – at least seen from a primate perspective. All other primates have a clitoris and urinary tract in the lower part of their genitals, and the mouth of the vagina above them, just below the anus. In people everything is the other way around: the anus lowest down, then the vagina and the urinary canal, and above this the clitoris.

The explanation is simple. Our last four-footed ancestral mother had the same backward-facing genitals as other primates. But when she became bipedal and acquired an upright skeleton and pelvis, the genitals were moved like a pendulum down and forward to finally sit at the front. The lower part thereby became uppermost, and the upper portion settled down below. I do not know if it has anything to do with bipedalism, but the distance between the clitoris and vagina is slightly greater in humans than in other primates.

How this fact can have been so overlooked is a mystery.

As a man I have difficulty is assessing the full consequences of the female genitals ending up inverted. But it is clear that when the anatomy for the primate female's sexual pleasure was sculpted, plausibly on the Sixth Day, there was no choice between vaginal or clitoral arousal: it was both. So long as the clitoris was turned backwards and situated below the vagina, then it was automatically stimulated during sex by the male's lower parts and scrotum, the latter especially developed in chimpanzees. This pleasing arrangement was thus disrupted at the division of the species when bipedalism turned the genitals upside down, so that the clitoris was no longer directly stimulated during sexual intercourse.

The womb and birth canal were also moved inwards. The birth canal had once led directly out from the womb, as in quadrupedal primates. But bipedalism turned it approximately 90 degrees to the womb, which has to straighten out just before a baby is expelled during birth. In its essentials this odd anatomical solution must also have been in place since the split from the apes.

The fact that many primate females seem to achieve orgasm as a result of numerous copulations suggests that the female orgasm's basic physiology is of very great antiquity. The sexual behaviour of chimpanzees, bonobos and other primates provides a clue that our last female quadruped ancestors enjoyed sex when they were in heat, and that they could experience orgasm through many short, repeated copulations. With the loss of oestrus and the transition to permanent female sexuality came the ability to also reach orgasm during individual but longer acts of sex. This in turn presumes that early human men were capable of copulating for longer than the few moments that the apes devote to the task. The fact that male chimpanzees often break off their brief sexual encounters without having achieved orgasm suggests that this is quite possible.

A new sexual behaviour

Even though the primate female's oestrus includes strong sexual arousal, the whole system is based upon her not being so satisfied with a single short copulation that her interest for sex will disappear before ovulation is over, and she is guaranteed to have been fertilised. In other words, reproduction through oestrus is not compatible with the female reaching a sexually relaxing orgasm after individual acts of intercourse. The primate female seems to experience a rather gradual sexual climax and perhaps first achieves orgasm after several short copulations in succession. This also fits with the difference in the speed of arousal between men and women, and with the often imperfect co-ordination of male and female orgasm that seems to be the heritage of our species. Despite the fact that the female primate does not need to reach orgasm in order to be fertilised, her ability to achieve it is evolutionarily deep-rooted. In terms of selective mechanisms this probably worked through orgasmic pleasure as an incentive for females to indulge in the kind of sex that led to fertilisation. The ability to experience orgasmic enjoyment may then have acquired a greater selective value when oestrus gave way to permanent sexuality.

I have suggested that our foremothers' aromatic and visual mating signals were knocked out as a result of bipedalism, with or without the contribution made by an aquatic life. The risk was then that the males would not be interested in mating during the short period of ovulation. On the other hand, selection saw to it that more females were born with constant sexual preparedness, along with ever more males who were ready to mate without the stimulus of the traditional oestrus signals. As the aromatic triggers and genital swelling disappeared, the woman's visual signals changed. Evolution towards a typically human sexual pattern would not have been possible if the female's temporary oestrus had not been replaced by permanent female sexuality and a greater ability to reach orgasm during individual but longer copulations, regardless of when they took place in the reproductive cycle. This assumes that early human men could complete longer acts of sex than primate males are often able to. The evolutionary selective factor may have been a female need for longer coitus when the clitoris now received less stimulation than before. The primate female's sexual arousal during oestrus and probably orgasm through repeated short copulations was therefore replaced by the same permanent sexuality as the male sex had always possessed, by female sexual enjoyment without a mating cycle, and the ability to reach orgasm through a few longer acts of intercourse.

Even though woman's hormonally-controlled temporary erotic scent apparatus has not entirely disappeared, it has nevertheless come to be almost totally replaced by permanent mating signals in the form of external body shape and movements. Men have in this way come to be the only primate males to be continually exposed to the erotic signals of the opposite sex. It is no wonder that men are on average more likely to be sexually stimulated by the sight of a naked individual of the opposite sex than other primate males and women. Perhaps it also explains why he is more sexually argumentative, tense and unpredictable than most other primate males.

The original primate oestrus and mating system thus turned into our uniquely human sexual behaviour, where women are just like men in their physiological readiness to mate any day of the year. Those who search for something that really separates us from most other animals can find a perfect example here. Finally we can simply note something about a reproductive system in which the female has no oestrus to speak of, does not clearly signal her ovulation, is always capable of sex and also gives out permanent sexual signals connected to reproduction: it functions far too well. If there is one thing that the human race has had no problem with, it is reproducing ourselves.

Neotene selection

Perhaps the special sexual qualities of the bonobos evolved first when the two species of chimpanzees went their separate evolutionary ways about 2.1 million years ago. Takayoshi Kano has noted that the bonobo's sexual behaviour is similar to that of young females among the common chimps, whose oestral urges extend a little beyond the period of ovulation compared with more mature females. Kano suggests that the bonobo's longer oestral activity can be seen in evolutionary terms as having arisen through a neotene process that pushed 'teenage' behaviour into adulthood. With reference to the straight skeletons and forward-facing vaginas of embryos and newborn infants among quadruped apes, I suggested above that bipedalism was evolutionarily achieved through a neotene process, and that the genitals moved to the front of the body as an anatomical side effect. The fact that the bonobo has a somewhat more upright body posture, a greater tendency to move on two legs, slightly less backward-facing female genitals, and a bit more cranial hair than the common chimp is very much in line with Kano's interpretation of neoteny. From this I would assume that the evolution of permanent sexuality in early human women was speeded up through the neotene selection process that created bipedalism.

Because the genetic gap is the same between humankind and both species of chimpanzees, the considerable similarities between humans and bonobos in terms of sexual behaviour can be ascribed to neotene parallel evolution. But the neotene qualities in the sexual habits of the bonobo, and their neotene anatomy, are nevertheless much less striking than they are in humans. Their female genitals are less backward-facing than those of the common chimp, but backward-facing none the less. Their sexual activities outside the period of ovulation lie roughly in between those of the common chimp and those of human women.

The penis

The human penis is on average bigger than that of most other primates, both in general and in relation to what the size of the testicles would suggest. When our last quadruped ancestors raised themselves up on two legs and their pelvises straightened up, the effects on the penis were not very dramatic. In a four-footed primate, in contrast to the vagina the penis is not oriented backwards. Situated under the body and facing straight down or obliquely forwards, the quadruped primate's penis is automatically pointed forwards or forwards and up, when he adopts the half-standing or standing position for sex.

Let us return to the situation when we became bipedal and the female genitals began to be moved forwards. For a time the vagina ought to have been more or less hidden between the legs. Having sex would then have been a rather difficult proposition, either from in front or behind. The smaller the penis, the harder it would have been for sperm to move as far as the egg in the womb, especially as the vagina had now moved to a position at a 90 degree angle to the mouth of the womb. The early man with a longer penis therefore acquired a reproductive advantage in this situation. An erect human penis is on average 30 per cent longer than the vagina. These may have been the extra centimetres that early men needed to get within shooting range at all during the crucial period when the female genitals were oriented neither backwards nor forwards. The large human penis would in that case have the same evolutionary background as so much else, our unique bipedalism.

There is one exception from the general primate pattern – the penis of the bonobo – which when erect is considerably longer than that of the common chimpanzee. It is actually longer than a human's, though thinner. This may not be coincidence. With its slightly straighter skeleton and less backward-facing vagina, the bonobo has, like humans, a propensity for intercourse both from in front and from behind. The great swelling of the skin around the female's genitals – up to fifty times its original size – places the male bonobo in roughly the same situation as early men found themselves in shortly after the division of the species, with the consequent need for an extra long penis.

The human penis lacks the small bone that keeps primate penises slightly extended even when they are not in action. This arrangement suits a quadruped creature that carries his equipment securely between four limbs. But for the early human male who had just raised himself up on two legs, it was bad news to wander through bushy forest with his fragile, newly enlarged and reproductively vital organ sticking straight out in front of him.

Even a possible life in the water would have brought problems. In this case the penis bone would have totally incompatible with an upright walk and would soon have been selected away. The male penis has probably had its unusual size (among primates) and flexibility since the time of the first early humans.

Bisexuality

Where animals are concerned we often take it for granted that their sexuality is exclusively directed towards reproduction and is therefore entirely heterosexual. Nor have I ever seen anything else suggested for early humans and their early modern descendants. But it can hardly have been so simple. As Bruce Bagemihl has recently shown in a major synthesis of the subject, homosexual behaviour is found among all kinds of higher animals and to the same degree in both sexes. As with masturbation, homosexual behaviour often appears in a form and context that does not much differ from human conditions. It is also quite clear that masturbation and homosexual behaviour in animals often concerns no more than the satisfaction of the sexual urge within the framework of a dominant heterosexual orientation. At the same time, however, a few individuals also seem to prefer more stable homosexual activities, which occasionally are quite simply connected to a long-term pairing between individuals of the same sex, as for example in certain monogamous birds. Homosexual behaviour occurs among all the extant close relatives of early humans: chimpanzees, bonobos, gorillas and orang-utans, and between females as well as males. The bisexuality of the bonobo has particularly attracted attention.

Because none of the great apes are monogamous, they similarly do not create permanent homosexual relationships. Nevertheless, a few individuals seem to be less heterosexually and more homosexually active than others. Among chimpanzees, the female's oestral urges and their attitude to free love ensures that homosexual behaviour and masturbation are always subordinate to their heterosexuality.

I therefore assume that bisexuality was not uncommon – not just among our last quadruped ancestors but also among early humans and all their descendents, all the way down to modern people. I would suggest that the majority of early humans were strongly heterosexual, but that both sexes also possessed a rather broad repertoire of homosexual behaviour as a general supplement to their sexual life.

I have proposed that bipedalism led to the disappearance of oestrus and oestral signals to make way for permanent sex, and that social rather than pair relationships began to form. Whether this affected the bisexual and homosexual behaviour of early humans is hard to say. It is quite possible that a sex life without oestrus gave individuals more room to cultivate rather more permanent homosexual tendencies. People were then a very long way from investing sexual behaviour with any kind of moral overtone.

8

INTELLECT AND LANGUAGE

The spoken word's potential for expressing emphasis and nuance has brought a very special quality to our social life and culture. But not only humans have language – most other creatures do too. Many animals mediate instinctively through scents, sounds and behaviour. Other animals with higher intelligence possess advanced communication systems.

The earliest evolution of human intellect, consciousness and speech is intimately connected, and should most appropriately be discussed in the same context. But how can we find traces of these things, when all sounds, thoughts and feelings disappear as quickly as they arise? How can we know if early humans had an inner consciousness or even if they thought at all, when we hardly know how our own intellect and intelligence work? But the origin of speech is so fundamental for our understanding of early human evolution that we cannot ignore it merely because so much about it is obscure. In any case, we have enough to go on to enable us at least to make hypothetical interpretations.

Brain and language

Although intelligence and speech evolved in close evolutionary partnership, and despite the fact that language alters and sharpens thinking, this does not mean that language is a prerequisite for cognition. In fact speech is a rather slow mechanism, as thoughts fly much faster than words. This also applies very clearly to the apes, whose natural communicative abilities with sound are negligible compared to their capacity for thought. Thinking is *not* grounded in language. The opposite is actually the case, as the spoken word could never have evolved if a foundation of elementary cognitive ability had not been present from the beginning.

The notion that modern language has no evolutionary prehistory, and that it suddenly just emerged among modern humans, is today utterly dead in scientific terms. Despite the complexities of the human brain it has no basic structures that cannot be found among other primates and higher mammals. In all its essentials human speech arose through an evolutionary upgrading of

106

what was already in the brain. Put simply, the brains of humans and mammals consist of three layers of different evolutionary age. The innermost and oldest is the so-called ganglion, the middle layer is the limbic system, and the outermost and youngest is the surface of the brain – the neocortex that all mammals possess. The primates have the largest neocortex, and humans have the biggest of all. Here we find the greater part of our analytical and logical intelligence and our capacity for speech. Almost all evolution in the human brain after the ape-stage has taken place in the neocortex.

The Broca and Wernicke centres are well-known areas in the left hemisphere of the brain with important functions related to speech and language. But there are others. Investigations indicate that almost every individual form of speech and linguistic understanding engages several different parts of the brain simultaneously. The same applies to thinking, emotional reaction, sight and hearing. Because human speech mediates thoughts and feelings, we can expect there to be connections in the brain between the functions of language, cognition and emotion. There are also clear structural similarities between linguistic functions and other forms of cognitive and sensory operations. We may note in passing the idea that we use only a small part of our brain capacity: this is a myth. The common comparison between the human brain and a computer is not particularly helpful either. In terms of working methods the similarities are really very few.

Studies of apes' mental and linguistic capacities, of their brains and those of the monkeys, lead us to believe that even our last four-footed ancestors possessed the brain structures for rudimentary linguistic communication.

In the late 1950s the American linguist Noam Chomsky presented his theory of *generative grammar*. He claimed that all languages have a common syntactic and grammatical core, and a common grade of complexity, and that this points to the presence of identical linguistic structures in everyone's brain from birth. Chomsky worked from the premise that people do not use language to copy others' statements, but instead to constantly create new meanings through new combinations of words. He also suggested that, even with only superficial linguistic influence, small children quickly and spontaneously absorb elementary grammatical structures from the language of their surroundings – including the ability to understand and construct statements that they have not previously heard. He drew the conclusion that humans have an in-built language programme in their brains, a kind of mental grammar. He even questioned the notion that people essentially think in their mother tongue. Chomsky's theory has not been uncontested but on the whole it has won strong support among modern linguists. A particular eye-opener in relation to the notion that there really are such common linguistic undercurrents is provided by a number of studies of children's speech development, sign language for the deaf, speech impediments caused by brain damage, and so-called pidgin and Creole languages.

Pidgin languages are newly created linguistic mixtures with limited simple functions – to facilitate trade, for example – and with a grammar hardly worthy of the name. A grammatical content is however present in so-called Creole languages, that developed as the next generation on from pidgin. Although Creoles were created quite spontaneously from elements of wildly differing languages, often by illiterate children, they quickly developed fully modern grammar and syntax. This is hard to understand in any other way than that all humans are the bearers of certain inherited basic structures for language.

Some scholars, with Terence Deacon at the fore, have however claimed that similarities between languages cannot lead us to common structures in the brain. They suggest instead that universal grammatical patterns depend upon all human languages having developed in the same direction under the same adaptive conditions. This idea has not been widely accepted. The cognitive researcher Steven Pinker has followed Chomsky to suggest that the inherited structures do not concern language, but basic thinking. We should therefore not think in any special language, but rather something he calls 'mentalese'. Guglielmo Cinque at the University of Venice has presented the results of a comparative analysis of no less than 500 different languages. He claims that the way in which adverbs are placed in sentences is common to all languages, and that this also is true for such linguistic elements as form, tense, aspect, modality and the main form of the verb. Cinque argues not only that all languages resemble each other but even that they are actually identical in this respect. The great differences that we perceive between different languages in terms of words and pronunciations would thus merely be superficialities.

Two American psychologists, Susan Goldin-Meadow and Carolyn Mylander, have presented a study on how four American and four Taiwanese deaf children developed sign language. The children's mothers, with respectively English and Mandarin as their native tongues, tried to use play to teach their offspring these languages, by talking to them and getting them to read their lips at the same time as they illustrated what they said with gestures and signs. In spite of this the children developed their own special sign language, which clearly deviated from what their mothers were trying to teach them. Although they ordered their signs in combinations that structurally had much in common with spoken language, these structures were not found in either English or Mandarin. The psychologists came to the conclusion that the children's way of handling combinatory elements was based on common genetic preconditions.

Independent of race and culture, everything suggests that people are bearers of certain common linguistic laws in the form of fundamental systems for the use of sound and basic grammatical rules, all anchored in congenital brain structures.

The neurologists William Calvin and the linguist Derek Bickerton claim that all animals that are able to interpret the world around them, for example by recognising tracks on the ground, also understand the concept of symbols.

If they also live a complex social existence as herd animals – like chimpanzees and gorillas with their shifting social relations and ever-changing alliances, reciprocal services, punishments and expectations – then they already possess the cognitive foundations for an elementary syntax. True language could therefore have arisen some time after our ancestors' brains had acquired sufficient capacity to handle slightly more complex systems of symbolic signals.

The realisation that there are certain common inherited components behind the basic construction of all languages, fixed in the make-up of the human brain, leads us to the conclusion that even modern speech has a long and unbroken biological and cultural tradition that links us with the most remote past.

Modern language

Through linguistics alone it is not possible to determine how long languages of modern types have been spoken. We can at least observe that there is nothing to suggest any change in the general structure and level of language over the last 5,250 years, which is at present the greatest length of time over which we can study linguistic development. Linguists therefore agree that the modern level of language arose before the oldest written evidence for it.

But the agreement stops there. Opinions differ widely as to how our modern linguistic capacity was attained, and when and how the evolution of language began. Not long ago it was thought that a spoken language could not be much older than the modern human in Europe – about 35,000 years. Now we know that modern humans have at least 200,000 years on the clock, not in Europe but in Africa. Many are therefore ready to allow modern language the same pedigree. A minimum is in any case the approximately 100,000 years that have passed since modern humans took the step from Africa to Eurasia. Because their competition removed all the older types of humans, the consequences are that all of humanity now has languages with the same degree of complexity and with the same basic structure.

In this context it is interesting to read the linguist Johanna Nichols' investigation of how long it may have taken for linguistic *differences* to arise. Based on a calculation of speed, by which a number of relatively stable grammatical elements have changed over time in different language families, Nichols suggests that it would have taken about 100,000 years for the world's current linguistic diversity to have developed from a single original common language.

Despite this, a number of researchers still maintain that a modern language first arose with the emergence of modern humans in Europe some 40,000–35,000 years ago. This is based on the fact that the oldest known archaeological evidence for a rich, 'fully modern' consciousness appears in Europe at this time. The latter refers to a sudden flowering of richer and more nuanced material culture in the form of finely made stone implements, composite

109

tools, frequent use of bone and antler, and a general expression of artistic and symbolic thinking, not least in the form of the extraordinary cave art.

As an archaeologist I find it unreasonable to demand archaeological proof of modern consciousness and modern thought processes in order to accept the notion of modern language forms at an earlier time. If one defines linguistic capacity on the basis of the material culture that happens to have been archaeologically preserved and discovered, then this is to deprive many later peoples of the modern speech that they obviously spoke. All known recent peoples on earth have spoken completely modern languages, regardless of their level of cultural development. When the Europeans reached Tasmania, the island's inhabitants possessed a stone technology and tool culture of such simplicity that a chimpanzee with a little training could have produced something similar. Nevertheless, in terms of intellect and language these people were just as well equipped as any Western archaeologist or linguist. If the acceptance of modern language in the distant past were to depend upon archaeological evidence for artistic expression and creativity, then this would deprive almost all early modern humans in Europe, Africa, Asia and Australia of developed speech. For the sake of consistency one would then be forced to conclude that the ancestors of modern Europeans must have become more stupid and lost part of their capacity for speech when the great artistic tradition ended with the last Ice Age about 12,000 years ago. But for some reason no one ever says this.

The more one examines the idea that modern language began in Europe, the weaker this argument appears.

Wild bonobos and gorillas in contrast to common chimpanzees, and wild orang-utans on Borneo in contrast to those in Sumatra, have an almost non-existent material culture. If one were to employ this difference as a factor in evaluating these groups' mental and social capacity, intelligence and latent linguistic talent, one would obtain a completely misleading result. We would go even more adrift if we assessed these groups' intelligence on the basis of their archaeological remains, because only the tool culture of certain West African common chimpanzees leaves such traces.

The fact that a particular cultural phenomenon presupposes a certain level of intellectual and cognitive capacity does not necessarily mean that the same cultural level cannot be attained if this phenomenon is absent, above all from the archaeological record. In the debate on humankind's earliest history, this form of logical error in argument is nevertheless repeated *ad infinitum*.

With arguments of this kind many scholars, led by Philip Liebermann, have tried to deprive the Neanderthals of a modern capacity for speech and intelligence. The Neanderthals populated Europe and westernmost Asia between 125,000 and 35,000 years ago. It is true that these people seem to have had a less varied and considerably more conservative cultural tradition than the later modern humans, with only negligible elements of what we perceive as art and other expressions of abstract and symbolic thinking. From reconstructions of the base of the skull, the throat and the location of the hyoid bone it has then been suggested that Neanderthals would have found it hard to produce certain sounds – especially the vowels a, i and u, and the consonants g and k – and that in general they were somewhat linguistically and intellectually challenged. Even though a long line of researchers has demonstrated that this argument relies on thin data, doubtful reconstructions and inaccurate premises, it has won strong support. The whole claim is also now contradicted by the find of a completely modern hyoid bone in a Neanderthal from Kebara in Israel. The Neanderthals' throats, air canals and sound production do not seem to have greatly differed from those of the modern human.

The fact that the Neanderthals' cranial capacity of around 1,750 cubic centimetres is more than any other human species has ever been able to boast of is usually explained by saying that this was merely an adaptation to their slighter greater body mass. (The Neanderthals had a compact, muscular and relatively short body shape typical of arctic peoples, as a biological adaptation to an ever-colder climate.) The slightly different form of the Neanderthals' brains has also been claimed to signal certain limitations in their overall ability and capacity for speech.

Even though brain size is only an approximate gauge of intelligence, it ultimately becomes a bit much when a larger brain is interpreted as a signal of lower mental capacity. A more reasonable view would see the big brains of the Neanderthals as an evolutionary effect of a very successful adaptation to a harsh environment, through selection precisely *for* intelligence and linguistic ability.

There is no doubt that the Neanderthals' looks have done them no favours. We really do have difficulty in imagining much between the ears of these people who looked like steroid-popping body-builders with sloping foreheads, massive eyebrow ridges, jutting chins, and arms and legs like gorillas. Different DNA studies have shown that Neanderthals appear to have belonged to an earlier, ultimately extinct branch of modern humanity – so now that we no longer need worry that we are descended from such King Kong look-alikes, the risk increases that we do not do them justice.

Be all that as it may. What I chiefly oppose is a manner of argument that renders it almost impossible to sensibly discuss the evolution of human speech. It is certainly possible that the Neanderthals and other late *erectus* people did not speak a fully modern language, or that they did so somewhat slower or more indistinctly. As I have argued above it is also possible that the missing element in the Neanderthals' intellectual toolkit was *not* the ability to think analytically, logically or in the abstract. Their cultural conservatism may instead have been an expression of a lack of creativity and curiosity as a result of having not undergone the same neotene cranial selection processes as modern humans.

Scientific controversies are sometimes like political debates or marital quarrels. From different starting points, values and language, people talk past one another, even though they are discussing the same subject. In relation to the origins of language, scholars have sometimes almost created contradictions where they do not in fact exist, simply by being unclear as to which linguistic level is in question. If by 'language' we mean language of a completely modern kind, then it is understandable that no one older than modern humans can have had language. But in the debate on language's origins and evolution a definition of this kind is meaningless.

The argument that modern language arose in Europe at the end of the last Ice Age is therefore weak. Everything suggests that this capacity is at least three to six times older, and first developed in Africa. Interesting in this context is the find made in 1995 at Katanda in eastern Zaire in Central Africa, of complex assembly tools of antler and bone including finely made harpoons remarkably like those from late Ice Age Europe. If the datings are secure then at 90,000 years old the African finds are more than twice as ancient as the corresponding discoveries from Europe.

Cranial fossils and archaeological material

Archaeology's only chance of interpreting the remote past is through direct or indirect association to something that we believe we already know, either from the present or from recorded history. The same applies when we interpret the remains of early humans. Our understanding of the biological and intellectual capacity of the earliest modern humans is often seen as unproblematic, because we can use ourselves as a point of reference. And for the oldest bipedal humans we primarily rely on modern apes for our comparisons. But what framework do we have for human evolution between this beginning and end, during the more than 2 million years between early *Homo* and late *erectus*, when our ancestors resembled neither apes nor modern humans? So long as the abominable snowman stubbornly refuses to reveal itself to science, we are left without any kind of living reference. The only things we have to illustrate a 'simpler' level of human evolution are the different stages of children's development, which have an obviously limited scientific value. I take this up here in order to explain why researchers have experienced such difficulty in getting to grips with *erectus'* intellectual, linguistic and social nature – a problem that is so hard that scholars have often simply ignored it altogether.

Those who see late Ice Age Europe as the time and place for the birth of the modern human spirit and language usually have little time for the question of *erectus'* abilities. This perspective has nevertheless been seriously called into question by new archaeological finds. Two such are the long wooden spears from Schöningen in northwest Germany, well dated to 400,000 years ago. They are about 2 metres long, very carefully shaped and made from specially selected hard cores of larch. In terms of size and proportions one of them is very similar to a modern sports javelin – thickest in the middle, finely balanced and evenly tapered towards the ends. At the point there is a slit for a thin stone blade. These spears were found together with stone tools and bone from a very wide variety of game, including wild horse bones with marks of cutting from stone tools. Later a further five wooden spears have emerged, and the find has also re-focused our picture of earlier discoveries. One of these, which seems to be the point of a wooden spear, was found as early as 1911 at Clacton in southern England, in layers of approximately the same age as those from Schöningen. The second find, a wooden spear in an elephant skeleton from the early Neanderthal period 125–115,000 years ago, was found in 1948 at Lehringen in Germany.

These finds have cast a very doubtful light on the claims for a late development not only of big game hunting, but also of an advanced consciousness and intellectual planning. The people who made and used the spears were late *erectus* or early archaic *sapiens*, that is to say the Neanderthals' ancestors who lived in Europe several hundred thousand years earlier than them. They point not only to the advanced use of organic material for tools and the ability to manufacture combined tools of stone and wood, but also the capacity to plan and pursue organised big game hunting long before many scholars thought this was possible. Some researchers have therefore suggested that the spears were not meant for throwing, but for use as stabbing weapons at close range. But there is no reason to believe that they took the time to create advanced throwing spears if all they needed was a simple thrusting stick.

These finds show that people in Europe at the border between late *erectus* and early archaic *sapiens*, with a brain volume of around 1,200 cubic centimetres, possessed an advanced intelligence and planning capacity, a meaningful depth of consciousness, and therewith probably a quite well developed capacity for speech.

At this time, about 400,000 years ago, people in Europe were making stone tools of fairly high technical precision. According to Thomas Wynn, the manufacturing process that the tools required presupposes operative thinking and processual decision-making of almost the same level as that needed for a developed spoken language. He suggests that these stone tools reflect a linguistic ability roughly equivalent to that of a modern 7-year-old child. Others argue that this is to overestimate the thinking behind such stone craftwork.

Jeffrey Laitman has suggested that there is a general connection between the indentations at the base of the skull and the preconditions for articulated speech. The more developed the linguistic ability the greater the throat, thus leading to a larger indentation of the base of the cranium. At the same time he argues that the older fossil skulls are, the flatter the base of the skull appears. On the basis of known cranial material he has felt able to conclude that humans must have had a relatively well developed speech capacity as long as 400–300,000 years ago.

Cartmill and colleagues have pointed out that the canals for the hypoglossal nerves in the skull – those that govern the work of the tongue – were almost fully developed at least a half million years ago, which they suggest indicates relatively developed speech. Others have questioned their interpretation.

According to fossilised skulls, half a million years ago the human cranial vault had already grown to such a size that Leslie Aiello and Robin Dunbar, on the basis of comparisons between brain and social behaviour among other primates, have estimated the human contact net to have embraced between 120 and 150 people. In their opinion this presupposes a relatively well developed spoken language.

Throughout the entire span of time between 1.6 and 0.5 million years ago, *erectus* made its universal handaxe – a systematisation of the earlier Olduvai handaxe tradition – in a surprisingly similar form over large parts of Africa and later also in Europe and western Asia. The handaxes were also residual cores deriving from the manufacture of stone blades. Handaxes were made 700,000 years ago in such standardised forms and proportions, especially on the same site, that they can only reasonably have been produced from a well-defined collective pattern. The question is whether such a precise cultural norm and such complex behaviour can be transferred from individual to individual and from generation to generation without the medium of a spoken language.

A few years ago a number of old finds of stone tools were published from the island of Flores in eastern Indonesia, one of the last islands before Australia. Some 900–800,000 years old, these tools can only have been made by *erectus*. The strange thing is that Flores Island never had a fixed land connection with any other area. Even when the world-ocean was at its lowest the nearest mainland was 20 kilometres away. As these matters stand, *erectus* was already capable of making and manoeuvring some kind of vessel and deliberately crossing bodies of water. This gives a quite new perspective on *erectus'* intelligence, application and ability to plan, just as for their ability to communicate.

Several independent sources thus suggest that up to half a million years ago early archaic *sapiens* had fulfilled all the anatomical requirements for modern articulated speech, and that the level of this communication might have approached that of our own. There are also implications that at least a million years ago *erectus* could speak a not completely undeveloped kind of language.

The earliest known human skull with a somewhat indented base belongs to an early, almost 1.8 million-year-old *Homo ergaster*. Laitman argues that the opening of the throat had the same position in the neck as in a modern 6-year-old, and that even at this date humans must be allowed a certain linguistic ability. Unfortunately no skulls with intact bases have been found from the immediately preceding period, and so we cannot yet say whether there were older ancestors with indented crania.

As common chimpanzees in the wild and several other animals have shown us, certain cultural experiences and skills can be mediated without a spoken language. However, it is hard to understand how the oldest stone tool making in eastern Africa, in all its systematics and complexity, could have been communicated solely through silent observation, demonstration and correction. Not least this applies to the 2.34 million-year-old finds from Nachukui in northern Kenya that have been discovered by the French archaeologists Helen Roche and an international team. Here we may perceive the presence of a knowledge-bearing spoken language, albeit not very developed. Because humans had been walking upright for more than 3 million years by this time, they almost certainly possessed far better throat anatomies for producing articulated sounds than any ape has ever had.

The suggestion that early humans had a richer and more varied repertoire of sounds than a modern chimpanzee finds support in studies of brain impressions in fossil skulls very much older than the earliest with indented bases. Prints on the inside of skulls of early *Homo*, *africanus* and *afarensis* all suggest brain structures that were clearly human in form. Brain impressions from *afarensis* show obvious signs of specialisation, which may reflect among other things the presence of mechanisms for central speech functions, usually localised in the left hemisphere of the brain. The same is implied by the fact that some of the next earliest known stone tools – about 2.5 million years old from Koobi Fora in Kenya – were principally made by right-handed people. These clear proofs of specialisation in the brain strengthen the idea that people at this time possessed a rudimentary speech. In addition there are impressions from the left hemispheres of both *afarensis* and *africanus* with a light swelling in the area of Broca's centre. Opinions are divided about this part of the brain, but it has been seen as the location of the motor functions and syntax of speech, and as the receptor for brain impulses that regulate hearing and feeling in the mouth, tongue and throat. Then we have Wernicke's centre, which appears to control among other things the reception of sound sequences and the differentiation of different individual's noises.

The brains of chimpanzees and some other apes also have small swellings where both Broca's and Wernicke's centres would be. Some researchers therefore claim that the light demarcation of Broca's centre on fossil human skulls does not tell us anything about early humans' ability to speak. But this reasoning can just as easily be reversed. The slight swelling of the chimpanzee's brain at the place for Broca's centre could reflect the considerable vocal ability that they definitely have. That some early human skulls have a clearer swelling at Broca's centre would in that case suggest that they possessed a linguistic ability bigger than that of a modern chimpanzee. This is not contradicted by the fact that the afarenes had slightly larger brains, weighed somewhat less and had slightly smaller body masses than chimps, even though the relationship between body size, brain size and intelligence is not absolute.

The different arguments put forward for the very early evolution of human speech are based on evidence of varying value. However, in combination the proofs are too weighty to be ignored.

Anatomical prerequisites

Most hypotheses on the origins of spoken language are based on an evolutionary situation in which speech in general possessed a positive selective value. But articulated speech is so unique that its birth must be sought in a very unusual evolutionary context.

Impressed as we are with our own linguistic abilities, we often underestimate those of animals. Many animals, especially higher primates, have quite complex communication systems, in which sounds form only one of several components. This suggests that it is more a matter of anatomical restrictions for the production of articulated sounds, rather than the ability to communicate in itself, that sets the limits for their potential to mediate through sounds. We now know that monkeys and apes have a throat and mouth that quite simply does not allow them to produce articulated and richly varied sounds. They have a narrow throat and a sort of lid that is located right next to a crude palatal vault, a flat palate, a primitive tongue and nostrils that cannot be closed as effectively by the palate. Chimpanzees can certainly produce a wide range of vowel sounds, but they cannot vary the form and size of the throat aperture and mouth sufficiently enough to pronounce articulated consonants and clear distinctions between nasal and oral sounds. Nor are their lip muscles made to form precise consonants, provide vowel range or produce clear sounds against the teeth.

The human throat goes deeper into the neck and is larger than that of the apes. There is room for a deeper pharynx and a greater distance between the roof of the mouth on the one hand and the throat and soft palate on the other. Our palate is also vaulted and provides space for a mobile tongue. This is how we can more easily form the consonants and clear vowel sounds that produce a varied and distinct speech.

The fact that quadrupeds, such as apes, cannot produce articulated sounds in any real sense thus has an anatomical basis. This suggests that the special evolutionary situation that articulated speech ultimately must derive from, was such that it produced the anatomical changes that made such language possible. And here we return to bipedalism.

Even though apes can move on two legs, they are essentially quadrupeds. They often switch between sitting, half standing and, especially in trees, stretched standing positions. The line of their bodies thus shifts continually between a right angle and the straight. In order to see downwards, forwards and upwards they must, depending on body position, bend their short necks backwards or forwards – something that limits the neck-room for their throats. The same space limitations are also produced by the need to separate the throat and windpipe so that the animal can breathe and eat at the same time.

Since becoming bipedal, early humans by contrast had a straight bodyline whether sitting or standing. To look up and down they needed only to move their bodies and necks a fraction backwards or forwards. This new anatomical situation reduced the need for powerful muscles and muscle platforms, which is supported by the fossil finds. What happened was that bipedalism made a space for the throat and palate to broaden in such a way that later made it possible to produce articulated sounds. Bipedalism is the mother of human speech.

To carefully follow a small child's development is very instructive in this context. A baby's throat is directly joined to the root of the tongue just as in a four-footed animal, and cannot therefore produce articulated sounds, just gurgling and babbling noises. But because the root of the tongue still covers the base of the throat, babies can also – like other mammals but in contrast to older children and adults – drink and breathe at the same time. We should be grateful for this baby's inheritance from our quadruped ancestors, for our species would otherwise have died out as soon as it arose. It is this heritage that allows the baby to suck and breathe at the same time, without filling its windpipe with milk. At around 3 months the throat slowly begins to sink and later take on an adult form. The first articulated sounds usually appear around the same time as a child begins to walk on two legs. This process can be seen as a speeded-up film of the long evolutionary process from a four-footed walk with accompanying unarticulated noises to an upright gait with its consequent anatomical potential to form articulated sounds.

A less happy effect of these unique changes in the throat is that hundreds of thousands of people the world over die every year through suffocation, after food or something else has become lodged in their windpipes.

The question must be when did these anatomical alterations to the throat begin, and at what speed did they progress. The fact that the afarenes had their heads located almost directly over their necks and spines, and that their neck was considerably less muscular that that of the chimpanzees, suggest that this process had already come a fair way by 4 million years ago, which is hardly surprising when one considers that bipedalism was then a couple of million years old.

Of course, effective spoken communication has a selective value for adaptation and survival. Since humanity's ancestors became bipedal, selection might very well have quickly begun the evolution of a larger and lower-sitting throat, with a bigger palate that allowed a little more variation and articulation of sound. Evolution of this kind may have progressed slowly for a long time before the throat had widened far enough down that it started to press on the base of the skull and bend it inwards. There is thus no reason to suggest that the earliest indented skull bases should mark the beginnings of development towards more articulated sound.

Apes and tools

Many believe that an important selective mechanism for the evolution of higher intelligence and communication in the higher primates has been their dynamic social interaction between individuals and groups. Dunbar and Aiello, for example, have shown that among higher animals and primates there is a clear connection between social group size – and thus social complexity – and the relative size of the neocortex that is principally connected with thinking. However, a question must be raised as to cause and effect.

For several million years after the division of the species, the brains of early humans were like those of modern chimpanzees, or only marginally larger. It was only with early *Homo* 2.5 million years ago that the brain began to grow at a slightly faster rate. Does this mean that early human intelligence stood still for more than 4 million years after the split from the apes?

By drawing an equivalence between brain volume and intelligence we may well have underestimated the mental capacity of early humans. One sign of this might be that the earliest humans were somewhat smaller and lighter than modern chimpanzees. Another signal is that brain impressions inside the crania of the afarenes indicate a vaguely human brain structure. There is thus some evidence to suggest that a couple of million years after the division of the species, early humans were slightly more intelligent than modern apes. In this case there would be no point in seeking the evolutionary factors behind the growth of intelligence within the timeframe of the afarene fossils that we currently have. Instead we are led once more back to the time of the last common ancestor.

The anatomical changes from a quadruped to a biped gait certainly brought with them problems of adaptation, for which intelligence clearly would have had a positive selective value. If there is anything to the aquatic hypothesis, then early humans also underwent no less than two demanding adaptations to new environments within a very short space of time: first from a purely wooded environment to the tidewater zone, and second back to the forests, albeit near to water. These shifts of environment, together with bipedalism, would have triggered a considerably greater selective pressure towards intelligence than anything that the ancestors of chimps and gorillas were exposed to within their rather stable biotopes after the division of the species. It is therefore quite possible that the split itself was a decisive catalyst for the beginnings of a slow evolution of intelligence.

Because the primitive working of stone is rather a demanding activity in intellectual terms, it is unlikely that the oldest stone tools represent the first manufacture and use of tools themselves. In all probability simple tools made of organic materials had long been in use, in roughly the same way as among common chimpanzees and orang-utans in the wild in Sumatra.

Even though common chimps are probably rather less talented than early humans, in the wild they exhibit at least 20 different types of planned and systematic tool use. In two thirds of instances this concerns the deliberate preparation of organic implements. Several of the tools have specific cultural traits that are specific to different populations. Some kind of tool use has been observed in at least 34 different groups of common chimpanzees spread over the entire species range in western, central and eastern Africa. In total, no less than 39 behaviours among common chimps in the wild have been defined as cultural. This is not a matter of tool culture alone, but also encompasses social behaviour and other forms of action. The interesting thing is that every chimpanzee settlement differs in some way from all the others. This means that one can in principle determine from which settlement a chimp has come on the basis of which kinds of cultural behaviour – or rather which combinations of behaviours – it displays.

One very common form of behaviour among chimpanzees is to throw and strike with branches and sticks, to throw stones at real or imagined enemies, and to use them as a threat within internal dominance displays. Much of chimpanzees' tool culture is however concerned with the acquisition of food. They use whatever happens to be in the vicinity: leaves, branches, twigs, shoots, vines, stalks, blades of grass, bits of bark and stones. There is also the well-known ant fishing of the females and infants. They select and break off a thin twig of a certain sort and thickness, which they then use to 'fish' termites and ants out of their nests – after which they happily lick the stick. Arnold Boetsch has observed that the twigs that West African chimpanzees employ are consistently longer than those used by chimps in East Africa, despite being used for exactly the same purpose. This appears to relate to the fact that they employ different kinds of grip, both to get at the ants and to eat them. It is hard not to see these differences as expressions of long-established variations in cultural behaviour. In a similar fashion, chimpanzees access the honey in bees' nests both on the ground and in trees. By poking with specially prepared sticks, and then smelling and feeling them, chimpanzees explore spaces that they could not otherwise reach. Some groups of chimps select crude stalks from fibrous plants, with which they scrape holes in trees that contain a fruity sap. They then take fibres that have fallen in the liquid while the hole is made, and suck the sap from them.

Another example of sophisticated tool use is when chimpanzees choose a leaf of a certain kind which they proceed to chew into a sponge-like lump, using it afterwards to soak up drinking water from holes in tree trunks and other inaccessible places. They can also use leaves as spoons to scrape out the last flesh from a hard fruit, or the last piece of brain from the skulls of their prey. A chimp will sometimes also use a leaf to remove dirt and filth from its body, and even to wipe its backside after relieving itself. Chimpanzees occasionally select leafy plants that are well known for their healing properties, chew them carefully and then press them to a wound. They may also chew and swallow a certain kind of leaf that appears to prevent intestinal parasites.

In Liberia, Guinea, the Ivory Coast and Sierra Leone in West Africa, wild chimpanzees use selected natural stones to crack nuts in a very human fashion. They place the nuts on a flat stone that they have chosen, and break the shell with an equally carefully selected stone or wooden club. As part of this deliberate planning they can carry their tools for hundreds of metres. This kind of behaviour has been observed in more than ten localities, but at only a few of them has it been seen to continue for a longer period and in a systematic form. According to Boetsch, who has studied this phenomenon in particular in the Tai region of the Ivory Coast, the infants try to acquire these skills by imitating their mothers. It also occurs that nut cracking mothers will deliberately teach their young by placing out both nuts and tools for them in an appropriate way, and when the infants make a mistake the mothers correct them – either by placing the nuts and tools in the correct positions, or actually by cracking the nuts themselves. A mother will intervene on average once every 5 minutes to help her infants in this task. In other words, the mothers analyse the youngsters' behaviour, and compare it with their own idea of how things should be done. There is thus an intention behind the teaching, with a predetermined idea of its objective.

This example of actively pedagogic teaching in wild chimpanzees is the only one known for any animal species. This kind of behaviour is not even especially common among modern humans in hunter-gatherer communities. The essentially cultural nature of this nut cracking is also indicated by the fact that it only occurs in West Africa, and there in at least a dozen geographical variations.

The conclusion is unavoidable: common chimpanzees in the wild are at least rudimentary cultural beings. The same is true to some extent for wild orang-utans' use of organic tools on Sumatra. A creature with the understanding of a chimpanzee is thus able to grasp the principles of working with a hammer and anvil, producing stone blades and then using them. As Frederic Joulien has shown, the mental processes required for the chimps' active teaching of nut cracking do not differ in principle from those required for the simple production of stone tools. Chimpanzees' nut cracking also sometimes results in the unintentional production of simple stone flakes. Experiments with stoneworking and chimps have demonstrated that when this occurs, the animals will then consciously begin to produce and use stone tools on their own. Even though this is influenced behaviour, the experiments – just like the spontaneous nut cracking – show that chimpanzees' intelligence is close to the level required to develop a stone technology on their own account.

We can take a look at the tame bonobo Kanzi, and his talents as a stoneworker. When Kanzi was given the opportunity to observe the stone technologist Nick Toth at work, he was himself inspired to begin working stone with the material that lay to hand. He then taught himself to manufacture sharp-edged blades, which he then used to cut a string that blocked the way to some food. After 2 months of labour without any help at all, Kanzi had learned to strike exactly the right pressure points on the stones, and to instantly pick out which stones were best suited for cutting. By contrast, he never succeeded in attaining the best angle for striking, which lies at 90 degrees. Toth suggested that this was mainly due to the fact that chimpanzees have more curved fingers and stiffer wrists than a human. It is not irrelevant that the intelligent Kanzi later noticed that it was both simpler and quicker to make the blades he needed by just throwing one stone at another. When he realised this he at once abandoned the more complicated manufacturing process.

Apes are not the only wild primates to use tools. In South America, Capuchin monkeys also exhibit a relatively varied and skilled use of tools, albeit not on a par with chimpanzees. They produce and use stone flakes and they employ unworked stones as cutting implements. In captivity they can also crack nuts with the help of bones that they have picked up, roughly as wild chimpanzees do with stone hammers. Asian Gibbons in the wild have also been seen to use tools. Even some other animals employ tools, such as marine otters and many birds. Californian sea otters make use of at least 14 different sorts of tools in no less than 30 different ways.

Seen in this light it may seem strange that neither wild gorillas, bonobos nor orang-utans on Borneo have been observed to manufacture tools. In captivity, by contrast, all apes learn to use them. The explanation may be that gorillas, pygmy chimpanzees and orang-utans have relatively stable access to food, whereas common chimpanzees often live in environments with a more uncertain and shifting availability of food and water. The tool culture of common chimps, which is primarily concerned with food acquisition, may have its foundations in the fact that they have to work harder for their sustenance while the others are more easily able to pick what they need. When mountain gorillas do not fish for angry little ants with a stick, but instead simply make a few sudden swipes with their hands, this is probably due to the fact that they have much denser and more protective fur under their arms. On the other hand, as Richard Byrne has shown, mountain gorillas' handling of prickly plant food such as thistles is extremely sophisticated, and includes a pattern of systematic and ordered action that is actually more complex than that exhibited by chimpanzees in connection with tool use.

There is a special form of systematic manufacture and use of tools that is common to all apes: the preparation of a bed for the night. Here all the great apes are very picky indeed. No one goes to sleep without first making up their own bed. Every night, and often even for short naps during the day, every adult individual quickly and efficiently bends and plaits a sleeping mattress of branches, twigs and leaves: the chimps between 5 and 15 metres up in a tree, orang-utans similarly up in the forest, and gorillas on the ground. The beds of apes are often ignored in discussions of their tool cultures, perhaps because they do not equate with our concept of a tool and because one suspects an element of in-born instinct. Nevertheless, this is still a question of the systematic making and using of implements with clear cultural traits. The tradition is passed on through the young, who every night for years on end watch and later imitate the actions of their mother. The cultural super-structure also emerges in the beds' appearance and placement, which often varies a good deal between different populations of the same species. The beds of apes are a good example of the familiar animal interactions of instinct, learning and culture.

Just like orang-utans on Sumatra, chimpanzees are among the few animals in the wild that selectively use tools for specific tasks. Chimps also employ both hands together in co-ordination when they use tools, and can take up several tools in succession to solve a particular problem. When it comes to organic materials for tools, wild chimpanzees practise all three of these fundamentals: the selective choice of raw material; its working up into a suitable form; and its use as a tool. For stone tools, chimpanzees apply a selective choice and use natural rocks that are of a shape most suited to their purposes. Some individuals are very careful indeed in their preparation and employment of simple tools in organic materials. As William McGrew has pointed out, there is also another layer of complexity in the tool culture of chimps, in that they sometimes use tools to make other tools.

Wild chimpanzees *are* thus to some extent cultural beings. They prepare and systematically use tools and, to a degree, they possess the ability to communicate experience and knowledge at an individual and generational level. This occurs partly through the intuitive acquisition of instincts and skills during childhood, and partly through the adults' conscious attempt to pass these on. The image of the chimpanzee as a cultural creator is supported by the fact that certain behaviours are specific to certain populations. The same applies to their repertoire of sounds.

Nut cracking chimps do not use tools arbitrarily. They spend time choosing both platform and hammer. When they move off to smash up roots, they often take along a proven hammer, which they have previously stored in a place they have memorised. Early *Homo* went one stage further. To make stone tools they not only chose stones of a certain size and shape, but also of particular kinds of rock – that is to say stones with special qualities. Sometimes they even collected the raw materials several kilometres distant. They therefore based their actions on previous knowledge of the properties, appearance and location of stones. When they later flaked off pieces to make one or more blades, this too was not random but followed a clearly discernable pattern. Behind these simple products one can thus perceive collective, communicated experience and a systematic planning that obviously surpasses what we find among chimpanzees. This suggests that early *Homo* possessed an instrument that permitted the passing on of stored skills beyond demonstration and imitation: a rudimentary and spoken proto-language.

It is often said that once the threshold of stoneworking had been crossed, then the growth of the brain was thereafter always intimately linked to cultural evolution. I suggest that this relationship extends much further back in time. The earliest stone tools do not mark the beginnings of our cultural tradition – this had older roots. Early humans had certainly long prepared and used organic tools and suitable natural stones. Even though such activity cannot be proven archaeologically, there is much to suggest that the human tool tradition is twice as old as commonly acknowledged.

Opinion has been divided as to the extent to which a spoken language is necessary for the creation of a simple material culture tradition. We now know that chimpanzees in the wild are able to do this without even communicating through sounds.

McGrew argues that the oldest finds of stone tools in Africa are so primitive that they might have been made by chimpanzees of the time. Thomas Wynn disagrees, and says that even though the mental equipment needed to make these tools was not greater than that of a chimp, it is still most probable that they were manufactured by *Homo*. The stone technologist Nick Toth argues that on purely anatomical grounds these tools could not have been made by chimpanzees. He also claims that the technology of the Olduvai tools is too complex to have been transmitted solely through imitation or silent demonstration. It required experience that must have been transferred from individual to individual over the generations, in a manner that could hardly have been possible without an elementary spoken language. Not even the earliest stone products were as simple as their appearance suggests. It is otherwise easy to think that these simple implements were made by picking up the nearest stone and bashing off a few flakes haphazardly.

Since the early humans of 4–3 million years ago were probably a bit brighter than modern tool-using apes, they were probably better equipped for the systematic use and production of tools. Several million years before the oldest stone implements they most likely used unworked stones as tools, while preparing and using other simple implements of organic materials. If chimpanzees can have a simple cultural tool tradition, then so could the early humans. I therefore assume that the earliest humans had a continuous, albeit limited, cultural evolution even before the time of the afarenes. In this case their brains would have been prepared over a very long period of time for the rather more demanding thought processes that stone tool production required. Only this kind of long-term foundation of intellectual and cultural capacity can explain how systematic stone working could 'suddenly' arise. Quite simply, it was not sudden at all.

Apes and language

Against our will we have been forced to concede that we do not have a monopoly on intelligence. Not only apes but also elephants, dolphins and other toothed whales have highly developed brains, a considerable intelligence and advanced communication systems, even over great distances. But above all we have had to change our perception of the great apes' intelligence and linguistic ability.

We once thought that apes could not learn to speak because they were too stupid. But during the 1960s and 1970s a number of experiments showed that, through intensive training in sign language and other symbols, adult common chimps, gorillas and orang-utans could learn to communicate with humans – and even with each other – with some success. It was then understood that it was the anatomy of their throats, not their brains, that hindered them from simple speech.

These studies also demonstrated that even though apes' syntactic skills are limited, they do not lack an understanding of syntax itself. Using sign language they could build sentences of two, three and sometimes more words, at times of some complexity. They could also learn the meaning of, and actively use, several hundred simple words and concepts. Even though their conversation mainly consisted of imperative messages, that is, expressions of concrete and direct desires and demands, they could also understand abstract concepts to some degree. Certain individuals even possessed rather advanced conceptual talents. This early phase of language training with apes also proved that they are not entirely incapable of forward planning. It was especially thrilling to discover that chimpanzees used their newly learned sign language for such purposes as cursing, lying to and making fun of their fellow creatures – other chimps as well as humans.

These early language experiments had methodological limitations. It took a long time to realise how misguided it was to begin speech training apes first when they were juveniles or adults, which for a human would prove a severe linguistic handicap. Especially important here is the work undertaken by Susanne Savage-Rumbaugh since the 1980s with young pygmy chimpanzees – first with the male Kanzi and later with others. Kanzi is the first ape to have had the opportunity to learn human language under almost the same conditions as a human child, that is to say spontaneously from babyhood and in his case from the age of 2 months. It began with the image-symbol training of Kanzi's foster mother Matata, something that only mildly interested her. One day when Matata was temporarily absent, it became clear that simply by being constantly present little Kanzi had learned – better than his mother – to understand spoken English and the principles of using pictorial symbols. Nobody had never made the slightest effort to teach him anything.

With the same kind of deliberate training as a human child receives, Kanzi was soon able to master a meaningful understanding of basic spoken English. As an adult Kanzi possessed a linguistic ability and comprehension far beyond what had been thought possible for an ape, roughly equivalent to that of a 2–3-year-old human child. Sometimes he even appeared frustrated that he could not communicate his thoughts quickly enough.

Primarily through Savage-Rumbaugh's work it has become clear that apes that make the acquaintance of human language spontaneously from babyhood not only understand and use language better than others but also faster. Kanzi's abilities cannot be dismissed by claiming him as a uniquely talented individual, because others have followed in his wake. It has also been shown that pygmy chimpanzees are more adept than common chimps in their handling of simple rules for connecting categories of objects and actions.

Attempts to teach human languages to apes have thus passed through several phases. First we tried to make the poor creatures speak in contradiction of their anatomical capacity to do so. Then came the more successful experiments with sign language and pictorial symbol languages, though primarily after the subjects had reached adolescence or adulthood, and only through organised training on human terms. It was not before the third phase that researchers grasped the way in which human children spontaneously learn languages right from the time they are babies.

The apes' abilities to comprehend modern human speech and to cope with linguistic symbols is therefore much greater than their vocal communication in the wild would suggest. Their potential for understanding syntactic nuances in spoken human languages is also larger than their own linguistic skills would imply. They have a latent capacity at a very basic level to communicate through human linguistic concepts, and they have a quite advanced ability to understand spoken human language. Experiments have also shown that apes command a considerable numerical understanding. Chimpanzees seem able to handle numbers of six to nine units. The bonobo Ai at the primate research centre in Kyoto can without problem cope with nine numerical units, and has no problem in understanding the order of difference between them. Even Rhesus macaques have shown themselves able to grasp up to nine numerical units. Chimpanzees, rats and certain birds also seem to be able to understand at least the basic principles of addition and subtraction.

There is a close structural similarity between speech and the language of natural gestures. It has also been found that human sign language is in principle constructed in the same way, and is as complex as, spoken language. Sign language and speech also appear to activate the same centres in the brain, such as Broca's and Wernicke's in the left hemisphere. Hiroshi Nishima has shown that when people who are born deaf use sign language, the same part of the right lobe is activated as for the understanding of speech. There also seems to be a connection between brain activity for language production and for manual activity like stone craftwork. It actually appears that certain functions for early language acquisition in the brain and nervous system of a human baby are also found in chimpanzees. Here we can also note Martin Sereno's studies of neurobiological mechanisms for sight functions in the brains of humans and animals. In apes and humans these are not concentrated in any special centre but instead spread among 20–25 different places in the brain. Sereno also argues that spoken language is regulated by essentially the same parts of the brain as steer sight functions. In which case, he says, only a slight rewiring of these functions would have been needed to trigger an early evolution of speech among the first humans.

Patrick Gannon has investigated the brains of eighteen chimpanzees and found that the *planum temporale*, the area of grey cells that is thought to control speech, was in seventeen cases larger in the left hemisphere in exactly the same proportions as in humans. Gannon and his colleagues have concluded that, neurologically, chimpanzees have what it takes for language.

Although we do not have information on wild chimpanzees' entire repertoire of sounds, we do know that they use at least 30 or so different sounds, which they vary and combine in many more meanings. Apes have a rich and expressive natural body language of gesture, which has not been intensively studied. It is clear, however, that chimpanzees' body language in terms of gestures, posture and facial expressions has obvious similarities with that of humans. One can observe chimpanzees laugh, greet one another with hugs and kisses after a period apart, beg a tasty morsel, seek comfort and reconciliation by putting out an open palm, or say 'no' by shaking their heads. One can also see chimps calm and comfort a frightened fellow creature by tenderly laying an arm round its shoulders, and observe a flock leader stifle a coming fight by raising his eyebrows a little.

A remarkable study of gestures among a group of five gorillas in a large animal park – who had never been exposed to language training – shows that in connection with play situations, sexual activities, group movements and conflicts they communicated with no less than 40 different, clearly meaning-bearing gestures. Astonishingly enough, when walking in single file they communicated through gestures back and forth along the line in up to eight waves, roughly like soldiers marching under order of silence.

Being bipedal, humans ought to have been able to develop an even more multi-faceted gesture language than apes. Irenäus Eibl-Eibelsfeldt has demonstrated that our basic pattern of facial expressions, posture and gesture is found in fundamentally the same form among all peoples throughout the globe, regardless of cultural context. He argues that in all its essentials the human body language is encoded in our genes.

Chimpanzees and gorillas have no problems in distinguishing all the sounds and nuances of sounds that are needed to understand human speech. This is not surprising. Their own rich repertoire of vowel sounds presupposes precisely that they can produce and interpret very fine variations of sounds. In fact most of the higher mammals have this vital ability. Male chimpanzees in the wild even seem to be able to vary their calls selectively in relation to their intended recipient.

The types of neurological mechanism that are required for the apes' complex communications through sound, gestures, postures, scent signals, behaviour and motor activities are an important part of the explanation as to why they can also handle human language at a basic level.

Linguistic experiments and other intelligence studies, together with research into the social life of the great apes, also show that they clearly possess an inner consciousness and an elementary understanding of themselves as individuals. They have a grasp of their own personality's relationship to the world around them that goes far beyond what is needed to maintain social relations within a flock. Chimpanzees not only have a basic notion of self-identity, but their social behaviour also indicates that they can to some degree place themselves in another's situation, even showing a kind of empathy. For example, a flock can deliberately slow its speed while on the move, in order to allow time for a wounded member to keep up. When a chimp has just lost a conflict of dominance, another chimp may come forward and comfort it with embraces and kisses. There are also examples of how an individual will carefully and consciously plan an aggressive act of revenge long (in some cases even years) after a perceived injustice. It is also clear that all the great apes perfectly understand the meaning of a proper noun, and that they can cope with personal pronouns such as I, my, and you. With sounds, gestures, body language and behaviour, chimpanzees possess the means of rich social communication.

Ordinary monkeys have a clear individual identity, and are good at reading and predicting other individuals' behaviour and reactions. But as Cheney and Seyfarth have shown, they are hardly aware of their own awareness, and they lack the apes' ability to place themselves in another individual's position, thereby also lacking elementary empathy.

On the other hand, a number of ordinary monkeys' linguistic abilities have also been re-evaluated. Studies of wild vervets, macaques, baboons and tamarids have indicated that they have a capacity for language that is greater than we had previously suspected, as we once took it for granted that their sounds expressed only instinctive feelings. Special studies by Cheeney and Seyfarth have proved that they are capable of communicating practical information through culturally transmitted and symbolically coded sounds, and that they can distinguish others' reflective behaviour from simple expressions of emotion. These monkeys also exhibit a basic but clear syntactic structure in the way that they repeat calls in phrases, and how these phrases are combined in sentence-like order. Ordinary monkeys' linguistic abilities are therefore much less limited than we thought.

There is thus much to suggest that the great apes have a latent capacity for language that is quite sufficient for a developed and articulated proto-language – if only the anatomical equipment for it had existed. Basic behaviour and qualities that we share not just with chimpanzees but also with more remote relatives probably go back to a common genetic heritage. The similarities between the communication powers of humans and apes cannot possibly be coincidental. There are thus good reasons for accepting that there is a close connection between the early evolution of language and other early human behaviour.

Latent linguistic capacity at the division of the species

From the early and middle Miocene there are fossil finds that show how already 10 million years before the split from the apes our probable ancestors had roughly the same size of brain as a larger monkey today.

The lack of fossils makes it hard to assess the intelligence and latent linguistic capacity among our last quadruped ancestors. And because we are almost completely lacking in fossils of the ancestors of modern chimpanzees and gorillas, we do not know very much about their evolution down to the present. Perhaps they lived for a long time in such a stable environment that they were only exposed to a limited amount of selective pressure towards intelligence and speech. In that case maybe the chimpanzee is only marginally more intelligent now than its ancestors were at the time of divergence. As we have seen, there is nothing to suggest that the earliest humans were less intelligent than modern chimps – if anything, the opposite is true. This would mean that their brain volume increased somewhat during the long span of time between the last common ancestor and the emergence of the afarenes.

The apes' limited anatomical potential for articulated speech and our own prejudices long prevented us from realising that a brain of 400 cubic centimetres has room for a considerable ability, not only to understand and express language, but also to comprehend basic abstractions, personal identity and numerical skill. If our earliest known bipedal ancestor possessed a sound communication and an ability to give and receive symbolic messages that was comparable to a modern ape's, then selection had good material to work with in order to slowly evolve an articulated spoken language.

The potential that I have discussed here included the following approximate components:

- a clear self-identity and personality;
- a rich and varied emotional life;
- some ability to imagine what was not present (things, individuals, actions);
- some planning ability;
- some problem-solving capacity;
- some numerical understanding;
- a rudimentary grasp of time;
- some ability to empathise with another individual's situation and feelings;
- a considerable capacity for learning;
- a hint of teaching ability;
- a considerable memory capacity;
- a rudimentary capacity for abstraction;
- some conceptual understanding;
- some ability to combine concepts in sequences;
- some perceptive capacity;
- some cognitive capacity;
- a limited grasp of syntax;
- a degree of semantic ability;
- a latent capacity for language, equivalent to that of a 2–3-year-old child;
- a considerable array of non-articulated sounds;
- a rich language of gesture;

- a rich body language;
- an advanced ability to vary sound nuances and to distinguish and interpret those of others;
- some ability for controlled sound communication;
- an ability to communicate at a distance.

All large modern apes possess most of these qualities. Even many ordinary monkeys in the Old and New Worlds have an elementary perceptual, cognitive, syntactic and semantic capacity, and a controlled sound communication involving the activation of different mechanisms in the neocortex to produce different sounds. In all probability even the earliest bipedal people could think according to the most basic of human linguistic laws, and possessed sufficient intelligence to by and by develop a rudimentary and articulated spoken proto-language.

We do not know when the anatomical preconditions for a more-or-less articulated speech emerged. However, we do know that bipedalism brought with it the basis for the evolution of the throat anatomy that was required to make articulated sounds. When one has been bipedal for 2 million years, then the throat really ought to have become adapted for the production of slightly more articulate sounds. The slow evolution towards an anatomy more suited to articulated sounds probably began fairly soon after the transition to bipedalism, and 4–3 million years after the division of the species early humans could probably produce more varied and better articulated sounds than modern apes. They may well have had a rudimentary spoken language at a level equivalent to the apes' capacity for symbolic expression, roughly equivalent to that of a modern child between the ages of 2 and 2.5 years. To accept that early humans eventually developed basic speech we must not assume that they were more intelligent than modern apes.

When and why did articulated speech come about?

In evolutionary terms, such unusual features in land-dwelling mammals as a spoken language, bipedalism, a lack of fur and the loss of oestrus can hardly have arisen independently of each other simply due to a general survival value. If things were that simple then all apes would long ago have evolved into two-legged, smooth-skinned blabbermouths who in addition never went into heat. What we need to look for is an evolutionary situation that is *not* characteristic of the apes, and which can at the same time plausibly have triggered a strong selective pressure towards speech. I can only see two such situations – one that was created by bipedalism as such, and another that the aquatic hypothesis is based upon.

Elaine Morgan has suggested that the seeds for the evolution of speech were sown in the actual adaptation to a life in water, when all of our gesture and body language would have been dislocated. And because creatures that waded

129

around in the waters would require a better rather than lesser means of internal communication, the only thing that remained was to improve vocal language. Selection favoured individuals with more and clearer sounds for giving and receiving information and social signals, which led to improved protection and assertion of themselves and those closest to them. In functional terms this was made possible by the fact that a life in the water provided an impulse for an upright gait that in turn allowed the evolution of the anatomical structures that were required for the formation of articulated sounds. The aquatic hypothesis would thus offer a logical evolutionary explanation not just for bipedalism, the loss of fur and other human qualities, but also for the origins of the first articulated speech.

The other evolutionary alternative is the traditional one in which our ancestors became bipedal on land. The changeable, rich environment close to water that early humans lived in after the split from the apes was considerably more attractive for dangerous land- and water-based predators than anywhere their last quadruped ancestors had inhabited. Another new problem was that the earliest bipedal humans would not have had the same dexterity as their ancestors when it came to rapidly climbing high up into the trees, partly for anatomical reasons and partly because their infants had trouble in clinging onto their bipedal and rather smooth-skinned parents. This confined women in particular to the ground, and thereby placed the whole flock in danger.

In other words, at the same time as the newly bipedal early humans lived under greater threat from predators than they had before, it was also more difficult to escape them. In this situation an improved communication facility in the form of more nuanced and clearer sounds for warning, information, social cohesion and practical planning would have had an absolutely vital survival value.

Proto-language

Our ancestors had been bipedal for 3–2 million years before the afarenes. Such a long period of upright walking should really have led to the changes in the anatomy of the throat that permitted the formation of more articulated sounds than a modern ape can produce.

I imagine that the things that our last primate ancestors had communicated through their social behaviour, body language, gestures and unarticulated sounds would later have begun to be expressed through a combination of behaviour, body language, somewhat more complex gestures and a slightly greater range of more articulated sounds. Soon came more sounds and sound combinations that began to take on the character of simple articulated words, and which in combination began to form what we might call a rudimentary spoken proto-language.

If this was the case then I guess that their vocabulary was dominated by nouns. Later on this may have expanded with a few basic verbs and personal pronouns, adjectives and prepositions. Case, gender, adverbs and declensions would still have been far away at this point.

A proto-language of this kind ought primarily to have been employed for simple social information of a practical nature, and to voice spontaneous social needs, relationships and emotions. Here I am thinking of such typical primate features as demands, wishes, requests, warnings, threats and submissive behaviour, but also a sense and feeling for fear, appreciation and the pleasure of being reunited with another – all things that chimpanzees with their limited means express in such clear ways. The concept of 'no' probably became part of the vocabulary long before the concept of 'yes'.

I want to stress once more that such a spoken proto-language does not presuppose a higher level of communication than that mastered by modern apes, and no more complex syntax and grammar than the latter demonstrate with the help of abstract symbols. Chimpanzees in the wild produce 'sentences' in the form of sequences of varied sounds. I assume that early humans came to be able to produce sequences of a few articulated sounds (phonemes) that can be compared to words. I further assume that they sometimes combined these in sentences of two or three words.

Simple imperatives and cries for assistance would certainly have formed the central components of the oldest articulated language: help, give me, stop it, go away, come here, don't come here, it's me that decides, sorry, let's be friends, be nice to me, I give up, I submit to you, yuck, look there, watch out, it hurts, I'm hungry, I'm sad, I'm scared, now I want to have sex, and so on.

All monkeys and herd mammals are good at identifying individuals. Chimpanzees can even recognise other chimpanzees in photographs. Since apes have a tangible sense of their own and others' identities, and can learn to understand the meaning of personal pronouns such as I, my, you and yours, then these kinds of basic pronomina may have entered the vocabulary rather early. Chimpanzees' strong group feelings and mistrust of outsiders of their own species, their family groups based around mothers with pre-pubertal infants and adult sons, together with their tendency to build personal coalitions imply that early humans later created expressions for concepts such as we, they and stranger. The fact that tame apes understand the principles of personal names should not, however, lead us to believe that early humans used names for each other. Common chimps are not averse to using an acquired symbol language to insult their fellow creatures. I imagine that early humans with the herd animal's typical ranking problems soon enough began to use certain already established 'words' in a new meaning as curses. When a close relative dies, chimpanzees can demonstrate strong and long-lasting emotional reactions, and a certain empathy with another wounded ape. It is probable that words to signify 'hurts' and 'is dead' entered speech early on.

Apes have clear perceptions about a large number of objects and pheno- mena in their surroundings, and in captivity they have learned to handle abstract symbols for hundreds of things. This ought to have made up one of the most common components of the earliest language. Primates in general are knowledgeable about hundreds of different plants, most of which serve as food. Many primates, chimpanzees among others, use sounds to inform others in the group when they have found a good food source, a pattern of behaviour with obvious survival value. Chimpanzees even use different barks for different food items. I assume therefore that a considerable array of simple nouns of this kind came to be included in the vocabulary. The same applies to general categories such as leaf, fruit, nut, flower and other important sorts of food. If they also, like chimpanzees, used certain selected plants as tools and medicine, then they would soon have given names to those too.

If chimps had been able to express themselves articulately, they would surely use words for a great many animal species. Obvious words for early humans would have included those for animals that they hunted, such as certain monkeys, gazelles and small game, and also for the bees whose honey they stole, not to mention ants, termites, beetles, caterpillars and other edible creepy crawlies. Chimpanzees and many other primates share humans' biologically founded respect for snakes. Early on we would have had words for unpleasantries such as snakes, spiders and scorpions, and for other dangerous creatures such as sabre-toothed cats, hyenas, crocodiles, hippos, buffalo and elephant, as well as for leopard and lion when these entered the scene in their present form, and not forgetting the rowdy but tasty baboon. I would remind us here of Cheney and Seyfarth's observations that even wild vervets use distinctive warning cries to designate dangerous animals such as leopards, eagles and pythons, each one triggering a special form of escape behaviour; this is very close to the employment of proper words.

Apes and many other animals possess an excellent spatial orientation based on a considerable capacity for collecting, sorting and storing information on natural changes in the environment. It is probable that several orientational nature- and place-names found a place in the linguistic repertoire of the early humans. These were probably joined later on by some elementary prepositions for spatial determination and daily life, concepts such as over and under, and informative situational terms such as here and there. They would soon have begun to use words for concepts such as close, far away, high and low.

Certain basic personal categories are obvious concepts for apes in the wild. Words for infant, girl, boy, woman, man and mother would soon have emerged in the early human language, though not a word for father before a relatively stable social monogamy emerged. And when we think of how conscious apes are of elementary parts of the body, 'words' for arm, hand, finger, leg, foot, toe, head, eye, ear, mouth, tooth, hair, skin and similar would have sooner or later crept into the proto-language. In the same category come well-known features like bed, tree, branch, twig, stone, water, rain, sun, darkness, light and so on.

The life of apes focuses to a large part around natural body functions. Concepts such as eating, weaning, being hungry, being full, being cold, being in pain, scratching, urinating, defecating and sleeping are all very present in their mental universe and must in the end having been formulated in sound by the early humans. It is not going too far to suggest that the early humans not only shared chimpanzees' interest in sex but also their complete lack of shyness in such matters. Sooner or later they would have created words for the sexual act itself, for vagina and for penis. I assume that early human women were just as interested in other births as modern female chimps are, and that they also made a word for 'having a child'.

Even if tame apes can understand simple concepts of time, I believe that it would have taken a long period before concepts such as yesterday, today, tomorrow, now, then and before were included in the early humans' mindscape in such a distinct way that they entered the first language. But they may have been formulated in words by early *erectus*.

The picture that I have sketched out here of the basic elements in the earliest spoken language is based almost entirely on the conceptual world of the apes, and on their emotional life, social behaviour, relationship to their surroundings and their ability to communicate. I would suggest that the early humans came to develop a vocabulary of at least a couple of hundred simple words. Here I have mostly just related the need for words for the apes' rather simplistic environment, and not to the much more multi-faceted lifestyle of the early humans in the forested belt around lakes and rivers close to the savannah.

Even if the early humans only expressed their most basic needs, emotions and thoughts through individual articulated vocal signals, words and the most simple word combinations, then they possessed a rudimentary spoken proto-language. In combination with gesture and body language, and the inarticulate sounds that they retained (and we still use them now), then this formed a more nuanced and effective system for practical and social communication than any ape ever possessed. When a proto-language of this kind first came into being, it was a tool for adaptation and survival without previous parallel in the animal kingdom. Only a proto-language of this kind, in my opinion, can explain the early humans' tangible ability to adapt themselves to new and changing biotopes, and their expansion over significant areas of tropical Africa. A simple proto-language may in itself have been an instrument for species success.

It is not easy to adopt a position as to when evolution towards an articulated language began, and with what speed it progressed. I nevertheless suppose that the first 3–2 million years after the division of the species were characterised by very slow development, which ultimately resulted between 4 and 3 million years ago in the afarenes acquiring a rudimentary proto-language of the kind I have tried to describe.

The degree of complexity one wishes to assign this earliest speech depends on when one thinks that it began. If, as I believe, the process started not too long after the split from the apes, then linguistic development proceeded at first very gradually indeed, and its syntax remained very simple for a long time. If it was as others have suggested, that the evolution of language did not begin until early *Homo* or early *erectus*, then a certain degree of complexity was attained in a much shorter time. There is much to suggest that intelligence expanded rapidly during the short period between 2.5 and 2 million years ago, when early *Homo* took the stage. It is possible that the level of language also rose dramatically then, and continued to keep pace with the evolution of *erectus'* brain. The spoken language became ever more multi-faceted and expressive. The groups of archaic *sapiens* who emerged in Africa, Europe and western Asia about half a million years ago ought to have possessed a relatively complex language, perhaps like that of a modern 6–7-year-old child.

If we equate humanity's long history with the passage of the minute hand round a clock face, then language of truly modern complexity emerged at a few minutes to twelve. But if we look at the whole process from the simple articulated verbalisation of the apes' communication and concepts through the rudimentary proto-language and on to modern speech, then this evolution went on almost round the clock.

The spread of language

Between 400,000 and 200,000 years ago, archaic *sapiens* was not far behind the modern human in terms of intelligence. They had a relatively complex social structure and they could communicate with a relatively nuanced and efficient spoken language. By this time humans had long existed on three continents: Africa, Asia and Europe. With such a wide distribution it was inevitable that humanity had divided into countless separate populations as a consequence of geographical and climatic barriers. In combination with differences in living conditions, this also created variations in terms of anatomy, body size, skin colour and features. Some scholars believe that they can see racial differences even in the skulls of late *erectus* and early *sapiens*, but this is much debated.

The archaeological material confirms that there were major cultural differences even during *erectus'* time. For example, in East Asia the old Olduvai tradition of stoneworking was retained long after the rest of humanity had progressed to a more advanced bifacial craft technique. Apart from this, cultural differences were probably expressed most clearly through products made from organic materials.

Tangible variations must also have emerged in terms of social behaviour and language. Despite its low level, a degree of linguistic division may already have occurred with early *erectus*. By the time of late *erectus* and archaic *sapiens*, we can count with certainty on a considerable variation with separate languages and language families. People in different places and on different continents could no longer understand each other's speech. We must therefore assume that language and culture were already contributing to the transformation of our species' in-born mistrust of outsiders into outright xenophobia. Modern languages and races in Europe and Asia are nevertheless hardly relics from *erectus*. According to the theory in which modern humans emerged in Africa and began to wander over to Eurasia about 100,000 years ago, the majority of late *erectus* and archaic *sapiens* in Europe and Asia were replaced by modern humans – roughly in the same way that in different parts of the world during the last millennium simpler cultures were suppressed by more complex ones. In this perspective it is also easier to understand the linguistic similarities that are found in the most widely separated corners of the globe.

9

WAYS OF LIFE AND SOCIAL STRUCTURE

Diet, nutrition and hygiene

In the debate as to which kinds of food are best for us, we are often as vegetarians and meat-lovers alike referred to some vague primordial human diet. But, there are many who say, we are neither one nor the other. If anything we are omnivores, we eat almost anything. And just look at our digestive apparatus, something in between a predator's short straight tubes and the cud-chewer's complicated system of intestines and stomachs. Of course, it is not really so simple. Our closest relatives have almost the same digestive tracts as we do, without being omnivores for all that. It is also easy to forget that our diet today depends to a large degree on our cooking abilities. By contrast to all other creatures we prepare most of our food.

Let us look a little closer at what our nearest relatives eat, what our ancestors probably did and did not eat, and what they did or did not cook along the path of their evolution. First we must draw a distinction between herbivores and herbivores. The great apes put away very different kinds of vegetarian food than do, for example, animals that chew the cud. Despite the fact that apes eat hundreds of different plants, their vegetarian choice still has clear limitations. From the rich tables of the tropical forest they pickily select sweet, calorie-rich and ripe fruits, young plants, tender leaves, shoots, buds and flowers. The occasional seed, nut, root and piece of bark slips down as well.

By contrast, and just like us, chimpanzees, bonobos, lowland gorillas and orang-utans avoid the cud-chewing animals' ripe leaves and plants, grass and twigs. Cud-chewers can efficiently process this kind of starchy food with their stomachs and intestinal systems that were specially designed to do just that. They are assisted by bacteria that neither apes nor humans have, very good at breaking down resistant starches. Unlike monkeys, apes and humans also lack the enzymes that can neutralise the acids in unripe fruit and ripe leaves. Through special adaptation to their marginal environment, mountain gorillas can also make do with ripe leaves, bark, fibre and such. That their eating habits do not reflect a fully rounded dietary adaptation is shown not least by their foul wind. The common chimpanzee is not as committed a vegetarian as the bonobo and the mountain gorilla. Now and again they may select a lighter meat dish *à la carte*, often a small monkey or rodent. Lowland gorillas occasionally catch a squirrel or a duiker, and orang-utans may eat young birds. All apes like insects, particularly ants.

In any case, the basic food of all apes remains fruit and fresh vegetables. For the common chimpanzee, the most carnivorous of all, vegetarian food makes up perhaps 95 per cent of the diet. It is mostly the females who eat insects, especially ants and termites. In terms of mass the insect diet does not count for much, but its importance as a source of protein explains the amount of time spent catching ants. At the same time it is primarily the males who hunt, and who eat most of the game. I therefore presume that the ant-catching of the females and infants, and the males' meat eating, form nutritional complements to one another, reflecting the fact that there are normally fewer plant species in the common chimpanzees' floral environment than in that of the bonobo, lowland gorilla and orang-utan. This kind of food probably does not completely satisfy their protein requirements, and matches the ant eating of the mountain gorilla in its equally low diversity home.

Just like humans, chimpanzees lack the ability to build up and store essential amino acids it their bodies. These are certainly found in the plant kingdom, but only rarely in any quantity within the chimps' special vegetarian diet. By contrast it is found in abundance in insects and other animals. The apes' sporadic meat eating and the delight that common chimps and mountain gorillas take in ants may therefore reflect a vital boost of amino acids, including phosphor and other elements. It is also relevant here that neither humans nor other primates can produce vitamin-C in their livers, an ability that was probably lost before the primates even evolved, perhaps through some mutation. This missing capacity would have proved fatal had the entire family of species not lived on food that was so rich in vitamin-C. It was only when our bipedal ancestors began to more consistently deviate from their original environment that this deficiency first would have created problems, perhaps around the time of early *Homo* or *erectus*.

A precondition for the apes' special choice of ripe fruit and tender plants is that in the tropical forests this kind of food is available virtually all year round. It is important to remember this when we consider the problems that humans encountered when they began to live in very seasonal environments in the northern hemisphere.

Even early *Homo*, and *Subhomo*, may on longer sojourns on the savannah have found it difficult to obtain enough fresh fruit and young plants. When early *erectus* began shortly afterwards to colonise more temperate areas with their tangible seasonal rhythms, they probably had a hard time finding plant food that gave them enough vitamin-C in the late autumn, winter and early spring. By contrast, the situation with regard to amino acids immediately improved.

Mark Teaford and Peter Ungar have recently compiled a synthesis of what the teeth and jaws of early humans can tell us about their diet. While data on early *Prehomo* is still sparse, their results primarily concern *anamensis*, *afarensis* and *africanus* during the period from 4.2 to 2.5 million years ago. First, marks of wear on the teeth and the proportions of the molars indicate that they ate a lot of fruit. The relatively small front teeth show that they could hardly bite through thick peel or the dense flesh around the larger seeds. At the same time the flat upper surfaces of the molars tell us that they also ate nuts, tender flowers and buds. The teeth of the early humans were less well suited to coping with meat, plant stalks and seed pods. The marks on their teeth confirm the picture of a varying vegetarian diet rich in fruit, with a successively greater amount of fibrous ground-growing plant foods. The same is implied by the fact that from *afarensis* onwards the jawbones of the early humans became steadily stronger. As far as I can tell, this tendency towards an ever-broader vegetarian diet that began around 4 million years ago reflects a life that was increasingly confined to the ground. This fits well with the way in which almost all fossils of *Prehomo* have been found in what was then a rich and diverse forested terrain.

I therefore suggest that early humans followed a mixed vegetarian diet that included a great deal of fresh fruit, juicy young plants, flowers, nuts and so on. Given their marked preference for lakes and watercourses, I would presume that this was also supplemented with certain aquatic plants, perhaps even shellfish and small fishes. We can also assume that early humans liked protein-rich insects such as ants and beetles, and sometimes even caught the occasional animal, not to mention taking advantage of the fresh offal left over from the kills of predators. Their consumption of raw meat was probably more limited.

The question is when did our ancestors begin to prepare meat by grilling or frying it over an open fire? A few early signs of fire use in Africa have suggested that we may have begun to do this almost 2 million years ago. A more realistic assessment, however, is that the first humans who more systematically grilled meat were advanced *erectus* about half a million years ago, and that the first to boil meat were modern humans as late as 30,000 years ago, if even then.

Something similar is implied by the cut marks on animal bones from areas where early *Homo* was known to exist, made by sharp stone stools and sometimes overlain by the tooth marks of predators. Occasionally it is the other way around, with cut marks on top of the tooth impressions. This suggests that they took advantage of animal remains left after predator kills, either having temporarily chased away the carnivore concerned, or waiting until it had left of its own accord. Early *Homo* may therefore have been a scavenger.

It is certainly easier to break down rotten meat than fresh, but eating a large quantity of it cannot have been good even for early humans. To the extent that they did scavenge, food was probably fresh, and especially from the softer tissues such as the heart, liver, brain, blood, marrow and the half-digested contents of the stomach and intestines – all nutritious sustenance that traditional cultures have always regarded as delicacies. Modern people often regard scavenging with disdain, as an occupation fit only for vultures, rats and hyenas. But exploiting fresh kills does not significantly differ from eating animals that one has brought down oneself. In fact it is possible that scavenging actively contributed to our ancestors abandonment of the tropical forests by compensating for what was the missing in terms of essential amino acids and vitamin-C.

It was worse about half a million years ago when people began to push further northwards into the Eurasian temperate climate zones, where sufficient quantities of tender plants were only available in spring and early summer, fruit and berries only appeared in the autumn and insect protein was hardly accessible in winter at all. Even if humans had already begun to grill meat over fire, the art of boiling was still far off which meant that it was difficult to break down the starches in full-grown plants. The only way to do this was to allow others to do what they could not do themselves, to break down the cellulose in the ripe vegetation. In winter, cud-chewing hoofed animals consume frozen grass, moss, bark, twigs and other things that their efficient digestion soon converts to dishes abounding in vitamin-C well suited for humans. I am speaking here of people eating the half-digested contents of plant-eating animals' stomachs and intestines. This is how the Inuit and other polar peoples have survived the arctic winter without getting scurvy. In its simplicity this method has a touch of genius, albeit not from the animals' perspective, and is an important precondition for the human colonisation of temperate and cold climates.

We should remember there that all people now living seem to be descended from those who left Africa as late as 100,000 years ago. Even though *erectus* in Asia and Europe was a keen meat-eater, modern humans cannot be the inheritors of their possible adaptation to a carnivorous diet. What is interesting here is the question as to what kind of diet *erectus* and early archaic *sapiens* maintained in Africa during the last 2 million years – something we know very little about. We have good reason to think that their food consisted mostly of fruit and other vegetation in combination with some meat. If nothing else we know that low-tech cultures in recent times have generally consumed more plants and less meat the nearer they have lived to the tropics (and vice versa). Even in sub-tropical and warm temperate areas, we find plants are more popular as food than meat, which only dominates in cold temperate and arctic climes. On the other hand, the animal fauna of the tropics was richer in earlier periods than in recent times.

It cannot be ruled out that we do possess a certain inherited adaptation to grilled meats, but our chewing and digestive equipment does not show much sign of this. At the same time we know that our closest relatives and primate ancestors were biologically well adjusted to a basic diet of ripe fruit, tender plants, shoots, nuts and roots, topped up with insects, rodents and offal. Similarly we know that *Prehomo* had essentially the same, though slightly expanded, eating habits. This is not unimportant when we consider that *Prehomo* represents more than 60 per cent of the bipedal human life on earth.

Seen in this context it should not surprise us that modern people seem to thrive on a diet based on fruit and vegetables – with or without a dose of meat and fish – always assuming that our vegetarian menu is diverse and varied, something that cannot always be said to be the case.

Those who claim that one must eat a lot of meat in order to get enough protein have probably never grappled with a gorilla, played tug-of-war with an orang-utan or arm-wrestled a chimp. This is probably a good thing, as the little chimpanzee is four to five times stronger than a human of the same body weight. A small female can lift a grown man with no difficulty at all.

The fact that our bodies react to boiled food by immediately increasing the production of white blood cells ought to tell us that this kind of sustenance was not on our original menu. It is also interesting to compare the differences in fat type and fat content between wild and tame animals. As a consequence of a more stable access to food and less exercise, the bodies of domesticated animals carry 25–30 per cent fat, compared to only 5 per cent for their wild cousins. At the same time wild animals have four to five times greater levels of polyunsaturated fat, more protein and fewer calories than domesticated animals. Because we started to eat the flesh of domesticated animals only yesterday in evolutionary terms, it is understandable that polyunsaturated fat seems to be more healthy than saturates, and that a large caloric intake can be a health problem.

People in all cultures tend to eat at specific times, perhaps most often fitted around activities and time-consuming food preparation. However, several studies show that we would feel better if we followed the example of our primate ancestors and the early humans – and the spontaneous behaviour of children – and nibbled away throughout the day instead of filling our stomachs on a few occasions.

An inheritance from our original fruit-sugar rich primate diet is probably also seen in our taste for sweet foods, that in the form of refined sugar has today brought health problems. So, even the candy industry has its evolutionary roots. The human body is also unable to build its own vitamin-D, maybe because our ancestors in the tropics got quite enough of this through sunlight. After a long period of debate, it is now supposed that the problem of vitamin-D that arose when humans colonised the darker northern latitudes was evolutionarily solved through a reduction of melanin levels in the skin, so that sunlight could penetrate. This ought to mean that the light, 'white' human races first appeared after modern people had left Africa, and first moved further north essentially no more than 40–30,000 years ago.

Of the main pillars in the modern Western diet – meat and fish, cereal products, milk and milk products, and fruit and vegetables – it is thus the latter that we are biologically best adapted to. Thereafter came an animal diet, and lastly cereals and milk products. The latter have only been consumed for a few hundred generations, and in places only for a very much shorter time.

Unsurprisingly, cereals and milk are responsible for a large proportion of our food allergies and ill health.

The question is why did early humans not leave Africa earlier, three, four or five million years ago – or even when they became bipedal – as they were already light on their feet even then. Why did we wait until barely two million years ago? I believe the answer is that *Prehomo*'s intellect and cultural skills were quite simply not up to the challenge of the cultural adaptations necessary to compensate for the loss of a tropical diet in a cold climate, and for our inherited environmental handicaps.

When the boundaries of human settlement later moved north, they probably did not move to a greatly colder climate, but instead followed the climate zones as they shifted north. In line with this, the earliest traces of human settlement in Europe seem to coincide with a global warm period. So long as they possessed only limited cultural capacities to deal with a colder climate and its dietary implications, then they were quite simply forced to turn back south every time the global temperatures became cooler. The first humans outside Africa were probably *erectus*. With a cranial capacity of 800–1,000 cubic centimetres they had left *Prehomo* intellectually far behind. They had already been making and using stone tools for more than half a million years, and they also used implements of wood, bone and other organic materials. All of this gave them a better chance of overcoming natural obstacles, asserting themselves and reproducing.

Many wild animals take care with their hygiene. Primates are experts at looking after their own and others' fur. It even occurs that chimpanzees in the wild will wipe themselves after defecating, especially if their stomachs are upset. The fact that many animals under natural conditions will maintain their cleanliness suggests a degree of inherited instinct, something that we should expect in view of the survival value of such behaviour. There are therefore good reasons for thinking that early humans too had an instinctive feeling for personal hygiene.

In one important respect the sanitary conditions of early humans differed from those of their last quadruped ancestors. The probable absence of fur brought with it the advantage that little bits and pieces could not fasten so easily on the body, but simultaneously the disadvantage that the dirt which had earlier been kept at bay by fur now stuck to the skin.

Subsistence and settlement

For tens of millions of years, that is from long before the origins of humanity down to very recently in evolutionary terms, our ancestors maintained a mobile subsistence strategy based on the principle of maximum reward for minimum effort. Nevertheless, there are major differences in how this was practised by apes and early humans on the one hand, and later hunter-gatherers on the other.

Infant apes do not require a permanent nest, because only one child is born at a time and the mother or group can carry it and give it all the protection it needs. In their search for food, apes move a certain distance every day and make a new bed every evening. Each individual, except of course weaning infants, picks its own food and consumes it on the spot. But this does not mean that apes wander around aimlessly. They deliberately move along paths and in relation to landmarks that they recognise, and they utilise resources that are well known to them. When did our ancestors abandon this primordial primate model for daily sustenance? When did we begin to practise the system common to later mobile hunter-gatherers, in which according to natural conditions or other factors they moved between different settlements for a period, using them as bases from which to collect food and other necessaries? A system of this kind is self-regulating in the sense that the base camp is moved when resources in that area have been exploited to the point where the transport of food and so on is no longer efficient. While apes are more or less daily nomads, lack base camps and sustain themselves individually, mobile hunter-gatherers move several times a year between different settlements that function as assembly points for the collection and transport of food and other resources to families and the collective.

That early humans were two-legged does not mean that they followed such a late human settlement strategy. The early woman's arms were full with carrying a child, so she was hardly any better equipped for transporting things than her quadruped ancestress had been with an infant that clung to her back. Early humans were hardly capable of making a leather bag, a woven basket or braided bands with which to carry small children, food and other things. We can expect such artefacts first of early *Homo* or early *erectus*. In all probability *Prehomo*, in their gallery forests close to water with little seasonal variation and a constant supply of vegetarian food, still practised a subsistence strategy like that of the primates. In the first instance early humans would thus have been unspecialised pickers, with individuals feeding their immediate needs as they slowly wandered in dispersed groups through the forests and along the beaches, with every day a new sleeping place in sight.

Even though *Prehomo*'s successor, early *Homo*, also seems to have primarily lived in gallery forest near water, their tooth patterns and wear marks show that in addition to fruit and fresh plants they also ate harder food like roots, root vegetables and a greater proportion of meat. It seems that they had also begun to move onto the savannah. If so, they may have begun to practise a simple gathering strategy. This is also suggested by the fact that early *Homo* transported selected stone raw materials several kilometres from where they found them, in order to work them somewhere else – perhaps a home base. We do not know if certain groups of early *Homo* stayed on the savannah for longer periods, but they probably used it mainly as an additional resource. Perhaps the whole group went there for short periods, or just for the day before returning to the forests at night. Another possibility is that the men, unburdened by small children, temporarily visited the savannah in order to later return to the others bringing roots, root vegetables, nuts and perhaps even meat.

Ever since the early 1960s when Jane Goodall discovered that common chimpanzees at Gombe in Tanzania quite regularly hunt, catch and eat small animals, the same has been observed elsewhere, among other places at nearby Mahale and at Tai in the Ivory Coast. What is interesting is the occurrence of systematically planned hunting, mostly of small monkeys like the colobus, and of young baboons. At Tai we even find organised hunting with beaters, in which different members of the hunting team have different tasks. It is almost only males who hunt and they also eat most of the catch, even though they may share a little with females and infants who ask for it. Even bonobos, lowland gorillas and orang-utans also hunt occasionally and eat small animals, though not to the same extent as the common chimps. These observations have shed new light on the question as to when and how our ancestors began to hunt. It seems likely that even the earliest humans hunted on a small scale.

They hardly hunted big game, however, and they were not even the great monkey hunters that the common chimpanzees can be. Even though the early humans were not totally out of their depth in trees – with their relatively long arms, long curved fingers and somewhat prehensile toes intact – they nevertheless walked truly upright. There is no way that they could have managed the daring and violent monkey hunts, 40 or 50 metres up in the treetops, which the chimpanzees excel in. On the other hand, they could catch the occasional young baboon and some other smaller ground-dwelling animals such as the lesser antelopes, and they could also pinch quite substantial pieces of large game that predators had killed.

The systematic distribution of food among adults is, as far as we can tell, unique to humans. Temporary individual food sharing does however occur among many animals. Chimpanzees can give food from mother to child, from sibling to sibling, and from male to female – the latter especially common after a successful hunt. Occasionally food may be shared between males, and given by adults to the elderly. Among bonobos food can also be given from one female to another, and from a female to a male. In general, chimpanzees seem to use food as a means of manipulating their environment, within the framework of a long-term and mutual give and take. As Craig Stanford has pointed out, hunting in this way possesses an important socio-strategic function in chimpanzee communities. But even spontaneous exchange also occurs among chimps, sometimes in an almost embarrassingly human way. In a photographically documented example, a passionate bonobo male steps out with his vital organ standing to attention, and successfully uses a tasty morsel to tempt a female into the bushes for a quickie.

Even though a simple gathering strategy may go back to early *Homo* or early *erectus*, it cannot be compared with the traditional patterns found in mobile hunter-gatherers, with their different cultural and social elements that require an advanced intellect. Many therefore argue that a traditional hunter-gatherer lifestyle is not much older than modern humans themselves.

It is possible that *Prehomo* exhibited the same inclination towards food sharing as modern apes. Early human men who got hold of a piece of meat almost certainly shared it sometimes with others in the group, especially women. But this was still a long way from the later form of systematic gathering with its established rules for the division of meat within a collective. This would have to wait until they began to cook food over an open fire, and until they could use language to express concepts of relationship. By that time we have arrived at developed *erectus* or archaic *sapiens*.

Hunting probably did not occur on any significant scale before the use of fire for food preparation. The human digestive system is quite simply not designed for breaking down large quantities of raw meat. The earliest secure evidence for the generalised use of fire is only some half million years old, and it is uncertain whether the practice was firmly established before 300–200,000 years ago. On the other hand at Koobi Fora in northern Kenya some 1.6 million-year-old traces have been found, that appear to indicate the deliberate use of fire together with stone tools of the early *erectus* type. Continued investigations may hopefully clarify this. So long as there is no indisputable proof of systematic big game hunting and a consequent use of fire for food production earlier than 500,000 years, then we must assume that such hunting first became common with archaic *sapiens*.

Advanced *erectus* and archaic *sapiens* probably developed a basic traditional strategy for hunting and gathering about half a million years ago, but a fully developed version would have to wait for another 200–100,000 years.

Population size

Chimpanzee flocks usually consist of 30–55 rather loosely connected individuals. This equates to roughly the same number of people in a major band of mobile hunter-gatherers. Now and again a larger number of individuals from different chimp flocks come together in a manner reminiscent of band meetings among mobile human communities. It is, however, hard to determine the natural size of the larger reproductive units among chimpanzees, because the groups available for study tend to consist of relatively small, isolated populations in environments that are steadily shrinking.

For mobile hunter-gatherers these kinds of larger social units may include between 300 and 500 people. But here too we only have data on isolated fragments of populations in marginal environments. In earlier times, when people lived in a more untouched world, these major reproductive groups, that equated to the number of individuals who exchanged genes in a long-term perspective, were probably larger. For animals a figure of 2,000 individuals is usually taken to represent the minimum for secure long-term reproduction. In settled small-scale human tribal societies, some 1,500 to

2,000 people are often linked by a common dialect or language, a good indicator of long-term reproductive community.

In my opinion, the earliest humans in gallery forests near water lived in loose flocks of 30 to 50 individuals. At least the same number of flocks together made up larger reproductive, and thereby also social and cultural, units of a couple of thousand individuals.

As is the case with other mammals among whom the males are bigger than the females, including modern people, early human women would have lived on average at least 10 per cent longer than the men.

Social organisation

There are few higher animals among which the adult individuals are loners who only meet when reproduction demands it. Most primates, and humans above all, are highly social creatures, shaped by evolution for a life spent in the company of others. There is much to suggest that one of the few exceptions among the primates, the rather solitary orang-utan, has become that way more through ecological necessity than natural inclination. People are highly social herd animals, just like our closest relatives the chimpanzees and gorillas.

It is typical of herd animals that their need for social proximity must be satisfied again and again. Lots of company at intervals does not really do it. Most people thus find it hard to cope with a long period of social isolation, and small children do not want to be left alone even for short periods. Still, we have a long way to go before we are as desperate as the African wild dog, which appears unhappy after only a few minutes' separation from the flock. Many humans certainly appreciate temporary solitude, as do common chimpanzees, but usually in the knowledge that there is a social collective to return to. It is no accident that solitary confinement has always been seen as the worst kind of imprisonment, and the hermit life the most refined form of spiritual self-denial.

Without our herd instinct, we humans would not have much of a social life beyond the demands of primary childcare and reproduction. It is the core of our social world, the force that programmes us for complex social interaction, and for life in a functioning society.

The family is in no way a human invention. All higher animals have something in the way of a family structure, with a primary function of securing reproduction. Among all mammals the breast-feeding mother takes centre stage, sometimes together with other females or with one or more males. Some mammals, including up to 10 per cent of primates and most birds, live in nuclear families. Most other primates practise a system of extended families, with a group of closely related females at the centre together with a leader male and sometimes young males. Because the infants of humans and apes are so dependent on adults for their food, care, protection and psychological security, their need for a family is all the greater. This must have been just as true for the earliest humans.

In later low-tech societies, every individual usually belongs to a nuclear family, an extended family or a family group, which in turn is part of a larger collective of relatives. In modern Western industrial society, however, families are frequently small, relatives separated and peoples' social contacts outside their workplace often rather limited. The fact that a large number of adults in their fertile years, along with old people and, in some communities, even children, live outside a real family system is an evolutionary anachronism of considerable dimensions. The greatest social problem of our time is the loneliness tormenting the solitary flock human.

Most of the primates apply male exogamy, which means that young males move to another group at puberty, while the young females stay in their childhood flock. Gorillas usually practise female exogamy, though its male equivalent is also found. All chimpanzees, though very few other primates, systematically practice female exogamy. This system has deep evolutionary roots, as seen in its unvarying implementation over the entire chimpanzee population, regardless of environment and independent of the fact that the different groups have long lived in isolation from one another. Female exogamy is also dominant among humans. Male exogamy, with settlements focused on the wife's family, is known from only 15–20 per cent of all traditional cultures, and in terms of the number of affected individuals the proportion is even smaller.

It can be very testing for a young female chimp to leave her mother, siblings and others near and dear, in order to move to a strange group, where she is at first met with suspicion and hostility from the other females. The fact that she still does this without any coercion shows that this behaviour is steered by strong evolutionary mechanisms. If a young female chimpanzee does not leave the flock before her first ovulation, there is a considerable risk that she will be impregnated by a close male relative, her father, an uncle or an elder brother. Due to their lives a little separate from the flock, these males in particular have not always been sufficiently imprinted through early close contact with the young female to hold themselves back when she is in heat. For the young female, however, the imprinting is strong enough to make her disinterested in sex with the groups' males, and to send her to the new ones in another group when her sexual drives are activated. Important here is the fact that the female's sex drive emerges in good time – 1 to 2 years – before her first ovulation, and that she generally leaves the flock for good. If the worst occurs in the form of some close male relative before the female has managed to leave, then there is seldom much harm done. As she has not yet had her first ovulation, she does not get pregnant. The few females who do not leave the home tend to instead slip away to another group when they are in heat. It therefore seems as though the hormonal mechanisms that regulate sexual attention also impel pubertal females to leave the close male relatives with whom they have grown up.

Because young chimps live much closer to their mothers than their fathers, a more effective shield against incest is created between mothers and sons than between fathers and daughters. It is thus a combination of imprinting through early close contact between adults and children, female exogamy, and sterility in early puberty that evolutionarily maintains the chimpanzee's system for avoiding incest and consequently ensuring their long-term reproduction.

The interesting thing here is that human woman are also usually sterile in early puberty. This is quite logical, since female exogamy, otherwise unusual among primates and mammals, is completely dominant in human low-tech societies. The phenomenon seems to have deep evolutionary foundations. From this perspective we can better understand why many recent low-tech communities in best 'South Seas' fashion have encouraged sexual freedom for youths in early puberty. At least while the advent of puberty is maintained at a more original level, that is to say, around the ages of 16–17 in humans, then young girls will seldom become pregnant in early puberty as their ovulation will not begin until later.

Imprinting through early close contact that was strong enough to prevent sexual congress between fathers and daughters can hardly have affected our ancestors before they began to practise both social and reproductive mono-gamy, or some kind of male harem system, that is to say a way of life in which fathers live permanently close to their biological daughters. Prior to that, they probably had much the same system for avoiding incest as the chimpanzees.

I would therefore assume that our last quadruped ancestors had a repro-ductive and social system that provided some limited degree of imprinting through early close contact between fathers and daughters, that their females first ovulated some time after their sexual drives were awakened, that they practised female exogamy, and that there was a life-long closeness between mothers, adult sons and brothers.

Among chimpanzees and bonobos, the immediate family consists of a mother and up to three infants, from newborn babies to as much as 10 years of age. Older females may also be accompanied by one or two young adult sons. Even though the males mostly socialise in groups of their peers, adult sons maintain a degree of social contact with their mothers, and through them also their younger siblings. Among bonobos the relationship is even closer between mothers and adult sons. For chimpanzees we find that imprinting through early close contact unites mothers, children and siblings in a collective, which is broken for the females when the daughters 'move away from home'. Sisters probably keep in touch if they should happen to move out to the same flock. Friendship and social alliances may also occur even between unrelated individuals. Adult male common chimpanzees tend to hang out together much more than adult females, probably because they have imprinted each other during their childhood games. When two females get together, it is usually because they share a social relationship to the same male.

A flock of chimpanzees is thus usually built up around a number of family units consisting of mothers, children, pre-pubertal youths and occasionally adult sons. For bonobos it is as common to find personal attachments between females as it is between males, despite the fact that the females have rarely grown up together. A chimpanzee flock will not only include brothers but also fathers, grandfathers and great-grandfathers, uncles and so on, many of whom are connected through imprinted relationships. Such a flock may also encompass familial relationships such as young aunts and cousins on the female side. Their exogamous system does always not prevent cousins from reproducing with each other. The same must have applied to the earliest humans.

The figures that we do *not* find in a chimpanzee flock are grandmothers, who normally live in a different flock to their grandchildren, and in practice also grandfathers and great-grandfathers, who though they are part of the flock are not subsumed in their own families. The absence of permanent pairing means that the parental mother–father relationship does not exist, and that imprinting through early close contact between fathers and children is very limited. Because the males often roam free among the different mother families, they are nevertheless included in a greater social community and contribute to the rearing of infants, though no more to that of their own children than to those of others.

Before we dismiss the chimpanzees' family system as undeveloped and primitive, it may be worth considering that it is one of the most common familial forms in the modern West.

Despite the fact that single partnership – *monogamy* – is formally practised in only 16 per cent of traditional human communities, and *polygamy* is found in around 80 per cent of them, it is nevertheless true that monogamy applies to most of the world's population while polygamy affects relatively few people. 'Marriage' to one person is by far the most common form of relationship throughout the world, whereas male polygamy is often confined to a small upper class. Female multi-marriage, that is, a woman with more than one husband, or *polyandry*, is practised in only a few percent of all known societies.

Multiple marriages for males among humans cannot have been common before the advent of later, sedentary societies with a surplus production and less egalitarian division of resources. It is all the more common among animals, for example the primates. Female harems are found consistently among gorillas and in a way among the solitary orang-utans too, who have reproductive rather than social harems.

In both animals and humans we find that polygamy follows either a strictly male or female line. Multiple marriages for men and women in the same group only occur in those few societies in which female polygamy predominates.

Among the animals, it is only the monogamous who ever celebrate a golden wedding, measured in animal years of course. Male harem leaders are always replaced after a few years, something usually explained by saying that fresh young blood sweeps aside the tired old men. That may well be true on occasion, but the primary reason is different. The main regulator of the system is that the harem leader and the young females, who are usually his daughters, are after only a few years mutually imprinted through early close contact, meaning that they avoid mutual sex. At the same time the older females, who have no such imprinting and to whom the male is unrelated, are becoming fewer. The male has therefore lost most of the motivation that once drove him to take over the harem. However powerful he may be, he cannot mobilise enough energy to defend his leadership, and he more or less gives up of his own accord. Imprinting through early close contact also explains why harem leaders are replaced so regularly within a species, but at different intervals for different species, depending on the age at which females attain puberty and how long they live. This regular replacement of leader does not take place in known human harems, where the imprinting effect is systematically avoided through female exogamy.

Why do humans not apply the same consistent multiple marriages for males as do gorillas, many baboons and certain langurs? Why do we not follow the chimpanzees and live in loose collectives without fixed pair relationships? Why are we as monogamous as we are?

The love life of chimpanzees is often called promiscuous, a term with such a negative overtone that it should be avoided. On the other hand, the technical term of *polygynandry* is a bit of a mouthful. I will speak instead of multi-pairing. All or most males participate in a free sexual life focused around the times when females come into heat. When a female chimp is in oestrus, she generally couples enthusiastically with many different males, except of course for her sons for whom she has been imprinted through early close contact.

This is therefore much to suggest that the earliest humans practised neither male exogamy nor a system of purely female harems.

The old picture of the sexually oppressed primate female is a thing of the past. Everything suggests that chimpanzee females and those of most other primates are just as sexually active as the males, and choose or reject their sexual partners to at least the same degree. We encounter the same pheno-menon among mobile hunter-gatherers and many other low-tech human societies. The same ought to have applied to early human females, even after they lost their periodic oestrus. Our last four-footed ancestors probably also employed a similar system for reproduction. If it was as I believe, that oestrus was replaced by permanent sexuality as an effect of the upright gait, then the love life of early humans probably began with the same kind of bacchanalia as we have seen among the bonobos.

For a long time it has been almost fashionable among scientists to interpret human infidelity as a natural biological reflex of a distant age, when every-body happily copulated with everyone else without risk of jealousy or social sanction. This may be somewhat of an exaggeration. Still, it is nevertheless clear that both sexes have a need for social contact with a large number of people, and a certain propensity for its sexual equivalent that results in a relative frequency of sexual relationships outside the framework of formal couples. This occurs in most societies, even those in which this kind of behaviour is formally discouraged. It is in this light that human monogamy, whenever it finally began, can be seen as more a matter of social and subsistence security than sexual monopoly.

In order to understand the strong position that social monogamy holds in human societies, we must consider the consequences of continuous multiple marriage. It is hardly an accident that this phenomenon is quantitatively rather rare in humans, and is not often applied consistently in the animal kingdom either. Systematic multiple marriage for males would mean that many men would have to get used to social and sexual celibacy. If half of all men had two wives, then the other half would have to go without; if a third of all men had three wives, then two thirds would remain single. Consistent multiple marriage for men would thus mean in principle that a large number of males would find themselves outside marriage and reproduction, with serious social consequences as a result. In many low-tech societies the problem is dealt with on the principle of age before beauty: the right to most wives is confined to mature gentlemen, while the young braves must wait until their elders have either become very elderly indeed, or else actually begun to pass on. In this way most men get a chance sooner or later.

If there were one thing that most male chimpanzees would have a hard time swallowing, it would be spending their lives on the sidelines as helpless witnesses to the sex life of the harem. So if the early human males even slightly shared the chimpanzee's enthusiasm for sex, a female harem system would have exacted a heavy price in the forms of tension and aggression between men and within society as a whole. But the shrinking canine teeth of the early humans firmly contradict this.

In certain groups of *Prehomo*, the men were almost twice the size of the women, if we have interpreted the bone material correctly and it is not a question of different species of varying stature. When it comes to mammals, such a size difference is usually seen as an evolutionary signal of powerful male competition for females. As a result, many researchers have argued that early human men lived in a milieu of strong rivalry for their women's attention. Richard Leakey has therefore suggested that the afarenes retained oestrus, that they practised female exogamy with residence in the man's family group, and that their society was heavily male dominated. When the size differential between the sexes later returned to normal for humans and chimpanzees, that is to say about 20 per cent, according to Leakey, this depended on reduced tensions between the men due to the sudden loss of oestrus. He argued that there was also a transition to male exogamy, with residence in the female's family group.

This rationale is unconvincing. To begin with, oestrus could not suddenly disappear in a puff of smoke, without special evolutionary cause. I have earlier suggested that the coming of bipedalism at the division of the species would have provided such an impetus. Second, the whole scenario is contradicted by our nearest relatives. Chimpanzees in fact combine a strong oestrus with minor size differences between the sexes, and consistent female exogamy. Among gorillas, the size difference is very large indeed, despite the fact that their oestrus is rather discrete and that they have only a very weak female exogamy. For many other primates with oestral reproduction, the size difference is roughly the same as for chimpanzees and humans. These examples demonstrate clearly that the large size difference between the sexes of afarenes was not connected with oestrus. In general, it is highly unlikely in evolutionary terms that male exogamy was ever common among our ancestors.

On top of all this, it is probable that male competition actually *increased* when oestrus disappeared.

There may be a slight connection between an upright gait and the evolution of social monogamy. So long as our ancestors were quadrupeds, their infants could ride on their mothers' backs and cling fast to their fur. But on two legs at least one of the mother's arms was occupied with holding a child, especially during transport. This must have created problems, for example in encounters with dangerous animals, in confrontations with other groups, in connection with food acquisition, and in the transport of objects over long distances. It also clearly handicapped the mother as a tree-climber, something that must to some extent have confined not just her but to a degree the whole flock to the ground. All this would have made early human women of fertile age more dependent on assistance from other individuals such as men, older people and larger children. In turn this placed rather more demand on the social cohesion of the group than had been the case before.

One suggestion has been that permanent sexuality in women made it easier for dominant men to control the sex drive of individual women, which led to increased sexual competition between men. These scholars have understood a permanent sex drive as the roots of male domination in human societies.

It is more likely that early human women, exactly like female chimps and bonobos, exploited their permanent sexuality to obtain protection, support and preference from different men – in the first hand, large, safe men. This may ultimately have led to a degree of selection in favour of bigger males, of the kind that we seem to see in the afarene skeletal material.

Another important size difference concerns the canine teeth. In apes and monkeys their large canines are primarily an instrument for physical violence, or the threat of it, within the social framework. Now fossil finds have shown that *Prehomo* had smaller canines than both modern and Miocene apes, and that they had shrunk to their present size by the time of late *Prehomo* and early *Homo*. This relationship totally contradicts the idea that marked size differences between the sexes were connected with increased aggression and violence.

The notion that the shrinking canines should result from less male sexual competition as a consequence of monogamy presupposes a degree of fidelity of which early humans were hardly capable. The monogamous male gibbon certainly uses his sharp canines to keep other males away from his partner, but the males of our closest relatives – the non-monogamous and sexually free competitive chimpanzees – rarely use their dangerous teeth on other males in order to obtain the upper sexual hand. This makes it even less likely that it was our sexual steadfastness that made *Prehomo*'s teeth grow smaller.

Male hierarchies among the apes are regulated by many other qualities besides strength and physical threat, such as self-confidence, mental strength, the provision of safety and a capacity for non-violence and cooperation with others. The same thing must have applied to the early humans. The most natural explanation is that the canines decreased in size because they had lost their original function, as a tool for violence in internal ranking disputes. But this presupposes that they had access to other means for such assertions. I have earlier argued that *Prehomo* had already begun to evolve a simple proto-language that was somewhat more articulate and expressive than the sounds of modern apes. I would suggest that this may well have soon begun to replace physical strength and large canines as a way of expressing will, threat and dominance. That the women's canines shrank at the same rate as the men's suggests that the level of aggression declined in society as a whole, and that the violent functions of the canines were superseded by something that *both* sexes had access to. It is hard to see that this could have been anything other than improved vocal communication. This would thus have contributed to the maintenance of social order not just between men but in society in general. Social monogamy was favoured by the same factors as made the canines shrink, that is to say, a rudimentary articulated communication in sound that gradually replaced physical violence in conjunction with conflicts, and which lowered the level of physical aggression in the whole community.

I assume that oestrus was replaced by permanent sexuality and considerable sexual freedom for both sexes, and that upright walking women found themselves physically exposed in a way that might have made large and protective men more reproductively advantageous. The latter would have favoured the evolution of males with powerful physiques. This would have been the case for much of *Prehomo*'s time. Social monogamy may have been a well-established order at least since *ergaster* or early *erectus* 2 million years ago – the first types of human with completely modern skeletons and that were ground dwelling to the same degree as we are. Even though we can hardly speak of strict sexual monogamy, more or less all men could have participated in reproduction on equal terms. With social monogamy then the selection towards tall men would have ceased, and the size difference between men and women would have returned to normal.

We have looked above at different changes that can be observed in connection with early *Homo* and early *erectus* – such as a growing brain, an extended childhood, elementary stone technology, the beginnings of base camps, a meatier diet, the start of savannah life, perhaps a simple gathering strategy and a probable boost to the evolution of spoken language. To this we can now add a normalised size relationship between the sexes, and maybe social and to some extent reproductive monogamy.

Even though chimpanzees are more egalitarian than many other primates, their hierarchies (especially those of common chimps) are more distinct than those of mobile hunter-gatherers. Chimpanzee society is marked by a continuous struggle for dominance. Among nomadic, chiefly monogamous hunter-gatherers the dominance problem is much less visible, society is less hierarchal and more peaceful. In my opinion this is connected to their access to and eager use of a modern, nuanced language for the solution of internal conflicts without physical aggression.

Now, of course, there are different monogamies. While monogamous couples in low-tech human societies generally live in groups together with pairs like themselves, among animals monogamous couples live totally separate from others under the severe control of the male. This is quite alien to the strong herd instinct that distinguishes chimpanzees, gorillas and humans, and by extension probably our last common ancestors. I therefore imagine that the early humans practised a social but hardly reproductive monogamy. It is hardly credible that naked early humans who formed social couples in groups of other couples, who lacked dwellings with privacy, and who furthermore had to cope with a new permanent female sexuality, could have lived up to any particularly high standard of sexual fidelity.

In this context and considering our heritage as herd animals, there is no other conclusion than that *Prehomo* lived in flocks of a number of women and men. Henry McHenry has also made the important observation that in a collection of bones of thirteen afarenes from Hadar in Ethiopia, who all seem to have died at the same time, both sexes are represented. This is natural if they lived in groups of both men and women.

I have trouble seeing how a society based on group-living monogamy in typical human fashion could function without a basic spoken language, which made it possible to peacefully mark and maintain the vital boundaries for what is and is not allowed.

There could have been no formal concept of blood relations before intellect, consciousness and speech had all reached a level that made it possible to formulate social connections in abstract terms. This may have occurred with late *erectus* or archaic *sapiens*.

Those who see monogamy as a latterday expression of a long social and moral evolution in human beings may think it wrong to describe early humans in such advanced terms. But monogamy is not a human invention. Almost one fifth of all primates practise it socially or reproductively, including the gibbons – our rather more remote relatives among the apes – along with a few spider monkeys and baboons. Despite the fact that even gibbons cheat a little, they live up to the ideal of a lifelong and sexually faithful partnership better than people do on average. Ninety per cent of all birds are socially mono-gamous, and even a few insects. Monogamy is in short not a cultural trait. It is a social order, compelled through a combination of subsistence related, eco-logical, demographic and biological factors.

Among the common chimpanzees, the female's status in the flock depends partly on the standing of the male(s) with whom she has special social relations. For bonobos on the other hand, the male's rank primarily rests on his mother's status in the flock. We must ask if the social standing of early human women changed with the transition to monogamy. While single partnership was more of a social nature, I would guess that women's status was rather variable before monogamy acquired overtones of sexual fidelity. Among chimpanzees there is considerable social mobility, and the domestic relationships between individuals and groups are often rather loose. Individuals move, and groups reform almost daily or by the hour. By contrast the boundaries between the different flocks are not normally crossed other than when young pubertal females emigrate. At the same time we find seasonal aggregations of several flocks, in a manner that reminds us of mobile hunter-gatherers.

Neither chimpanzees nor mobile hunter-gatherers have strong leader figures. Even if there is a socially dominant male in every flock of chimps, he does not dictate and control in the same decisive way as we find among some of the other primates. This is even truer for mobile hunter-gatherers. One person in the group – usually a man – may assume command in a crisis, but in general they have no leaders at all. Just as for chimpanzees, who this person is depends less on physical strength and aggression and more on such qualities as experience, self-confidence, security, tolerance and a steady, friendly demeanour. Especially interesting here is Frands de Waal's observation that a flock leader among chimpanzees will consistently decline to take sides when he intervenes to stop a quarrel, even when it involves relationships and friendships that concern him personally.

The males' greater physical strength, more boisterous behaviour in general and their more prevalent aggression is enough to ensure that a leader of a group of common chimpanzees is always male. But in a different way the females still dominate, mainly through their strong influence over infants of all ages and over adult sons. At the same time it is mostly the females who transmit cultural traditions to the next generation. Even if the females are less sociable than the males, at least in East Africa, they still possess a certain talent for commanding the social stage. And when a female is in heat, there are no limits to her social standing. On the other hand, this does not happen very often. Among common chimpanzees, it is therefore the males who dominate in a physical sense and on average are to be found slightly higher up the social scale, but the females have a greater social and cultural influence. This relationship was probably very similar for at least the earliest humans.

Bonobos are among the few mammals with socially dominant females, where a female occupies the highest social rank in the entire flock. The male's status is actually dependent on that of his mother, and he inherits her social position. Like the gentleman he is, he does not utilise his physical superiority even if attacked by an angry female.

In common chimpanzees the sexual roles are more clearly linked to physical and functional differences. The females breast-feed continuously for 3 or 4 years, they have constant contact with their young and take the primary responsibility for their care and upbringing. The males provide leadership, protection, the guarding of the flock and its territory, as well as going out hunting. These activities presuppose that they roam over a wider area than the females, who are hindered by their infants. Again, this was probably also the case among the earliest humans.

It is hard to say to what degree the division of labour between the sexes and their social dimension among common chimpanzees reflects in-born instinct or the indirect expression of physical and physiological differences. For example, sterile and childless female chimps have been observed to join the males on hunting expeditions. Often the males and females communicate better with one another than they do with their own sex.

Neither male chimpanzees nor patriarchal male gorillas oppress or bully females physically, mentally or socially. When the social system is in equilibrium, the sex roles of chimpanzees rest more on practical mutual consideration than on dominance and social competition. I imagine that something similar was true for the early humans.

Social norms and morality

Flock mammals tend to be tolerant and friendly towards the infants of the group, regardless of kinship. Adults can certainly be rough in their child raising, but they do not deliberately harm the young. This is a deep-rooted instinct in us humans too. Nevertheless, as a result of our late developing complex social structure, we are alone in often deviating from this pattern. Happily liberated from advanced intelligence and complex culture, it would never occur to the apes to give their children the insensitive upbringing and cruel treatment of which human civilisation has so often shown itself capable.

We are not the only ones who can feel and express strong emotions. Many higher animals seem to experience feelings like terror, fear, sorrow, relief, happiness, calm and anger that are strikingly like our own. Apes and a few other animals can fall into deep depressions in connection with the death of a close relative, which in its expression is very human. Such emotions in people seem to be regulated by the oldest parts of the brain.

Thanks to our intelligence and linguistic ability, we can analyse our feelings and experiences, and rationalise them together with other people. This gives us a better chance of coping with emotional crises and unnatural situations than other higher mammals, which are psychologically very vulnerable. The apathy, blank expressions and resignation that one sees in the residents of even the better zoological prisons speak plainly. I will not even mention all our concentration camps for chemical experimentation on animals.

Animals are frequently perceived as incapable of placing themselves in another individual's situation. But still, higher mammals display an instinctive concern for small infants, and often those of others. Some social herd animals such as dolphins and other whales, elephants and apes are also quite obviously capable of elementary empathy even with adults, which presupposes a certain ability to imagine how other individuals are feeling. Up to a point, even some of the higher primates like macaques and baboons seem able to predict others' emotional reactions and act accordingly. A great many animals can thus in some sense be ascribed a theory of mind. Just as in humans, among chimpanzees we find varying degrees of generosity and regard for their fellow creatures.

The adoption of children was once seen as an expression of empathy that only humans could muster. But adoption occurs among many animals too. If a mother chimpanzee dies, her motherless infant will be taken care of by others. That this is often an adolescent sister or brother is a direct expression for the feeling of belonging that a close upbringing provides. But we should note that chimpanzees can also adopt infants who are not their kin.

No human society, however 'primitive', lacks a concept of morality. We should not expect anything else. The fundamental norms of social behaviour actually have nothing at all to do with religion and culture. No social life can function without common conscious or unconscious rules. As a result all higher animals have strict, tacit norms for social behaviour. This naturally applies in particular to social herd animals such as primates, elephants, dogs, lions, cetaceans and many others, together with social insects like bees, wasps, ants and termites. They are steered by both instinctive and acquired understandings of what they can and cannot do in the context of social life. The great cultural differences between human communities cannot hide the fact that the basic norms of our social behaviour are founded in no small degree on our collective evolutionary heritage.

Superficially, chimpanzee society can give an impression of a stormy sea of argument, greed, tenderness and playful free time. But as Frands de Waal has shown, a clear pattern runs through it all: positive actions are generally repaid with equally positive ones, and negative acts are also usually repaid in kind, both in the short and long term. This can take the form of sharing food, cleaning another's fur, building and maintaining alliances, or giving support in conflicts. This concern for reciprocation appears clearly in an unwillingness to provide for those who do not themselves share what they have. As a human it is not hard to recognise oneself.

Many of the higher herd animals' unspoken social norms form the basis of the fundamental universal framework for social behaviour that characterises human societies regardless of religion, culture or nationality. It is self-evident that the earliest humans also lived in accordance with an unconscious social rulebook of this kind. Humans differ from other beings through their use of culture and speech to embroider, motivate and formally define their norms of social behaviour. It is difficult to say when the human race began to attain the degree of inner consciousness and linguistic expression that this presupposes. It hardly took place before early *erectus*. A good deal of what we understand as basic universal morality was thus in existence long before modern humans came into being approximately 200,000 years ago. On the other hand, there was hardly any reason to extend and formulate such general moral codes before the advent of sedentism and the so-called higher religions, in other words during the last 10,000 years. Humans seem to be alone in thus adding a cultural component to their natural system of social norms.

I have assumed that *Prehomo* lived in flocks consisting of a number of blood-related men and a roughly equal number of generally unrelated women. Men were generally socially cohesive through imprinting by early close contact, while the women were generally not. *Prehomo* may have begun to practise mono-gamy in the social sense at an early stage, while at the same time maintaining a liberal view of sexual freedom. I nevertheless imagine that women and men in a pair relationship may have developed personal ties. The sexual relations of early humans may thus have been rather variable. There are also good reasons for believing that such social partnerships would not have lasted if those involved did not find them satisfactory.

I have suggested that male competition for influence, leadership and to some extent sex may have been regulated with the help of a proto-language. This of course does not rule out the occurrence of physical violence, but this relied on muscle power – the arms and hands – rather than the teeth. Internal male aggression was kept at a manageable level not least through imprinting as a result of early close contact. By contrast there is every reason to think that suspicion and aggression between different flocks may on occasion have been considerable, precisely because their external relations were governed by men who were not imprinted in this way.

Domination, aggression and violence

Even the most democratic human societies have a hierarchical structure, and are not free from aggression and violence connected to power and status. At least when viewed remotely, the history of the higher cultures is one long catalogue of conflicts, wars, violence and brutality. Many people have there-fore found it hard to avoid the conclusion that humanity is naturally evil, a notion that can be glimpsed even in the biblical Creation story. In our own time, we have long cherished the idea that violence is primarily an expression of different social and cultural conditions. The question is then as to which evolutionary inheritances lie behind these manifestations, and by which func-tions these are triggered.

Most animals are disinterested in the suffering of others, but at the same time animals are never intentionally cruel and there is nothing in their behaviour to suggest in-born badness. There are no grounds for believing that humans are an exception to this. Most people are rarely aggressive or violent, they are not cruel and never come close to killing another person. But as always when considering the civilised human, there are no simple explanations. The cultured person's behaviour varies across a broad scale in imperceptible coalition with our biological and social heritage, cultural influence and the natural world.

The herd instinct has programmed us for a functional life in social groups with social cooperation. Its mechanisms for reciprocal care provide the basis of our tendency for tolerance and altruism towards people other than our close kin, and also constitute the evolutionary framework for human morality. But at the same time every individual of every species, by simple virtue of the fact that their ancestors stood the test of evolution, is marked by an intense self-focus that in turn varies in strength according to the patterns of the individual biological spectrum and the influence of environmental factors. Life in a flock society is therefore dependent on two opposing and biologically deeply rooted instincts: one that promotes peace, collaboration and concern, and another that rewards self-centredness, egoism and aggression. It is in this field of tension that we humans live our lives.

The social ranking among herd animals does not serve an end in itself, and its primary function is to ensure social stability and security in the group. For animals, with their limited linguistic range, controlled aggression inevitably becomes a social instrument. The ranking game can at the same time act as a medium for competition over food resources. In males rank can also bring with it differential access to reproductive favours, and in females it can clear a path to genetically, socially and economically attractive males. Among chimpanzees, violence can even be triggered by personal animosity and a simple desire for revenge.

Most primates are herd living, hierarchic and more or less territorial. Even though many species are quite peaceful, fights can easily break out. The internal struggle for dominance primarily involves males, though females can also participate. Male aggression against females is less common but does occur, as does the reverse. Physical violence between females is uncommon, and serious violence against small infants is very rare. Bonobos have a clearly much lower level of aggression than common chimps.

The flock life of animals thus cannot function without a certain degree of hierarchy based on complex inherited behaviour, of different strengths from one individual to another. Coincident with the drives for domination and ascension of the social ladder, we find the capacity for submission, to move into line with authority, and to obey. Though hierarchical tendencies are weaker in chimpanzees, especially bonobos, than in other primates, they are still clear. Without access to a nuanced language, then ranking can only be maintained and changed through varying degrees of threatening and aggressive behaviour, or outright physical violence. Sometimes this may be a demonstrative play to the gallery, and sometimes may depend on more subtle methods.

As de Waal has shown, chimpanzees have a very strong drive towards reconciliation after argument, something that is central to their social life. In its essentials this is also found in humans, though expressed instead through speech.

Alliances are also very important, in which two or more individuals stick together in order to assert themselves against a higher ranking creature. This concerns a long view system of services and reciprocations, usually but far from exclusively offered on the basis of kinship. Among, for example, chimpanzees, macaques and langurs conflicts often develop along lines of kinship, regulated by imprinting through early close contact – in much the say way as in small scale, low-tech human societies and sectors of more complex ones. Among primates, just as in humans, personality type and social heritage can affect ranking. I assume that similar factors shaped the milieu of the early humans too. Direct and aggressive ranking competition in common chimpanzees and gorillas often plays itself out among males, whereas the internal ranking of females is often governed by their relationship to the males. The exception is the bonobo, as we have seen, with males who to a large degree inherit their social standing from their mothers. Mating competition among male chimpanzees is comparatively mild, even more so among their bonobo cousins, and it rarely leads to serious disagreement. The male alliances of chimpanzees tend to be more opportunistic, changeable and status oriented than those of the females.

Among both primates and humans, aggression between relatives is relatively low level, not least as a direct effect of mental imprinting through early close contact. The same evolutionary mechanisms contribute to the fundamental way in which we humans block and tone down our aggression in some quarters but not in others.

The male and female ranking systems are thus at one and the same time distinct and co-ordinated. But because the flock leader is male among most of the primates, the status systems of the females tend to be somewhat devalued by comparison with those of the males. The same occurred in most known human societies, and it was probably also true in the time of the early humans. Social behaviour in individual historical and modern people, and also at the level of groups and societies, almost certainly reflects this kind of evolutionarily anchored ranking system.

In common chimpanzees, violence is occasionally unleashed by males against females, by females against other females, and by males against adolescents of both sexes. But among primates in general, male violence against females and the young is usually comparatively mild. It has no comparison with the brutal violence against women and children that we find in higher human cultures and modern societies, with all the cultural disturbances that have caused male primate behaviour to spin out of control. Similarly the brutal rapes that are committed all over the world have no parallel among the primates, even if rape does sometimes occur in animals. Rape in humans seems to relate more to psychological and social problems than it does to sexual need. Among primates and mammals in general, the image of aggression and physical violence is statistically dominated by the male sex. The same sad pattern is found in all known human societies, irrespective of their cultural level and degree of complexity. To claim that this sexual distinction does not include a strong biological component would be to place oneself under a very considerable burden of proof.

Even though common chimpanzees normally maintain rather peaceful social relations, their nervous temperament, short fuses and lack of a spoken language often contribute to the rapid escalation of arguments and fights, which afterwards pass just as quickly. The fact that everyday human society generally functions without these kinds of constant physical scuffles and threats is in large measure due to our advanced speech. The social development of small children is enlightening here. Before they acquire a command of language as a means of coping with sudden crises, such as arguments with children of the same age, they find themselves in the same situation as chimpanzees and reply with the same dramatic emotional reactions and physical aggression.

For primates and many other herd animals that lack an effective array of symbolic signals, there remains only aggression and the threat of it, albeit often mild and ritualised. It is the primates' main instrument for asserting and protecting themselves, working their way up, guarding their position, expressing dominance, and demanding respect and submission. To this is added a whole battery of more sophisticated media in the form of postures, movements, glances, facial expressions, noises, spatial locations and social alliances. I suspect that the same was true for our last quadruped ancestors, but that the importance of the physical gradually declined during the age of the early humans in tandem with the evolution of a proto-language.

Another example can be found in the primates' upbringing of infants. Chimpanzees exhibit great patience with rowdy youngsters and try to control them with restrained measures. But if this does not work, then in the absence of a nuanced and expressive language then they have no choice but to turn to mild violence. In the same way, Prehomo's and early Homo's methods of coping with unruly children would have changed as their spoken proto-language developed, so that the physical last resort was suppressed in favour of verbal rebuke.

In general terms the routines of dominance are less aggressive and are expressed in gentler forms in stable human communities than among chimpanzees, including bonobos. I would explain this by reference to humanity's unique ability to deflate social tensions, acquire prestige and express wishes, demands and threats through a spoken language instead of physical aggression. This entire process is strikingly exemplified by the contrast between the often mildly neurotic chaos in a group of common chimps and the relative calm and constant talk in a band of mobile hunter-gatherers.

Despite the dynamism in chimpanzee society, a certain equilibrium is the norm, and aggression is commonly manifested in gentle forms. It is primarily when the system is subjected to external stress, population pressure and diminishing resources that stronger internal aggression is triggered off. This later returns to a state of relative stability. This is in other words a sensitive system.

We encounter similar rank and dominance games in all known historical and modern complex societies, chiefly among men and mainly regulated verbally. They occur in all contexts outside the nuclear family: at the workplace, in the board room, in the schoolyard and university, in politics, the church, the military, in business, the sports world and so on. The only thing new is that the borders now only occasionally follow lines of kinship.

Much of the male violence in historical societies was triggered through the strengthening of our original herd-based aggressive behaviour with cultural factors. An inherited need for assertion enhanced by exaggerated ideas of manly prestige and honour proved fertile soil for aggression almost everywhere in patriarchal, low technology and archaic historical cultures, whether in Homeric Greece, Celtic Europe, the Viking Age North, feudal Europe or Japan. It concerns a masculine culture of violence that overall reflects a primate aggressive pattern, but with its control mechanisms disabled by cultural factors.

Typical for many flock primates, not least chimpanzees, is suspicion of strangers of their own species. In this respect humans are model primates. As strongly as we support our own groups and collectives (through nationalism, patriotism and so on), we can muster an equal distrust of all that is foreign to them, always ready to suspect the worst. This is inflated by cultural, linguistic and superficial physical differences.

In a sense, the human dislike and fear of the unusual can be compared to the phobias that make us afraid of snakes, spiders, heights and so on. Evolutionarily based on a respect necessary for survival, alertness and caution escalate into uncontrolled fear. Unsurprisingly, practical experience suggests that the treatment of these maladies through gradual exposure to their object is a method that also works against xenophobia.

Most mammals and birds have some kind of system for controlling territory, often due to subsistence necessity. Low technology human societies also lay claim to land in some way, in the form of shared, exclusive or direct rights of exploitation or ownership, which superficially reflect inherited behaviour. The rather approximate concept of territoriality that we meet in mobile hunter-gatherers is not unlike that of chimpanzees and other primates. I view the strict territorial concepts of many later sedentary societies as hefty cultural enhancements of more original and flexible notions of land use.

Primates' instinctive suspicion of foreign members of the same species, and the concomitant promotion of the interests of their own communities, can be seen as the intuitive equivalents to our verbal formulations of 'us' and 'them', charged with an ethnic overtone with the help of language.

The territorial behaviour of chimpanzees can sometimes lead to aggression that has lethal consequences. Over a period of years in the 1970s at Gombe in western Tanzania, Jane Goodall observed how a group of males deliberately attacked and killed one member after another in a neighbouring group, with the clear intention of eliminating it completely (and they eventually succeeded). Japanese researchers seem to have noted something similar also in the Mahale region a little further south along the east coast of Lake Tanganyika.

On the other hand, such behaviour seems in general to be rather rare, and probably depends on special catalysts. I note that in both instances this occurred in isolated populations that were ecologically severely pressed. Nevertheless, these examples clearly show that chimpanzees are quite capable of committing systematic, premeditated and lethal violence against outsiders of their species, in a way that chillingly reminds us of human warfare.

In order for the threat of violence to be taken seriously in a flock of primates, it must on occasion be followed through. Then again, long-term security and reproduction would be endangered if such violence too often led to serious injury. Internal aggression must in other words be kept within the tolerance level of the group. Evolution has dealt with this problem through the development of ritualised forms of aggression, together with instinctive blocks and control mechanisms against severe violence. As soon as the defeated party ritually signals submission, the opponent instinctively reins in his or her violent behaviour. These blocks are stronger in animals that have muscular physiques and sharp teeth. Controlled aggression of this kind is an efficient means of social expression.

With such a carefully designed inclusion in our evolutionary baggage, one would have thought that we humans would have been well off. It is clear in this context that we do in fact have inherited blocks against killing our own kind. The principles of 'thou shalt not kill' apply to any society. Most people do not fight or try to kill one another. The problem is simply that civilised society has become so complex that these inhibiting mechanisms have been dislocated, and the balance in this delicate system has been disturbed – if it has not in fact been permanently out of order for thousands of years now.

When a man behaves with more than common brutality, we say thoughtlessly that he acts like an animal. In fact he behaves like a person. Ironically enough, it is precisely the same culture that we claim *separates* us from the animals, which removes our blocks against serious aggression.

For more than 30 million years as unarmed primates, our ancestors expressed their aggression principally through ritualised threatening gestures, shouts, stamping, pushing, smacking and controlled bites. All this was meant to scare and put others in their place, rather than to seriously injure or kill. Evolution has fitted our inhibitions against violence to what we were originally capable of inflicting with our physical strength and teeth. Our patterns of aggression are in other words evolutionarily tailor-made for a life without artificial weapons.

Because submissive behaviour and close physical contact sets off in primates their blocks against continued violence, the same ought to have been true for our last primate ancestors and the earliest humans. Soon the latter were able to add articulated verbal threats and pleas for mercy. The problems came with cultural progress. Even a simple sharp-edged stone tool used at arm's length, or a club at twice the distance, could kill before signals relating to submission and close contact had any chance to trigger the inhibitions that would stop violent behaviour. Later on, when real ranged weapons such as stabbing and throwing spears, bows and slings came into use, the instinctive blocks against lethal violence took another step backwards through the lack of physical close contact, and the difficulty of showing or understanding submissive behaviour in time. The greater the distance involved, the more ineffectual were our in-born blocks against violence. The knowledge that an opponent holds as lethal a weapon as you leads only to increased fear. It is critical to strike first. An incautious move, a moment's distraction, and the consequences could be catastrophic. For millennia this fear of others' uncontrolled use of weapons has forced us into an ever more vicious circle. Instead of triggering natural instincts for submission, artificial weapons only create more violence. Biological evolution would never throw up something so insane, and here we can say that culture has truly slipped up.

Prehomo could almost certainly throw stones with a degree of accuracy, and swing a tree branch with dexterity. Early *Homo* had sharp stone tools and could make a simple club. I would imagine that the path towards a more violent human behaviour might have begun on a minor scale with early *Homo* and *erectus*. Already some 1.5 million years ago, *erectus* had well-made and sharp-pointed hand axes, and for several hundred thousand years now we have had access to sharp-bladed stone knives. Skilfully formed, long-shafted throwing spears have been around for at least 500,000 years, spear throwers for 20,000 years, and the bow and arrow for 15,000 years – all of them efficient and lethal ranged weapons. In purely functional terms we have therefore long been well equipped to disturb our species' natural barriers against serious violence.

Because our compassion for an opponent as a fellow human decreases with distance, ranged weapons mean that conflict is depersonalised. The overtones of intimacy and ritual restraint that distinguish the fighting methods of herd animals, and for that matter also certain low-tech traditional human cultures, became transformed in complex archaic societies into an unemotional slaughter at some remove. Modern battle is today often a matter of blind killing at long distance, in which opponents do not see each other and in fact hardly know who their adversaries are.

Nomadic hunter-gatherers are comparatively peaceful but not entirely free from violence, either internally or externally. The temporary and serious settling of scores between individuals and groups may have begun quite early. Skeletal remains from the end of the early Stone Age and from different parts of the world bear witness to fatal injuries caused by human hand. For tens of thousands of generations, the Mark of Cain has been burned into the foreheads of humanity, or perhaps more accurately into the foreheads of men.

It is remarkable that for almost the entire period from the division of the species down to the advent of settled agrarian societies, human beings could make war only with hunting weapons and their fists. During this whole time, perhaps with some exceptions, no weapons were made specifically to kill people. This indicates that violence was still not a dominant part of our experience. The invention of weapons with which to kill each other was civilisation's contribution.

Human beings thus very clearly reflect the flock-living primates' behaviour when it comes to cooperation, assertion of status and territory. The same is true for conflict resolution, but there we have seriously messed up the system.

Much of what we see as typically human in terms of social organisation and behaviour, whether it functions well or not, seems to rest significantly on a biological predisposition with roots that partly go back to the time of the early humans. When we add an anatomy and physiology that is basically the result of biological evolution, then our debt to them becomes clear indeed. It is the only heritage we have, and we must take care of it. The more we take it seriously, the better chance we have of understanding ourselves, our society, our culture and our history.

BIBLIOGRAPHY

A selection of monographs

Abitol M. M. (1996) *Birth and Human Evolution: Anatomical and obstetrical mechanisms in primates*, Westport, Conn.: Greenwood.

Abramson P. R. and Pinkerton S. D. (eds) (1995) *Sexual Nature, Sexual Culture*, Chicago: University of Chicago Press.

Aiello L. and Dean C. (1990) *An Introduction to Human Evolutionary Anatomy*, London: Academic Press.

Aitchison J. (2000) *The Seeds of Speech: Language origin and evolution*, Cambridge: Cambridge University Press.

Aitken M. J., Stringer C. B. and Mellars P. A. (eds) (1993) *The Origin of Modern Humans and the Impact of Chronometric Dating*, Princeton, NJ: Princeton University Press.

Alcock J. (1993) *Animal Behavior. An evolutionary approach*, Sunderland, Mass.: Sinauer.

Alexander R. D. (1987) *The Biology of Moral Systems*, New York: Aldine de Gruyter.

Angela P., Angela A. and Tonne G. (1993) *The Extraordinary Story of Human Origins*, New York: Prometheus.

Arsuaga J. L. (2002) *The Neanderthal's Necklace: In search of the first thinkers*, New York: Four Walls Eight Windows.

Avital E. and Jablonka E. (2000) *Animal Traditions: Behavioural inheritance in evolution*, Cambridge: Cambridge University Press.

Axelrod R. (1987) *The Evolution of Cooperation*, New York: Basic Books.

Badcock C. (1994) *Psychodarwinism*, Edinburgh: Edinburgh University Press.

Bagemihl B. (1999) *Biological Exuberance. Animal homosexuality and natural diversity*, London: Profile Books.

Betzig L. (ed.) (1997) *Human Nature. A critical reader*, New York and Oxford: Oxford University Press.

Bickerton D. (1990) *Language and Species*, Chicago: University of Chicago Press.

—— (1996) *Language and Human Behavior*, Seattle: University of Washington Press.

Blackmore S. (1999) *The Meme Machine*, Oxford: Oxford University Press.

Boaz N. T. (1997) *Eco Homo. How the human being emerged from the cataclysmic history of the earth*, New York: Basic Books.

Boehm C. (1999) *Hierarchy in the Forest. The evolution of egalitarian behavior*, Cambridge, Mass.: Harvard University Press.

Boesch C. and Boesch-Achermann H. (2000) *The Chimpanzees of the Tai Forest. Behavioural ecology and evolution*, Oxford: Oxford University Press.

Boesch C., Hohmann G. and Marchant L. F. (2002) *Behavioural Diversity in Chimpanzees and Bonobos*, Cambridge: Cambridge University Press.

Bourke A. F. G. and Franks N. R. (1995) *Social Evolution in Ants*, Princeton, NJ: Princeton University Press.

Boyd R. and Silk J. (1997) *How Humans Evolved*, Scranton, Pa.: W.W. Norton.

Brown D. E. (1991) *Human Universals*, Philadelphia: Temple University Press.

Byrne R. (1995) *The Thinking Ape. Evolutionary origins of intelligence*, Oxford: Oxford University Press.

Byrne R. and Whiten A. (eds) (1988) *Machiavellian Intelligence. Social expertise and the evolution of intellect in monkeys, apes, and humans*, Oxford: Clarendon Press.

Calvin W. H. (1996) *Cerebral Codes: Thinking a thought in the mosaic of the mind*, Cambridge, Mass.: MIT Press.

Carstairs-McCarthy A. (1999) *The Origins of Complex Language: An inquiry into the evolutionary beginnings of sentences, syllables, and truth*, Oxford: Oxford University Press.

Cavalieri P. and Singer P. (eds) (1993) *The Great Ape Project*, New York: St Martin's Press.

Cavalli-Sforza L. L. and Cavalli-Sforza F. (1995) *The Great Human Diasporas. The history of diversity and evolution*, Reading, Mass.: Addison-Wesley.

Chaline J. (1994) *Une famille peu ordinaire*, Paris: Seuil.

Chaneux J.-P. and Chavaillon J. (eds) (1996) *Origins of the Human Brain*, Oxford: Clarendon Press.

Chomsky N. (1965) *Aspects of the Theory of Syntax*, Cambridge, Mass.: MIT Press.

—— (1988) *Language and Problems of Knowledge. The Manuaga lectures*, Cambridge, Mass.: MIT Press.

Conroy G. (1997) *Reconstructing Human Origins. A modern synthesis*, New York/London: W.W. Norton.

Coppens Y. and Senut B. (eds) (1991) *Origine(s) de la Bipédie chez les Hominidés*, Paris: CNRS.

Corballis M. C. (1991) *The Lopsided Ape. Evolution of the generative mind*, New York/Oxford: Oxford University Press.

—— (2002) *From Hand to Mouth: The origins of language*, Princeton, NJ: Princeton University Press.

Corballis M. C. and Lea S. E. G. (eds) (1998) *The Evolution of the Hominid Mind*, Oxford: Oxford University Press.

Crow T. J. (2002) *More on Human Evolution. The speciation of modern* Homo sapiens, Oxford: Oxford University Press.

Daly M. and Wilson M. (1988) *Homicide*, New York: Aldine de Gruyter.

—— (1998) *The Truth about Cinderella. A Darwinian view of parental love*, London: Weidenfeld & Nicolson.

Dawkins R. (1976) *The Selfish Gene*, Oxford: Oxford University Press.

—— (1989) *The Selfish Gene*, new edn, Oxford: Oxford University Press.

—— (1999) *The Extended Phenotype. The long reach of the gene*, revised edn, Oxford: Oxford University Press.

Deacon T. W. (1998) *The Symbolic Species. The co-evolution of language and the brain*, New York/London: W.W. Norton.

Diamond J. (1992) *The Third Chimpanzee: The evolution and future of the human animal*, New York: HarperCollins.

—— (1997) *Why is Sex Fun? The evolution of human sexuality*, London: Weidenfeld & Nicolson.

Dixson A. F. (1998) *Primate Sexuality. Comparative studies of the prosimians, monkeys, apes, and human beings*, Oxford: Oxford University Press.

Donald M. (1991) *Origins of the Modern Mind. Three stages in the evolution of culture and cognition*, Cambridge, Mass.: Harvard University Press.

Dugatkin L. A. (1997) *Cooperation Among Animals. An evolutionary perspective*, New York: Oxford University Press.

Dunbar R. (1988) *Primate Systems. Studies in behavioural adaptation*, London: Chapman and Hall.

—— (1996) *Grooming, Gossip and the Evolution of Language*, London: Faber and Faber.

Durant J. H. (ed.) (1989) *Human Origins*, Oxford: Clarendon Press.

Durham W. H. (1991) *Coevolution. Genes, culture and human diversity*, Stanford, Calif.: Stanford University Press.

Eccles J. S. (1991) *Evolution of the Brain. Creation of the self*, London: Routledge.

Ehrlich Paul R. (2000) *Human Natures: Genes, cultures, and the human prospect*, Washington DC: Island Press.

Eibl-Eibesfeldt I. (1989) *Human Ethology*, New York: Walter de Gruyter.

Ellison P. T. (2001) *On Fertile Ground: A natural history of human reproduction*, Cambridge, Mass./London: Harvard University Press.

Fichtelius K.-E. (1985) *Hur apan miste pälsen och kom upp på två ben*, Stockholm: Akademilitteratur.

Fichtelius K.-E. and Wilsson L. (1999) *Om människan. Ursprung, särställning, vägval*, Jönköping: Brain Books.

Fisher R. (1930) *The Genetical Theory of Natural Selection*, Oxford: Clarendon Press.

Fleagle J. G. (1988) *Primate Adaptation and Evolution*, San Diego, Calif.: Academic Press.

Fletcher D. J. C. and Michener C. D. (eds) (1987) *Kin Recognition in Animals*, New York/Chichester: John Wiley.

Flohr A. K. (1994) *Fremdenfeindlichkeit. Biosociale Grundlagen von Ethnozentrismus*, Wiesbaden: Westdeutscher Verlag.

Foley R. A. (1987) *Another Unique Species. Patterns in human evolutionary ecology*, London: Longman.

—— (ed.) (1991) *The Origins of Human Behaviour*, London: Unwin Hyman.

—— (1996) *Humans Before Humanity*, Oxford: Blackwell.

Foley W. A. (1997) *Anthropological Linguistics. An introduction*, Malden, Mass./Oxford: Blackwell.

Fossey D. (1993) *Gorillas in the Mist*, Boston: Houghton Mifflin.

Fouts R. (with Mills S. T.) (1997) *Next of Kin: What chimpanzees have taught me about who we are*, New York: William Morrow.

Frank S. A. (1998) *Foundations of Social Evolution*, Princeton, NJ: Princeton University Press.

Gadagkar R. (1997) *Survival Strategies. Cooperation and conflict in animal societies*, Cambridge, Mass.: Harvard University Press.

Gamble C. (1993) *Timewalkers. The prehistory of global colonization*, Gloucester, UK: Alan Sutton.

Gazzaniga M. S. (1994) *Nature's Mind. The biological roots of thinking, emotions, sexuality, language, and intelligence*, London: Penguin.

Gibson K. R. and Ingold T. (eds) (1993) *Tools, Language and Cognition in Human Evolution*, Cambridge: Cambridge University Press.

Goodall J. (1986) *The Chimpanzees of Gombe*, Cambridge, Mass.: Belknap Press/ Harvard University Press.

Gould J. S. (1977) *Ontogeny and Phylogeny*, Cambridge, Mass.: Harvard University Press.

Griffin D. R. (1992) *Animal Minds*, Chicago: University of Chicago Press.

Griffin M. and Griffin J. (1993) *Being Human: Putting people in an evolutionary perspective*, London: J. M. Dent.

Groves C. P. (1989) *A Theory of Primate and Human Evolution*, New York: Oxford University Press.

Gullan P. J. and Cranston P. S. (1994) *The Insects. An outline of entomology*, London: Chapman and Hall.

Hager L. (ed.) (1997) *Women in Human Evolution*, London: Routledge.

Hauser M. D. (1996) *The Evolution of Communication*, Cambridge, Mass.: MIT Press.

Hausfater G. and Hrdy S. B. (1984) *Infanticide: Comparative and evolutionary perspectives*, New York: Aldine.

Heltne P. G. and Marquardt L. A. (eds) (1989) *Understanding Chimpanzees*, Cambridge, Mass.: Harvard University Press.

Henke W. and Rothe H. (1994) *Paläoanthropologie*, Berlin: Springer Verlag.

Hepper P. G. (1991) *Kin Recognition*, Cambridge: Cambridge University Press.

Hölldobler B. and Wilson E. O. (1990) *The Ants*, Berlin: Springer Verlag.

Hoogland J. L. (1995) *The Black-Tailed Prairie Dog. Social life of a burrowing animal*, Chicago: University of Chicago Press.

Howells W. (1993) *Getting There. The story of human evolution*, Washington DC: Compass Press.

Hrdy S. B. (1977) *The Langurs of Abu: Female and male strategies of reproduction*, Cambridge, Mass.: Harvard University Press.

Ingold T. (ed.) (1988) *What is an Animal*, London: Unwin Hyman.

Isaac G. (ed.) (1997) *Koobi Fora Research Project*, Vol 5: *Plio-Pleistocene archaeology*, Oxford: Clarendon Press.

Itoigawa N., Sugiyama Y., Sackett G. and Thompson R. (eds) (1992) *Topics in Primatology*, Vol 2: *Behavior, ecology, and conservation*, Tokyo: University of Tokyo Press.

Johanson D. and Edgar B. (1996) *From Lucy to Language*, London: Weidenfeld & Nicolson.

Johanson D., Johanson L. and Edgar B. (1994) *Ancestors. In search of human origins*, New York: Villard Books.

Johnson J. and Odent M. (1994) *We are all Water Babies*, Limpsfield, Surrey: Dragon's World.

Jones S., Martin R. and Pilbeam D. (eds) (1992) *The Cambridge Encyclopaedia of Human Evolution*, Cambridge: Cambridge University Press.

Kano T. (1992) *The Last Ape. Pygmy chimpanzee behavior and ecology*, Stanford, Calif.: Stanford University Press.

Kappeler P. M. (ed.) (2000) *Primate Males: Causes and consequences of variation in group composition*, Cambridge: Cambridge University Press.

Karmiloff K. and Karmiloff-Smith A. (2001) *Pathways to Language: From fetus to adolescent*, Cambridge, Mass.: Harvard University Press.

Katz L. D. (2000) *Evolutionary Origins of Morality. Cross-disciplinary perspectives*, Thorverton, UK: Imprint Academic.

Kelly R. L. (1995) *The Foraging Spectrum. Diversity in hunter–gatherer lifeways*, Washington DC: Smithsonian Institution Press.

King B. J. (2000) *Origins of Language: What non-human primates can tell us*, Conyers, Ga.: Premier Book Marketing.

Knight C. (1991) *Blood Relations. Menstruation and the origins of culture*, New Haven, Conn./London: Yale University Press.

Knight C., Studdert-Kennedy M. and Hurford J. R. (eds) (2002) *The Evolutionary Emergence of Language: Social function and the origins of linguistic form*, Cambridge: Cambridge University Press.

Knutsson H. (1995) *Slutvandrat. Aspekter på övergången från rörliga till bofasta samhällen*, Uppsala: Societas Archaeologica Upsaliensis.

Kohl J. V. and Francoeur R. T. (1995) *The Scent of Eros. Mysteries of odor in human sexuality*, New York: Continuum.

Krebs J. R. and Davies N. B. (1993) *An Introduction to Behavioural Ecology*, 3rd edn, Oxford: Blackwell.

Laland K. N. and Brown G. R. (2002) *Sense and Nonsense. Evolutionary perspectives on human behaviour*, Oxford: Oxford University Press.

Landsberg M. E. (ed.) (1988) *The Genesis of Language. A different judgement of evidence*, Berlin/New York: Mouton de Gruyter.

Leakey M. and Harris J. M. (eds) (1987) *Laetoli: A Pliocene site in northern Tanzania*, Oxford: Clarendon Press.

Leakey R. (1994) *The Origin of Humankind*, New York: Basic Books.

Leakey R. and Lewin R. (1992) *Origins Reconsidered. In search of what makes us human*, London: Little, Brown.

Lewin R. and Foley R. (2004) *Principles of Human Evolution*, 2nd edn, Oxford: Blackwell.

Lieberman P. (1991) *Uniquely Human. The evolution of speech, thought, and selfless behavior*, Cambridge, Mass.: Harvard University Press.

——— (1998) *Eve Spoke. Human language and human evolution*, London: Picador.

Ljungberg T. (1991) *Människan, kulturen och evolutionen. Ett alternativt perspektiv*, Nyköping: Exiris.

Lumsden C. and Wilson E. (1981) *Genes, Mind and Culture. The coevolutionary process*, Cambridge, Mass.: Harvard University Press.

——— (1983) *Promethean Fire: Reflections on the origin of mind*, Cambridge, Mass.: Harvard University Press.

McGrew W. C. (1992) *Chimpanzee Material Culture. Implications for human evolution*, Cambridge: Cambridge University Press.

McGrew W. C., Marchant L. F. and Nishida T. (eds) (1996) *Great Ape Societies*, Cambridge: Cambridge Univesity Press.

McKinney M. L. (ed.) (1988) *Topics in Geobiology: A multidisciplinary approach: Heterochrony in evolution*, Vol 7, New York: Kluwer Academic/Plenum.

McNamara K. (1997) *Shapes of Time. The evolution of growth and development*, Baltimore, Md.: Johns Hopkins University Press.

Manning A. and Dawkins M. S. (1998) *An Introduction to Animal Behaviour*, 5th edn, Cambridge: Cambridge University Press.

Marks J. (2002) *What it Means to be 98% Chimpanzee: Apes, people, and their genes*, Berkeley, Calif.: University of California Press.

Martin R. D. (1990) *Primate Origins and Evolution. A phylogenetic reconstruction*, London: Chapman and Hall.

Maryanski A. and Turner J. H. (1992) *The Social Cage. Human nature and the evolution of society*, Stanford, Calif.: Stanford University Press.

Matano S., Tuttle R., Ishida H. and Goodman M. (eds) (1992) *Topics in Primatology*, Vol 3: *Evolutionary biology, reproductive endocrinology, and virology*, Tokyo: University of Tokyo Press.

Maynard Smith J. and Szathmáry E. (1999) *The Origins of Life. From the birth of life to the origin of language*, Oxford: Oxford University Press.

Megarry T. (1995) *Society in Prehistory. The origins of human culture*, Houndmills, Basingstoke: Macmillan.

Mellars P. (1996) *The Neanderthal Legacy. An archaeological perspective from Western Europe*, Princeton, NJ: Princeton University Press.

Mellars P. and Gibson K. (1996) *Modelling the Early Human Mind*, Cambridge: McDonald Institute.

Mithen S. (1996) *The Prehistory of the Mind. A search for the origins of art, religion and science*, London: Thames & Hudson.

Morbeck M. E., Galloway A. and Zihlman A. L. (eds) (1997) *The Evolving Female. A life history perspective*, Princeton, NJ: Princeton University Press.

Morell V. (1995) *Ancestral Passions. The Leakey family and the quest for humankind's beginnings*, New York/London: Simon & Schuster.

Morgan E. (1972) *The Descent of Woman*, London: Souvenir Press.

—— (1982) *The Aquatic Ape*, London: Souvenir Press.

—— (1990) *The Scars of Evolution. What our bodies tell us about human origins*, London: Souvenir Press.

—— (1994) *The Descent of the Child. Human evolution from a new perspective*, London: Souvenir Press.

—— (1997) *The Aquatic Ape Hypothesis*, London: Souvenir Press.

Morris D. (1967) *The Naked Ape. A zoologist's study of the human animal*, New York: McGraw-Hill.

Napier J. R. and Napier P. H. (1985) *The Natural History of the Primates*, London: British Museum/Cambridge University Press.

Nishida T. (ed.) (1990) *The Chimpanzees of the Mahale Mountains. Sexual and life history strategies*, Tokyo: University of Tokyo Press.

Nishida T., McGrew W., Marler P., Pickford M. and de Waal F. (eds) (1992) *Topics in Primatology*, Vol 1: *Human origins*, Tokyo: University of Tokyo Press.

Nitecki M. H. and Nitecki D. W. (eds) (1994) *Origins of Anatomically Modern Humans*, New York: Plenum Press.

Noble W. and Davidson I. (1996) *Human Evolution, Language and Mind: A psychological and archaeological inquiry*, Cambridge: Cambridge University Press.

Nowell A. (ed.) (2001) *In the Mind's Eye: Multidisciplinary approaches to the evolution of human cognition*, Ann Arbor, Mich.: International Monographs in Prehistory.

Ozinga J. R. (1999) *Altruism*, Westport, Conn.: Praeger.

Parker S. and McKinney M. (1999) *Origins of Intelligence. The evolution of cognitive development in monkeys, apes and humans*, Baltimore, Md.: Johns Hopkins University Press.

Parmigiani S. and vom Saal F. S. (eds) (1994) *Infanticide and Parental Care*, Newark, NJ: Harwood Academic.

Pepperberg I. (1999) *The Alex Studies: Cognitive and communicative abilities of Grey Parrots*, Cambridge, Mass.: Harvard University Press.

Pinker S. (1995) *The Language Instinct. The new science of language and mind*, London: Penguin.

—— (1999) *How the Mind Works*, London: Penguin.

Potts M. and Short R. (1999) *Ever Since Adam and Eve. The evolution of human sexuality*, Cambridge: Cambridge University Press.

Primack R. B. (1993) *Essentials in Conservation Biology*, Sunderland, Mass.: Sinauer.

Quiatt D. and Reynolds V. (1993) *Primate Behaviour. Information, social knowledge, and the evolution of culture*, Cambridge: Cambridge University Press.

Relethford J. H. (1994) *Fundamentals of Biological Anthropology*, Mountain View, Calif.: Mayfield.

Renfrew C. and Zubrow E. (eds) (1995) *The Ancient Mind. Elements of cognitive archaeology*, Cambridge: Cambridge University Press.

Ridley M. (1993) *The Red Queen. Sex and the evolution of human nature*, New York: Viking.

—— (1997) *The Origins of Virtue. Human instincts and the evolution of cooperation*, New York: Viking.

—— (2003) *Nature Via Nurture. Genes, experience, and what makes us human*, London: Fourth Estate.

Rightmire Ph. (1990) *The Evolution of 'Homo erectus'*, Cambridge: Cambridge University Press.

Roede M., Wind J., Patrick J. M. and Reynolds V. (eds) (1991) *The Aquatic Ape: Fact or fiction. The first scientific evaluation of a controversial theory of human evolution*, London: Souvenir Press.

Rose S. (2003) *Lifelines. Life beyond the genes*, Oxford: Oxford University Press.

Runciman W. G., Smith J. M. and Dunbar R. I. M. (eds) (1996) *Evolution of Social Behaviour Patterns in Primates and Man*, Oxford: Oxford University Press.

Russon A. E., Bard K. A. and Parker S. T. (eds) (1996) *Reaching into Thought: The minds of the great apes*, Cambridge: Cambridge University Press.

Sapolsky R. M. (1997) *Junk Food Monkeys, and Other Essays on the Biology of the Human Predicament*, London: Hodder Headline.

Savage-Rumbaugh S. and Lewin R. (1994) *Kanzi: The ape at the brink of the human mind*, New York/Chichester: John Wiley.

Savage-Rumbaugh S., Shanker S. G. and Taylor T. J. (1998) *Apes, Languages and the Human Mind*, New York/Oxford: Oxford University Press.

Schick K. D. and Toth N. (1993) *Making Silent Stones Speak: Human evolution and the dawn of technology*, New York: Simon & Schuster.

Shepher J. (1983) *Incest. A biosocial view*, New York: Academic Press.

Sherman P. W., Jarvis J. U. M. and Alexander R. D. (eds) (1991) *The Biology of the Naked Mole-Rat*, Princeton, NJ: Princeton University Press.

Small M. F. (1993) *Female Choices. Sexual behaviours of female primates*, New York: Cornell University Press.

—— (1995) *What's Love Got to do With It? The evolution of human mating*, New York: Anchor Books.

Smolensky P. and Prince A. (1997) *Optimality Theory. Constraint interaction in generative grammar*, Cambridge, Mass.: MIT Press.

Smuts B., Cheney D., Seyfarth R., Wrangham R. and Struhsaker T. (eds) (1987) *Primate Societies*, Chicago: University of Chicago Press.

Sober E. and Wilson D. S. (1998) *Unto Others. The evolution and psychology of unselfish behavior*, Cambridge, Mass.: Harvard University Press.

Sommer V. (1996) *Heilige Egoisten – Die Sociobiologie indischer Tempelaffe*, München: C. H. Beck.

Stanford C. (1998) *Chimpanzee and Red Colobus. The ecology of predator and prey*, Cambridge, Mass.: Harvard University Press.

Steele J. and Shennan S. (eds) (1996) *The Archaeology of Human Ancestry. Power, sex and tradition*, London: Routledge.

Stringer C. and McKie R. (1996) *African Exodus. The origins of modern humanity*, London: Jonathan Cape.

Susman R. L. (ed.) (1984) *The Pygmy Chimpanzee. Evolutionary biology and behavior*, New York: Plenum Press.

Sussman R. W. (2002) *Primate Ecology and Social Structure*, Vol. 3: *Old World monkeys and apes*, Needham Heights, Mass.: Pearson Custom.

Symons D. (1979) *The Evolution of Human Sexuality*, New York/Oxford: Oxford University Press.

Tattersall I. (1998) *Becoming Human. Evolution and human uniqueness*, New York: Harcourt Brace.

—— (2002) *The Monkey in the Mirror. Essays on the science of what makes us human*, San Diego, Calif.: Harcourt.

Taylor Park S., Taylor Park K. and Gibson R. (eds) (1990) *Language and Intelligence in Monkeys and Apes. Comparative developmental perspectives*, Cambridge: Cambridge University Press.

Thornhill N. (ed.) (1993) *The Natural History of Inbreeding and Outbreeding. Theoretical and empirical perspectives*, Chicago/London: University of Chicago Press.

—— (1997) *Misplaced Desire: An evolutionary examination of incest*, New York: Basic Books.

Tobias P. (1991) *Olduvai Gorge*, Vol 4: *The skulls, endocasts and teeth of* 'Homo habilis'. Cambridge: Cambridge University Press.

Trivers R. (1985) *Social Evolution*, Menlo Park, Calif.: Benjamin/Cummings.

Uddenberg N. (1998) *Arvsdygden. Biologisk utveckling och mänsklig gemenskap*. Stockholm: Natur och Kultur.

Vrba E. S., Denton G. H., Partridge T. C. and Burckle L. H. (eds) (1996) *Paleoclimate and Evolution with Emphasis on Human Origins*, New Haven, Conn./London: Yale University Press.

de Waal F. (1989) *Peacemaking Among Primates*, Cambridge, Mass.: Harvard University Press.

—— (1996) *Good Natured. The origins of right and wrong in humans and other animals*, Cambridge, Mass.: Harvard University Press.

—— (1998) *Chimpanzee Politics: Power and sex among apes*, revised edn, Baltimore, Md.: Johns Hopkins University Press.

—— (ed.) (2001) *Tree of Origin. What primate behavior can tell us about human social evolution*, Cambridge, Mass./London: Harvard University Press.

de Waal F. and Lanting F. (1997) *Bonobo. The forgotten ape*, Berkeley, Calif.: University of California Press.

Walker A. and Leakey R. (eds) (1993) *Equality Beyond Humanity. The Nariokotome 'Homo erectus' skeleton*, London: Fourth Estate/Harvard University Press.

Walker A. and Shipman P. (1996) *The Wisdom of Bones. In search of human origins*, London: Weidenfeld & Nicolson.

Vauclair J. (1996) *Animal Cognition. An introduction to modern comparative psychology*, Cambridge, Mass.: Harvard University Press.

Westermarck E. (1891) *The History of Human Marriage*, London: McMillan and Co.

Whiten A. and Byrne R. (eds) (1997) *Machiavellian Intelligence II*, Cambridge: Cambridge University Press.

Wills C. (1994) *The Runaway Brain. The evolution of human uniqueness*, London: HarperCollins.

Wilson E. O. (1975) *Sociobiology. The new synthesis*, Cambridge, Mass.: Harvard University Press.

—— (1978) *On Human Nature*, Cambridge, Mass.: Harvard University Press.

—— (1992) *The Diversity of Life*, Cambridge, Mass.: Belknap Press/Harvard University Press.

Wind J., Chiarelli B., Bichakjian B. and Nocentini A. (eds) (1992) *Language Origin: A multidisciplinary approach*, New York: Kluwer Academic.

Wolf A. (1995) *Sexual Attraction and Childhood Association. A Chinese brief for Edward Westermarck*, Cambridge: Cambridge University Press.

Wolpoff M. and Caspari R. (1997) *Race and Human Evolution. A fatal attraction*, New York/London: Simon & Schuster.

Wood B. (1992) *Koobi Fora Research Project*, Vol 4: *Hominid cranial remains*, Oxford: Oxford University Press.

Wrangham R. W., McGrew W. C., de Waal F. B. M. and Heltne P. G. (eds) (1994) *Chimpanzee Cultures*, Cambridge, Mass.: Harvard University Press.

Wray A. (ed.) (2002) *The Transition to Language*, Oxford: Oxford University Press.

Wright R. (1994) *The Moral Animal*, New York: Little, Brown.

A selection of journals

American Anthropology
American Ethnologist
American Journal of Physical Anthropology
American Journal of Primatology
American Naturalist
American Scientist
Animal Behaviour
Annual Review of Ecology and Systematics
Behavioral Ecology
Behaviour. An International Journal of Biology
Behavioural Ecology and Sociobiology
Bioessays
Bioscience
Current Anthropology
Current Biology
Discover

Ethology (formerly *Zeitschrift für Tierpsychologie*)
Ethology, Ecology & Evolution
Ethology and Sociobiology
Evolutionary Ecology
Folia Primatologica
Homo
Human Biology
Human Ethology Bulletin
Human Evolution
Ibis. The International Journal of Avian Science
International Journal of Primatology
Journal of Animal Ecology
Journal of Anthropological Archaeology
Journal of Avian Biology
Journal of Biological Anthropology
Journal of Ethology
Journal of Evolutionary Biology
Journal of Human Evolution
Journal of Insect Behavior
Journal of Molecular Biology
Man
Molecular Biology and Evolution
Molecular Ecology
Natural History
Nature
New Scientist
Oikos. A Journal of Ecology
Philosophical Transactions of the Royal Society. Biological Sciences
Primate Ethology
Primates
Proceedings of the National Academy of Sciences, New York
Proceedings of the Royal Society, London. Biological Sciences
Science
Scientific American
The Auk. A Quarterly Journal of Ornithology
The Behavioural and Brain Sciences
The Condor. An International Journal of Avian Biology
The Quarterly Review of Biology
The Scientist
The Wilson Bulletin
Trends in Ecology and Evolution

INDEX

abstract thinking 110, 124
Acheulean stone technology 59, 62
adoption: humans and animals 24, 156
Afar, Ethiopia 60, 75, 78
Africa 20, 44, 47, 59–63, 75, 80–2, 133–5,
   138–41, 145; Acheulean stone tool
   tradition 59, 62; advanced *erectus* 59; first
   humans leaving 59, 94; hand axe
   tradition 114; *Heidelbergensis* leaving 60,
   63; modern humans appearing 60, 109,
   134–5; modern humans leaving 88;
   oldest stone tools 123
aggression 7, 10, 30, 35; blocks against
   162–3; early humans 160; herd animals
   157–62; male 9, 160; modern humans
   157; ritualized 162; social insects 33
Ai (bonobo) 125
Aiello, Leslie 114, 118
Allia Bay, Kenya 52, 144
altruism 37, 157; evolution of 12–17, 25,
   38–90, 93
America 2, 28
amphibians 18
ant-dipping: chimpanzees 119, 137
antelopes 55, 143
ants 11, 33–4, 132, 137, 156; *see also* social
   insects
apes 5, 7, 38, 46–7, 52, 54, 64, 67–8, 107,
   112, 151–3; age of 44; canine teeth as
   instruments for hierarchical aggression
   151–2; consanguinity with humans
   42–3; diet 135–7; emotions and
   empathy 155–6; genetical distance to
   humans 41; hands free for work 66;
   human-like features of embryos 82–3;
   inhibitions against sex 24; knuckle-
   walking 45; lack of fossil finds of 75, 76;
   lack of subcutaneous fat 71; language
   capacity 116, 123–9; ovulation 89,
   95–6, 98, 103; present occurrence 41–2;

qualities distinguishing from humans
   73–4, 77; sexual behaviour 102; split
   from humans 41, 44, 50, 66, 70, 80; tool
   use 117–23; unable to produce
   articulated sounds 116
aquatic hypotheis of bipedalism 70–9, 84,
   70–5, 77–8, 84, 118, 129
Aramis, Ethiopia 52
archaic *sapiens* 60, 62, 87, 113, 134–5;
   see also Homo Heidelbergensis
Ardipithecus 48, 51–2
Ardipithecus ramidus kadabba 51–2
Ardipithecus ramidus ramidus 52
Arnarsson, Ulfur 41
Asfaw, Berhane 55
Asia 2, 43–4, 47, 59, 61–3, 78, 87, 110,
   114, 134, 139
Australia 2, 60, 110, 114
Australopithecus 47–8, 52, 54
Australopithecus aethiopicus 57–8
Australopithecus afarensis 52–4, 56, 85, 115,
   138
Australopithecus africanus 47, 54, 56, 115
Australopithecus anamensis 52, 158
Australopithecus bahrelghazali 54
Australopithecus boisei 57–8
Australopithecus crassidens 58
Australopithecus garhi 55, 58
Australopithecus praegens 52
Australopithecus robustus 57–8
Awash, Ethiopia 51, 54–5
Axelrod, Robert 13

baboons 89–91, 127, 143, 149, 153,
   156
Bagemihl, Bruce 105
Bahr-el-Ghazal, Chad 54
Bateson, Pat 19
bears 67
beavers 15, 19, 72

bees 11, 34, 156; *see also* honey bees; social
 insects
beetles 132, 138
Bermudez de Castro, J. M. 87
Bickerton, Derek 108
biological heritage: humans 3–11
biologism 9–10
bipedalism 5, 80–1, 86, 90, 96, 102–3,
 116–17, 129–30, 150; neoteny and 76,
 83–5, 88; origins of 51, 64–70, 75–80,
 93–4, 97, 99
birds 18, 21–2, 30–2, 35–6, 145, 161
bisexuality: in apes and other animals 105
Bodo, Ethiopia 60
Boehm, Christopher 38
Boesch, Christophe, 120
Boetsch, Arnold 119
bonobos 8, 45, 75, 154, 156, 160;
 aggression 158; breast-feeding 95, 155;
 diet 136–7; family structure 146–8;
 female exogamy 146; food sharing 143;
 genetic similarities with humans 42–3;
 genital swelling 89, 98; hierarchal
 structure 154; homosexual behaviour 24,
 90, 105; hunting 137; inbreeding
 avoidance 146–8; language capacity
 124–9; lesbianism 24, 96; material
 culture lacking in the wild 110;
 menstruation 95–6; neotene evolution
 85–6, 103–4; oestrus 95, 97; present
 occurrence 41–2; sexual behaviour 96–7,
 99–101, 103–4, 149, 151; testicle size
 93; tool use 120–2; *see also Pan paniscus*;
 pygmy chimpanzees
Borneo 71, 110, 121
bows 163
Boxgrave, England 62
brain 7–8; language and 107–9
breast-feeding: chimpanzees and bonobos
 95, 155; early humans 155; hunters and
 gatherers 95; modern societies 95
Broca's centre 107, 125; in *afarensis* and
 africanus 115; in chimpanzees 115
Brunet, Michel 50, 54
Burma 20
Byrne, Richard, 121

Calvin, William 108
camels 7
canine teeth, reduction of 85–6, 150–2
capuchin monkeys: tool use 121
caring for young, evolution of 30–2, 37, 40
Cartmill, Matt 113
caterpillars 132
cattle 7

Caucasus 63
Central Africa 41–2, 119
Central America 2, 60
Ceprano, Italy 62
cetaceans 156
Chad 50–1, 54
cheetahs 19
Cheney, Dorothy 127, 132
chicken 7
chimpanzees 7, 46, 51, 53–4, 73, 84–5,
 103, 110, 114–15, 140, 145; aggression
 158, 161–2; ancestors of 44, 49, 64–5,
 70, 78; Broca's centre 115; diet 136–7,
 143; division of labour 155; empathy
 127, 156; family structure 146–8; female
 exogamy 23–4, 146; food-sharing 4–5,
 143, 156; genetic distance to humans 41,
 86; genetic diversity 20; genital swelling
 89, 98; hierarchal structures 153–5;
 homosexual behaviour 105; hunting 91,
 143, 155; incest avoidance 23, 146–8;
 infanticide not common 28–9, 92;
 inhibitions against sex 23; knuckle-
 walking 45; language capacity 123–9;
 menstruation 95–6; numeric capacity
 123–9; oestrus 23, 95–7, 151; orgasm
 100; penis 104; present occurrence 41–2;
 reciprocal behaviour 158; respect for
 water 72, 75; sexual behaviour 89–94,
 96, 100–1, 149–52; size difference
 between sexes 151; social behaviour
 158–9; sterility in early puberty146;
 symbolic thinking 108–9; territorial
 behaviour 162; testicle size 93; tool use
 4, 117–23; transport capacity 67;
 upbringing 160; violence 159–60, 162;
 war-like aggression 5; *see also Pan
 troglodytes*
China 61–2
Chomsky, Noam 107–8
Cinque, Guglielmo 108
Clacton, England 113
Clarke, Ronald 53–4
climate change 81–2
coal tits 31
coevolution of genes and culture 5, 13–14,
 37, 39
cognition 106, 110; *see also* consciousness
colobus monkeys 26, 143
Congo 41–2
consciousness 110, 126, 157
Costello, R. K. 98
crabs 73
crayfish 73
Creol languages 107–8

crocodiles 80, 132
Crompton, Robert 76
cuckoos 31
curiosity in humans, neotene evolution of 86–8
Czechoslovakia 62

Danaqil, Eritrea 60, 74, 78
Dart, Raymond 47
Darwin, Charles 7–8, 12
Dawkins, Richard 10, 13–15, 37, 39
Deacon, Terrence 108
Diamond, Jared 91
diet: apes 136–7, 143; early humans 80, 85, 136–43
Disotell, Todd 44
dive reflex of babies 72, 74
division of labour 67, 155
Dmanisi, Caucasus 61
DNA analyses 31, 33, 42, 60, 79
dogs 86, 156
dolphins 123, 156
dominance 9, 40; drives for 31, 33, 158
duikers 137
Dunbar, Robin 114, 118

eagles 132
Egypt 20
Eibl-Eibelsfeldt, Irenäus 126
East (eastern) Africa 43–5, 50, 56, 58, 60, 63, 115, 119, 154
East (eastern) Asia 60, 62
elephants 38, 60, 68, 71, 78–9, 113, 123, 156
empathy: elementary in some herd mammals 156; evolution of 39; lack of in monkeys 127
encephalisation quotient 50, 53, 56, 58–9
England 62, 113
Eritrea 60
erotic signals, evolution of permanent 97–100
Ethiopia 51, 53, 55, 60, 63, 74
Eurasia 59, 87, 104, 135, 139
Europe 2, 43–4, 47, 59, 87–8, 112–13, 135, 139, 141; Acheulean stone tool tradition 62; archaic *sapiens* 134; celtic 161; feudal 161; hand axe tradition 114; modern humans appearing 60–1; Neanderthals in 110; Viking Age 161
exogamy: bonobos 146; chimpanzees 23–4, 146–7; early humans 148; gorillas 146; human societies 18, 21–2, 40, 146, 150–1; last quadrupedal ancestor 45, 147; other animals 18, 21–2, 24, 146

family structure: apes 146–9; early humans 145–55
fatty glands 72
Fejej, Ethiopia 53
Fichtelius, Karl-Erik 71, 73
Finland 63
fire, use of 5, 138–9, 144
fish 18, 33, 73–4, 138
Fisher, Ronald 12, 37
flock instinct 7, 158; *see also* herd instinct
Flores, eastern Indonesia 62, 114
flycatchers 31
food sharing: bonobos 143; chimpanzees 4–5, 143, 156; early humans 93–4, 144
foramen magnum 83
France 50, 62
free will 6, 8–9, 11
Freud, Sigmund 8, 21–2
fur, absence of (loss of) 65, 69, 71, 74, 79, 90, 93

Gaeth, Ann 79
Gannon, Patrick 125–6
gazelles 132
genetic bottle-necks in evolution: animals 19; humans 86
Genghis Khan 2
genital swelling: human loss of 95–9; primates 89
genitals: backward-facing in apes and monkeys 97, 100; female 73; forward-facing in humans 71
Germany 62–3, 113
gibbons 28, 41–2, 91–2, 121, 151, 153; *see also Hylobates*
goats 7
Goldin-Meadow, Susan 108
Gombe, Tanzania 147, 162
Gona, Ethiopia 55
Goodall, Jane 143, 162
Gorilla gorilla beringei 41
Gorilla gorilla gorilla 42
Gorilla gorilla graueri 41
gorillas 43, 73, 75, 140, 145, 148–9; aggression 159; ancestors of 44, 65–5, 78, 78; diet 136–7; genetic distance to humans 41; genital swelling lacking 89; knuckle-walking 45; language capacity 124, 126, 128–9; material culture lacking in the wild 110; oestrus 151; present occurrence 41–2; size differences between sexes 151; symbolic thinking 108–9; tool use 121; *see also Gorilla gorilla beringei; Gorilla gorilla gorilla;*

Gorilla gorilla graueri; low-land gorillas; mountain gorillas
Gran Dolina, Spain 62
Greece 62, 161
ground squirrels 15, 26
group selection 38
Guinea 119

Hadar, southern Ethiopia 53, 58, 153
Haile-Selassie, Yohannes 51
Hamilton, William 12–13, 15–17, 38
Hamiltons rule 16
hamsters 15
hand axes 62, 114
Hanuman langurs 26–9
Hardy, Alistair 70–3, 75–6, 79
Hawaii 20
herd animals 7, 109, 131, 145, 153, 156
herd instinct: in animals 7, 36, 39, 145; in humans 7, 36, 39, 145–6, 153, 156
herring gulls 30
Herto, Ethiopia 60
hierarchal structures: chimpanzees 154–5; early humans 7, 154–5; modern humans 10, 157
hippopotamus 26, 51, 68, 71, 78–9, 132
holok 42
hominids 5, 48
hominins 48
hominoids 48
Homo antecessor 64
Homo erectus 48, 57, 59–62, 68, 85, 92, 112–14, 134–5, 137, 142–4, 152–3, 157; language capacity 111, 133–4; meat eating 139
Homo ergaster 53, 59–61, 85, 87; first human outside 141
Homo habilis 48, 59, 61
Homo Heidelbergensis 60, 62–3
Homo rudolfensis 48–59
Homo sapiens 58, 60, 62
Homo sapiens sapiens 60, 87
Homo sp. 49–50, 55–8, 61, 69, 77, 84, 91, 112, 137, 143, 152; canine teeth of modern size 151; definition of 48; diet 142; fundamental changes 152; human brain structures 115; increase of intelligence 38; inner ear of modern type 54; neoteny and 85–7; tool making 67 122; *see also* archaic *sapiens*; *Homo antecessor*; *Homo erectus*; *Homo ergaster*; *Homo habilis*; *Homo Heidelbergensis*; *Homo rudolfensis*; *Homo sapiens*; *Homo sapiens sapiens*

homosexual behaviour: animals 105; female bonobos 96, 105
honey bees 31; *see also* bees; social insects
Hoogland, John 29
Horn of Africa 43, 56, 74
horses 7, 85, 113
Hrdy, Sara Blaffer 26, 101
human heritages from the apes 6–11
human universals 8
humanity, definition of 4–5
Hungary 62
hunters and gatherers (gathering) 6, 93, 95, 120, 141–4, 149, 152–4, 160–1, 163
hyenas 132
hygiene: animals 141; early humans 141
Hylobates 42
hypothalamus 7

Iberian Peninsula 82
Ice Age 61, 81, 88, 110, 112
Ileret, Kenya 59
imprinting through early close contact 18–25, 28–33, 38, 44, 147–9, 157; *see also* Westermarck effect
inbreeding: blocks against 34–6; historical examples 20–1; social taboos against 18, 20–1
inbreeding avoidance 20, 75; animals 17–20; humans 18–21; early humans 17–19, 21
incest: humans 24, 30
incest avoidance: humans 18–25, 30, 34; bonobos 23, 146–7; chimpanzees and 23, 146–8
inclusive fitness 12
Indonesia 61–2, 114
infanticide 25–31, 91–2; animals 26, 28–9; chimpanzees 28–9; Hanuman langurs 26–7, 29; humans 30; mental blocks against 27; prairie dogs 28–9
insects 18, 33, 74, 137, 152; non-social 35; *see also* social insects
Isernia, Italy 62
Israel 61–2, 111
Italy 44, 62, 75
Ivory Coast 119, 143

Japan 60, 161
Java, Indonesia 61–2
Java Man 61
Jesus Christ 2
Johansson, Donald 53, 64
Johnson, Virgina 101
Joulien, Fréderic 120
Jung, Carl Gustav 8, 28

Kanapoi, Lake Turkana, Kenya 52
Kano, Takayoshi 85–6, 103
Kanzi (bonobo) 120–1, 124
Katanda, eastern Zaire 112
Kebara, Israel 111
Kenya 51, 55, 58–9, 114, 143–4
Kenyanthropus platyops 55, 85
Kenyapithecus 44
Kimeu, Kimoya 59
kin selection theory 6, 12–14, 90–2;
    critique of 14–17, 25–9, 31–8
Köhler, Meike 44–5, 75–6
Koobi Fora, Kenya 59, 115, 143
Koro Toro, Chad 54, 58
Kromdrai, South Africa 58

labour division 93
Laetoli, Tanzania, footprints 53–4
Laitman, Jeffrey 113–14
Lake Baringo, Kenya 51–3, 58
Lake Tanganyika, Africa 162
Lake Turkana, Kenya 52, 55, 59, 88
language: articulated 5, 116–17, 129–30,
    133–4; evolution of modern 109–12;
    latent linguistic capacity of last
    quadrupedal ancestor 127–9; universal
    patterns 107–9
langurs 149, 159
lanugo 72
last quadrupedal ancestors 43–5, 49, 68, 70,
    90, 94, 98, 128, 141, 149; aggression in
    160; backward-facing vagina 97;
    imprinting through early close contact
    147, 149; possible lack of attraction to
    water 78; potentials for communication
    107, 130
Leakey, Mary 54
Leakey, Meave 52, 55
Leakey, Richard 59, 150
Lehringen, Germany 113
leopards 132
lesbianism see homosexual behaviour
Li, Yu 76
Liberia 119
Lieberman, Philip 110
limbic system 7, 107
Lindblad, Jan 71
Linnaeus (von Linné, Carl) 7, 47
lions 29, 88, 132, 156; genetic diversity 20;
    infanticide 26
Longgupo, central China 61
Lorenz, Konrad 8, 86
loss of fur: humans 70–1, 75–6, 79,
    84–5
Lovejoy, Owen 67

low-land gorillas 75, 88; genetic diversity
    20; hunting 136–7
Lucy 53, 56, 64–5
Lumsden, Charles 13, 37

macaques 99, 125, 127, 156, 159;
    inhibitions against sex in 24
McCabe, Justine 23
McGrew, William 122–3
McHenry, Henry 153
Madagascar 20
magpies 31
Mahale, western Tanzania 162
Makaamitalu, Ethiopia 58
Malawi 59
mammals 6, 26, 28, 34, 69, 81, 99, 145,
    154; aggression by males 160; curiosity
    86; exogamy in 21–2; flock 155; higher
    155–6; imprinting through early close
    contact in 22, 36; inbreeding avoidance
    in 18, 36; land 71–3; monogamy 92;
    neocortex 107; ovulation 96; social
    complexity in 35
martins 31
Masters, William 101
Matata (bonobo) 124
Maurer, Germany 62
Maynard Smith, John 12
Mayr, Ernst 37
Mediterranean, the 81
Mendel, Gregor 37
menstruation: chimpanzees and bonobos
    95–6; hunter-gatherers 95; modern
    societies 95–6
mice 15
Miocene period 43–4, 49, 65, 73–5, 82,
    127, 151
Modjokerto, Indonesia 61
molluscs 80
monkeys 28, 66–7, 72, 98–9, 107, 116,
    129, 136, 143, 151; empathy is lacking
    127; infanticide 26; inhibitions against
    sex 24; language capacity 127
monogamy: in animals 17, 22, 28, 30–1, 67,
    92–4; social in early humans 92–4, 132,
    148, 150–4, 157
Monte Bamboli, Tuscany, Italy 44
morality, origins of 17, 37–8, 155–8
Morgan, Elaine 68–9, 71–3, 84, 129
Morotopithecus 44
mountain gorillas 41, 121; ant eating
    121, 137
Moyà-Solà, Salvador 44–5, 75
mussels 51, 73
Mylander, Carolyn 108

Nachukui, Kenya 115
naked mole rats 19, 33–4, 36
Nariokotomo, Kenya 59
natural selection 12, 19, 21, 81
Neanderthals 60, 63, 113; intelligence 87,
  110–11, 113; lack of neotene traits of
  skull 86–7; language capacity 87,
  110–11
Near East 3, 63
neocortex 107, 118
neoteny: and evolution of archaic *sapiens* 60;
  and evolution of bipedalism 76, 82–5,
  88; and evolution of bonobos 85–6,
  103–4; and evolution of brain 83,
  85–6; and evolution of domestic dogs
  86–7; and evolution of *Homo* 85–6;
  and evolution of modern humans
  86–8; *see also* pedomorphosis;
  peramorphosis
Nepal 27
nepotism 17, 40
New South Wales, Australia 60
New World 26, 129
Nichols, Johanna 109
Nishima, Hiroshi 125
nuclear family 40, 67, 93–4, 145–6, 161;
  animals 145
nut cracking: chimpanzees 66, 119–22
nutrition, 136

Oedipus: complex 21; myth 25
oestrus: bonobos 95; chimpanzees 23, 96–8,
  102, 149; loss of in early humans 89–94,
  97–103, 129, 149–50; modern humans
  95–6
Old World 26, 63, 129
Olduwai, Tanzania 59, 114
Olduwan stone technology 59, 61–2, 123,
  134
Omo, Ethiopia 57
Orang-utans 41, 89, 110, 140, 145, 148;
  Borneo 42; diet 136–7, 143; food-
  sharing 4–5; language capacity 124, 129;
  Sumatra 42; tool use 118, 121–2; *see also*
  Pongo pygmaeus
Oreopithecus 44, 75–6
Oreopithecus bamboli 44–5, 76
orgasm: apes and monkeys 100–1; humans
  101–2
Orrorin tugenensis 51
otters 72
ovulation: apes 89, 95–6, 98, 103; early
  humans 90–1, 95–6, 103; modern
  humans 95
oysters 73

Pakistan 61
Pan paniscus 41
Pan troglodytes 41
Pan t. schweinfurtii 41
Pan t. troglodytes 41
Pan t. vellerosus 41
Pan t. verus 41
Paranthropos 49
parental care 12, 34; evolution of 30–2, 35
pedomorphosis: and human evolution 82,
  85–6
penis: length of bonobo 104; length of
  chimpanzee 104; length of human 104;
  loss of bone in human 104–5
peramorphosis: and evolution of human
  brain 83, 85–6
permanent sex in humans, evolution of 149,
  151
Persia 20
Peru, Inka empire 20
phenotype matching 15–16
Pickford, Martin 51
pidgin languages 107–8
pigmentation 77–8
pigs 7, 71
Pinker, Steven 108
planum temporale 125
Pleistocene period 82
Pliocene period 75, 82
polyandry 148
polygamy 22, 27–8, 93, 148; chimpanzees
  67
polygynandry 149
Pongo pygmaeus 42
population size: early humans 144–5;
  efficient size for inbreeding avoidance
  22
prairie dogs 26, 29
praying mantis 35
Prehomo 48–50, 54, 57–8, 138–42, 144,
  150–3, 157, 160
primates 22, 28, 39, 71–2, 91, 93, 114,
  117, 121, 142; communication 116;
  exogamy 21, 146; group size related to
  social complexity 118; hygiene 142;
  imprinting through early close contact
  22; inbreeding avoidance 18–19;
  infanticide 29; knowledge about food
  plants 132; monogamy 153; neocortex
  107; norms for social behaviour 156;
  oestrus 102–3, 151; ovulation 96, 98;
  polygamy 148; sexual behaviour 97, 149;
  sociality 145; violence as a social
  instrument 157–64; vitamin-C not
  produced 137

proboscis monkey 72
proto-language 157, 160; reconstruction of 130–4
pygmy chimpanzees 41, 121, 124–5, 158
pythons 132

Ramirez-Rozzi, F. V. 87
rape: animals 159; modern societies 159
rats 125
reciprocal altruism 13–14, 16–17
Renzidong, China 61
reproductive altruism 25, 31–2
reproductive fitness 12–13
reproductive success 8, 17
reptiles 18, 33
rhinoceros 61, 68, 71
Rift Valley, East Africa 56
right-handedness: early *Homo* 115
Riwat, Pakistan 61
Roche, Helen 115
Rose, Steven 38
Rwanda 42

sabre-toothed cats 61
Sahara 44, 88
Sahelanthropus tchadensis 50
Savage-Rumbaugh, Susanne 124
savannah hypothesis 65–70, 76, 79
Scandinavia 62–3
Schagatay, Erika 71–2
Schöningen, Germany 112–13
sea cows 79
seals 71, 84
selfishness, social evolution of 37, 39–40
Senut, Brigitte 51
Sereno, Martin 125
sexual behaviour: apes 89–93, 98–9, 102; bonobos 96–7, 99–101, 103–4; chimpanzees 89, 91, 93, 96–9, 100–1, 103–4; early humans 89–90, 92–4, 97–105; evolution of permanent sex 89–100; monkeys 98–100; primates 98–9, 100–3
sexual dimorphism 53, 151; *see also* size difference between sexes
Seyfarth, Robert 127, 132
sheep 7
shellfish 73–4, 138
Shepher, Joseph 23
Short, Roger 93
siamang 42
Sierra Leone 119
Sima Atapuerca, Spain 62
size difference between sexes: chimpanzees 151; early humans 53, 151; gorillas 151

slings 163
snakes 132, 161
social insects 11, 15, 18, 25, 33–6, 156; lack of social complexity 35
social norms: early humans 156–7; flock animals 155–6
social structure in human societies: basic evolutionary components 39–40
sociobiology 8–11, 13–14
South (southern) Africa 47, 53–4, 56–60
South America 121
South East Asia 42
southern Asia 60
Spain 60, 62
spears 112–13, 163
speech: anatomical prerequisites of in humans 116–17; *see also* language
spider monkeys 153
spiders 18, 33, 35, 161
Spoor, Fred 54
squirrels 137
Stanford, Craig 143
starlings 31
sterility in early puberty: chimpanzees 146; humans 147
Sterkfontein, South Africa 53–4, 56
Stewart, Caro-Beth 44
Stone Age 2–3, 7, 163; northern Europe 2
stone tools 55, 87, 113, 118, 123, 138
subcutaneous fat 68–74, 77, 79
Subhomo 48–50, 54–7, 77, 137
subsistence strategies: apes 141–4; early humans 141–4; hunters and gatherers 141–4
Sumatra 42, 110, 118, 120, 122
Swartkrans, South Africa 58
sweat glands 65, 68–74, 77, 79
Sweden 2, 71
swimming ability in humans, evolution of 72
symbolic thinking 110; apes 108–9
Szalay, F. S. 98

Tabarin, Kenya 52
Tai forest, Ivory Coast 143
tamarins 127
Tanzania 59, 143, 162
tapirs 71
Tasmania 110
Taung, South Africa 47
Tautavel, France 62
Teaford, Mark 137
termites 11, 33, 132, 156
Terra Amata, France 62
territoriality 7, 161–2

testicles, size of: apes 93; humans 93
Thornhill, Nancy 20
Tobias, Phillip 53, 70
tool use: apes 117–23; other animals 121
Toros-Menalla, Chad 50
Toth, Nick 120
tree swallows 31
Trivers, Robert 13, 17
Tugen, Kenya 51
Tuscany, Italy 44

Ubeidiya, Israel 61–2
Uganda 42
Ungar, Peter 137
upright gait 71, 74, 78–9, 82, 117, 130,
    149, 151; see also bipedalism
Uraha, Malawi 59

vagina: backward-facing in apes and
    monkeys 83–5; forward-facing in
    animals 84; forward-facing in ape
    embryos 103; forward-facing in early
    humans 74, 82–5, 97–8; upside-down
    in humans 101
Venta Mircena, Orce, Spain 61
vervets 99, 127
violence 10, 157; inhibition against 27–9,
    162–3; male 9; modern humans 9–10,
    157; primates 157–64
Vrba, Elisabeth 85

de Waal, Frands 154, 156, 159
Walker, Alan 59

war-like aggression: ants 5; chimpanzees 5,
    9, 162; humans 9
warning cries: animals 25
warthogs 68
wasps 33–4, 156
weapons: preventing natural blocks against
    lethal violence 163
Wernicke's centre 107, 125; in afarensis
    and africanus 115; in chimpanzees
    115
West (western) Africa 42, 64, 119–20
West Asia 134–5
Westenhöfer, Max 70
Westermarck, Edward 22
Westermarck effect 22–3
whales 38, 71, 79, 84, 123, 156
Wheeler, Peter 69
White, Tim 52, 55, 60
wild dogs 34, 145
Williams, George 13
Wilson, David Sloan 38
Wilson, Edward O. 10, 13–15, 37, 39
Winkler, Paul 27
Wolf, Arthur 23
wolves 19, 34
Wynn, Thomas 113, 123

xenophobia: chimpanzees 161–2; humans
    161

Yanmou, southwestern China 61

Zaire 112